Human Bandwidth™
Awakening the Extraordinary Within

Gunnar Nilsson

Steve,

    May you continue to expand your
Awareness as you read & experience this book.
May you continue to share your energy to
empower others

Gunnar

RAPID CREEK PUBLISHING

Grateful acknowledgement is made to:

Excerpt from *Your Biography Becomes Your Biology* by Caroline
Myss, an interview conducted by Michael Toms of New
Dimensions Radio and published in full at http://www.myss.com

John and Jane Byrnes for Katie Byrnes' profile.

Excerpt from *Wherever You Go There You Are* by Jon Kabat-Zinn,
© 1994 by Hyperion

Excerpts from *Strength To Your Sword Arm: Selected Writings*
(Holy Cow! Press, 1992) Copyright by the estate of Brenda Ueland
and reprinted by permission of the publisher. All right reserved.

Excerpt from *Discounting Dynamo* by John Huey
(*Time*, December 7, 1998) ©1998 Time Inc.

Excerpt from *Man's Search for Meaning* by Viktor E. Frankl.
© 1959, 1962, 1984, 1992 by Viktor E. Frankl. Reprinted by
permission of Beacon Press, Boston.

Published by Rapid Creek Publishing, 2650 Jackson Blvd.,
Rapid City, SD 57702
http://www.human---bandwidth.com

Printed in the United States of America

ISBN 0-9716368-0-X

10 9 8 7 6 5 4 3 2 1

This book is dedicated to you, the reader.

May you come to experience yourself as a fully alive human being —

recognized for who you truly are

and for who you can become.

Acknowledgements

My deep appreciation and love goes first to my wife Jan, for her courage, and for her love, support, and patience in writing this book. I want to thank my children Kirsten, Laura, and Erica for their input, love, feedback, and energy.

Thank you Dave Ellis for your early advice and Doug Toft for helping transform a business manuscript into this book. Many people have contributed ideas and suggestions including Jim Stuart, Susan Olsen, Gary Gesme, Jim Thompson, Ellen Romeiser, Scott Paseltiner, Pat Wolsko, Michael Schiesser, Tom Wolsko, Paul Gipson, a collective thank you to my clients and the thousands of people with whom I have worked and to the preceding generations who helped to weave our social fabric. Thanks Marilyn Blythe and Kirsten Maxwell for your support, organizing, and research. Thanks to Sandrine Larsen and Yvonne Decker for your word processing. Thanks Kim Oslund Hadd for your creativity in the layout. This book was a marathon for me, and Mary Maisey-Ireland and Larry David were there for me during the last eight grueling and exhilarating miles. I would like to extend heartfelt hugs to Mary and Larry who masterfully and lovingly edited the text and energized me in the process. Thank you, God, for the 100+ 4:00 a.m. wake-up calls and the lessons of life.

A special thank you is extended but not limited to dozens of healthcare professionals whose combined knowledge and insights contributed to portions of this book, including: Adam Romeiser Jr., M.D., Jay Munsell, M.D., Dohyan Choe, Dean Deng, Charles Lo, M.D., Jeff Maurus, M.D., Deepak Chopra, M.D., Barry Arnason, M.D., James Quinlan, M.D., Jonathan Gilbert, M.D., Frank Martini, M.D., Caroline Myss, Ph.D., Lew Birkmann, M.D., Ingrid Dilley, Margaret McIntyre, Pamela Kihm, and Jody Speckman. Our involvement with many of these healthcare professionals resulted from Jan's MS diagnosis in 1989 and our subsequent journey and search for treatment and therapies.

I would like to further acknowledge people who have contributed and supported me in many ways for which I am and will be grateful: Mildred Kohler, Jimmy Wang, Carol Howles Keddie, Fred Erler, Elaine Grauer, Jim Galley, Art Weimer, Malcolm McLean, Bob Linehan, Val Linehan, Lynne Twist, Evelyn Laster, Mike Kucinic, Tony Brown, Ramkrishna Bajaj, Robert Chester, Randy Powell, Gus Busing, Tom Henrich, Rami Henrich, Tony Danielson, Patricia Wolsko, Helen Wolsko, Tom Wolsko, Sue Wolsko, Michael Reid, Arlene Reid, Howard Goldman, Tom Drucker, Gary Lester, Bob Lindmark, Rick Lindmark, Gary Lindmark, Barbara Gazzolo, Sally Danielson, Carl Ivey, Ollie Matson, Lalita Banavali, Joan Holmes, Curt Danekas, Jerry Reinsdorf, Dorothy Parkander, Monte West, Charles Frazier, Chuck DiFrancesca, Joanne Vetterick, Ike Sewell, Pat Debonnet, Ingrid, Thorsten and Sigrid Lindmark, Leo, Ella, Tommy and Kenth Nilsson, Howard Ross, Penelope Bell, and Julie Eyres.

Lastly, thanks Mom & Dad for giving me life.

Table of Contents

An Invitation

One of our primary societal imperatives is to improve the world's standard of living. Generally we think of this from a socio-economic perspective.

Human Bandwidth, Awakening the Extraordinary Within invites or perhaps provokes one to bring this imperative closer to home by examining your personal standards of living from a core or essence perspective. It is intended to be the **beginning** of an inquiry into the nature of human awareness and your basic human capacities.

I ask you not to read this book but to experience it. Engage your senses, emotions, and spirit as well as your mind and brain by participating in the exercises and keeping a journal of your insights. Postpone drawing conclusions. Allow the messages within to permeate all levels of your being. Upon completion of the book, move into action.

You have substantial human capacities which, when tapped, will alter your life. You can do and be whatever you imagine. *Human Bandwidth* can awaken you to your extraordinary nature.

Thank you for joining me on this journey.

CHAPTER I:
Bandwidth—
Key to Extraordinary People & Organizations

What lies before us and what lies behind us are but a small matter compared to what lies within us.
— Ralph Waldo Emerson

Helen Abby • Sandra Abby • Wodie Accord • David Abrams • Mike Adelamn • Len Adell • David Ahlstrand • Bob Ahrens • Jim Aikman • Ronald Aldinger • Liz Allen • Michael Allen • Brian Alm • Roy Altman • Manny Alves • Don Ammerman • Marjorie Ampulski • Jan Amsinger • Alex Anagnost • Paul Ander • Arlis Ander • Ann Anderson • Arnie Anderson • Cathy Anderson • Danny Anderson • David Anderson • Edith Anderson • Jack Anderson • Ken Anderson • Kirk Anderson • Martha Anderson • Rick Anderson • Ronald Anderson • Tim Anderson • Sven Andersson • Karin Nilsdotter Anderson • Danny Anderson • Alan Andreini • Peaches Andreini • Jane Andrew • Eric Anttila • Larry Armstrong • Barry Arnason • Zachary Arnell • John Artec • Harry Arvanis • Richard Asch • Lynne Asche • Roger Ashman • Jean Augustine • Carol Austin • Harvey Austin • Paul Axtell • Dolores Ayala • Norman Ayer • Gladys Babich • Steve Babich • Don Bacich • Mona Backman • Keith Bailey • Ramkrishna Bajaj • Madhur Bajaj • Vimla Bajaj • Dick Baker • Ken Baker • Kendall Baker • Ruth Baker • Sharon Balais • Tom Baldwin • Bob Ball • Cole Balough • Lolita Banawali • Sheldon Barat • Philip Baratta • Beverly Barber • Brian Barber • Dave Barder • Bill Barth • Brenda Barnes • Denny Barrett • Sally Barrett • Jim Barton • Mary Barentine • Charles Bashaar • Carol Bashaar • Bill Basenett • Maureen Mullen Battle • Sean Battles • Aleen Bayard • Michael Bayles • John Beacon • Karen Beacon • Rob Bearman • Diane Beatty • Mike Beatty • Dr. Berlin • Leslie Beck • Dan Beck • Jean Beck • Warren Beck • Lee Beck • Christy Beckmann • Fred Behnken • Al Behring • Kathryn Behring • Liz Behring • Mike Behring • Debra Belander • Penelope Bell • Les Bell • Bill Bennett • Carol Bennett • Mike Bennett • Mabel Benson • Betty Benton • Jim Benton • Conrad Bergendorff • Jack Berg • LaVonne Berg • Sheri Berto • Sven Bergman • Kerstin Svendotter Bergman • Don Bergsrud • Dick Bergsud • Sue Bergsrud • Ed Bernheim • Joe Bernot • Brette Bensinger • Peter Bensinger • Carol Bettendorf • Paul Bettendorf • Bob Biedron • John Biggs • Marie Biggs • Kateri Biggs • Melanie Biggs • John Bjork • Carl Bjorklund • Myrtle Bjorklund • Randi Larson • Charmaine Bjustrom • Ed Blaine • Gene Blaho • Lil Blaho • Gene Blaho • Kathy Blaho • Nancy Blaho • Cheryl Blaho • Laurie Blaho • Tom Blasczyk • George Bledsoe • Faron Blessing • Bonnie Block • Doug Block • Richard Block • Terry Bluhm • Dixie Blumeyer Winterland • Marilyn Blythe • Tom Blythe • Ann Boaden • Helen Bobak • Emerson Bodell • Ellen Bodell • Valerie Bofinger Peterson • Brenda Bogan • David Bogan • Charles Bogan • Barbara Bolling Rimington • John Bolm • Karen Bolm • Bill Bolsen • Bill Bomberry • Deb Bomberry • Barbara Bopp • Ruthane Bopp • Peter Bourne • Michael Borkovitz • John Borling • Betty Borling • Carl Bornsen • Jerome Bosch • Barry Boscoe • James Bosler • Jon Bottorff • Linda Bower • Jim

LIFE IS A GIFT!

Morrie Schwartz was a professor of sociology and psychology at Brandeis University in suburban Boston. Insatiably curious, Morrie's life was his laboratory. He routinely conducted his experiments in the classroom, at home, on the dance floor, with groups and individuals, in meditation, and sometimes in formal research.

Known to millions of people through *Tuesdays with Morrie*, his is a tender story. As he succumbed to Amyotrophic Lateral Sclerosis (ALS) or Lou Gehrig's Disease, his last months were chronicled by one of his former students, Mitch Albom. In the book and in several interviews on *Nightline* with Ted Koppel, Morrie shared his life's purpose and his dying days. He was committed to living life fully regardless of his circumstances.

Most of us are fearful of death, and that fear tends to hold us back from living "full out." By powerfully and publicly sharing his last months, Morrie Schwartz allowed us a glimpse of the possibility of death as a natural expression of a life fully lived.

Seven years prior to reading *Tuesdays with Morrie*, I paid a last visit to my friend Jon Hobart, an attorney and fraternity brother who was dying of ALS in Memphis. I had seen him in the summer, sitting in a wheelchair and talking, mentally as sharp as ever. Now, just four months later, he lay in bed, unable to move or speak. He could barely move his lips to mouth words. Jon's normally functioning brain and mind were trapped inside a dying body.

After greeting him with a hug, I stepped back. "Thanks for coming," he mouthed. "It's great to see people. I spend most of my time with the birds." As I turned to see several birds bouncing around on the ground outside his bedroom window, he continued "You know, I never paid attention to the birds—and so many things. Now all the simple things bring me joy."

Morrie and Jon died of the same illness, and they shared something else. Each learned and taught others much in the last year of his life. Morrie's public sharing of his dying and Jon's private sharing of his spirit were both extraordinary. Although I had known Jon since we were eighteen, I had never really connected with his spirit or inner being. My visits with Jon and his wife, Sondra, were unforgettable. They penetrated my heart. As I read *Tuesdays with Morrie*, I smiled, laughed, cried, and re-experienced what I'd learned from Jon: **life is a gift to be lived fully.**

A couple of years later I gave a copy of *Tuesdays with Morrie* to my good friend Bob Connell. He finished it early one morning, and then sat crying on his living room sofa. He and Jon Hobart had been friends since childhood. When Bob shared how the book affected him, I felt a deep, unmistakable connection to both Bob and Jon. This connection transcended years of friendship, both good times and tough times.

Sadly, I needed this wake-up call—a friend, my age, deteriorating, dying—to begin feeling on a deeper level and examining my own life. I had experienced other deaths before, as well as my own close calls, but those experiences had only a short-term impact. Soon I was back to taking life for granted, asleep to the value, the purpose, and the gift that is my life .

Intellectually, I knew I wasn't seizing the day. My marriage was good, my kids were great, and my career pursuits, for the most part, were successful. But something was definitely missing in my experience, and I knew it. My search for answers was coupled with a curiosity about the nature of life and learning. I read personal growth books. I attended workshops, seminars, and experiential programs.

Then came the second wake-up call. A year after Jon contracted ALS, my wife Jan was diagnosed with Multiple Sclerosis (MS). I went into shock. Why Jan? Why now? Where is this headed? (There isn't a cure for MS.)

We were suddenly living on a roller coaster. Our entire family was caught up in the swirl of uncertainty. Our three daughters faced an over-whelming health crisis, as well as the possible loss of their mother. Jan talked with Jon Hobart, and although his words were encouraging, his rapid deterioration frightened her.

When Jon died, we projected our worst fears into Jan's situation, even though the probability of her dying anytime soon was very slight. Gradually, and to different degrees, each of us became aware that we had a choice. We could be victims of Jan's illness. Or, we could respond to this new reality as an opening. We began to distinguish the razor-thin line separating problems from possibilities.

We were no longer an ordinary family. As the progression of MS made its reality inescapable, each of us opened to the possibility of living life from an extraordinary perspective. Kirsten, Laura, and Erica grew up quickly, as they gave up their self-centeredness, took on more of the household responsibilities, and learned to care for Mom. I reconstructed my business affairs so that I could be home most nights, and I learned to serve. And Jan reached deep inside herself, took a stand for her health, relinquished many of the tasks and pleasures that were her dominion, and learned to allow us to care for her.

EXTRAORDINARY PEOPLE CONTRIBUTE TO ALL OF US

As part of my ongoing research, I read books and research articles and spoke with doctors, scientists, clergy, and eastern medical practitioners. Over the years, Jan has worked with doctors of ancient Chinese and Korean medicine, neurologists, medical intuitives, and spiritual healers.

From my position as an observer, and sometimes as a participant, I saw threads connecting these seemingly divergent approaches. I began to make similar connections between people such as Albert Einstein, Michael Jordan, Sam Walton, Caroline Myss, Dr. Dohyan Choe, Dr. James Lo, Dr. Deepak Chopra, Michael Walter, Tony Danielson, Jon Hobart, and Morrie Schwartz.

Each one, in his or her own unique way, contributed to Jan and to me. Directly or indirectly, the energy, spirit, creativity, love, support, and experience of each person came through. We could feel in each person his or her diverse and unlimited capacities. Such insights opened us up in the face of Jan's illness to the possibility of who we could be.

Any extraordinary moment or experience, when shared, can encourage and inspire us to expand our own capacities. I suspect that you too have been inspired by extraordinary human beings. Their energy seems to transcend their words and actions, reflecting directly who they are. These people expand our sense of human potential. They awaken us to the possibility that we can be happy, whole, creative, fearless, and loving—not just on occasion, but every day of our lives. There have been many such people throughout history.

During my lifetime, I have interacted with tens of thousands of people as a student, relative, athlete, spouse, parent, friend, employee, entrepreneur, educator, change agent, board member, CEO, son, and human being. In recent years, I have worked with leaders and organizations in business, non-profit organizations, and academia to develop and transform the capacities of people.

Through observations, interactions, roles, and life experiences, I became aware of certain common qualities that seemed to significantly impact the level at which people live their lives. These qualities are not the result of special training, genetic advantage, secret weapons, or a silver bullet. **These people simply find more frequent access to a wider range of their potential—their human bandwidth.**

Each period of human development has given us people who, at least periodically, operated at unusually high bandwidths. These people were leaders, elders, scholars, teachers, scientists, artists, doctors, nurses, caregivers, explorers, merchants, widows, orphans, inventors, soldiers, farmers, fishermen, heroines, entrepreneurs, craftspeople, bankers, servants, clergy—to name a few.

Many of the names are familiar: Socrates, DaVinci, Gutenberg, Mozart, Marco Polo, Joan of Arc, the Wright Brothers, Eleanor Roosevelt, Thomas Edison, and Einstein. Millions more go unmentioned in the history books, the unsung heroes of each generation. Such people were the trim tabs or leverage points of their era. They were the spark plugs, the creators, generators, and leaders. More importantly, they were the people who contributed to others at the most basic levels of caring, sharing, teaching, and nurturing. Collectively, their discoveries, inventions, sacrifices, and every day contributions created quantum shifts in society.

Each generation of humanity has benefitted from and built on the contributions of exceptional or extraordinary people from earlier generations. Today, hundreds of thousands, maybe millions, are contributing to the enhancement of human existence. To a large extent, these people are operating on high bandwidth, although they aren't necessarily aware of it. If asked, most would point to something outside themselves as the source of their creativity, leadership, courage, service, or contribution.

The fact that you are reading this book demonstrates your interest in developing your own basic human capacities—your bandwidth. Hopefully, you won't need the kind of wake-up calls that I did in order to discover your extraordinary potential. What is yours to discover is the fact that you will live your life more fully, and contribute more effectively to others, when you contact the breadth of your whole being.

Consider the possibility that you are a human being who is unaware of your exceptional nature. You have had many extraordinary moments in your life, but perhaps you've never connected them to see the reservoir of extraordinary-ness in yourself. Pause for a few minutes and take yourself on a chronological tour of your childhood.

You might begin with preschool or kindergarten. Recall your experiences and the faces of your classmates. Remember playing, parties, trips, vacation, scouts, teams, music lessons, picnics, beaches, hiking, biking, learning to read, write, type, add, subtract, multiply, and divide. Recall the faces of friends, extended family, teachers, coaches, and neighbors.

Visualize those times that were extraordinary. Make some notes so you can start to appreciate your exceptional moments and begin to see the source and patterns of those moments and experiences. Later in the chapter, we will continue the journey into your extraordinary nature.

HIGH-PERFORMANCE IS NOT THE SAME AS BEING EXTRAORDINARY

Before we move on to discuss bandwidth, I want to make a distinction between exceptional people and high-performing people.

Simply put, high performers are people who excel at some activity. High-performance and performance culture are commonly-used terms to describe people and organizations who achieve great results in school, sports, business, or other human endeavors, relative to their contemporaries.

Exceptional people are often high performers, but they go beyond the application of skill and technique to a whole other level of existence. **Exceptional or extraordinary people live from a self-created state of expanded capacity or higher bandwidth.** They're able to connect with an intelligence and energy that transcends their minds and manifests in their performance and contribution to the world. They discover the **source** of performance and creativity.

The ancient Chinese called these people "evolved individuals." You could say they are accomplished, expanded, highly developed, or transformed in one or more areas of their life.These are people who are masterful in areas such as leadership, organization, relationships, teaching, art, invention, research, thinking, discovery, and caring. However, such people are not necessarily "masters." They may be totally inept, for instance, at balancing a checkbook or staying in shape physically.

In a nutshell, extraordinary or exceptional people are high-energy people who give or share energy with others. They are creative, insightful, knowledgeable, compassionate, courageous, funny, masterful, caring, loving, empathetic, wise, serving, inventive, adventurous, thoughtful, and inspiring. And they give of who they are to you and others in their lives. They live in the PRESENT MOMENT— the here and now—with much greater frequency than do ordinary people. They are growing or expanding rather than contracting or resisting. They have a greater awareness of their inner capacities. They are able to transform these capacities into conversations and actions that make a difference.

Some people will scan this book for hints on how to be "successful" human beings. Entire industries have sprung up around measuring and improving productivity, performance, test scores, etc. Millions of books and articles offer "how to's"—prescriptions for success at investing, travel, health, and almost any activity you could name. Thousands of experts offer consulting or workshops on improving performance in every facet of life. Strategies, planning, and prescriptions for action are the recommended paths to performance enhancement.

While I applaud these efforts and praise high performers, that is not the purpose of this book. I am suggesting a different approach to greater achievement.

Consider this premise: **Through accessing our entire bandwidth, we tap into a limitless source of energy and creativity which goes beyond the cultivation of performance, strategy, and technique.** When you focus exclusively on improving your strategy or technique, you limit your possibilities to only that which you plan to do or say. Technique involves a repetition of strategies inherited from the past. By accessing your entire bandwidth, you go beyond the limitations of your mind and its pre-conceived notions. The possibilities for what you might do or say become limitless.

Through this book, you may discover your potential to be exceptional and to live an exceptional life. Begin by understanding the notion of human bandwidth.

IMAGINE THAT YOU EXIST AS BANDS OF ENERGY

Human bandwidth refers to all the capacities of a human being working in harmony or unity. These capacities converge in language and manifest in daily conversations, actions, and symbols. As a synonym for bandwidth, we can also look to a dictionary definition of the word *capacity*: "potential; possibility; ability; capability; capable of development into actuality; being something that may or may not occur."

Human bandwidth is a metaphor drawn from electronics, where bandwidth is technically defined: "A range within a band of wavelength, frequencies, or energies, especially a range of radio frequencies that is occupied by a modulated carrier wave." Or, "the data transfer rate of an electronic communications system." (The word bandwidth can also refer to the amount of mental space available to deal with an issue. This is not my meaning in this book.)

Consider that you are a field of energy within an infinite universal energy field. Within your personal field, you have multiple capacities, or bands of energy. For purposes of this book, I have chosen to focus on six of these bands.

We are born into this world with basic human capacities or energies—human bandwidth. Families, schools, culture, gender, and other influences tend to contain, override, or diminish these capacities.

BANDS OF HUMAN ENERGY

Spirit

Brain

Mind

Senses

Emotions

Body

Rediscovering and accessing these capacities can be our best gift to ourselves—and to the world. By doing so, we can shift from resignation to active choice making. We can transform from common to exceptional, from ordinary to extraordinary.

SEE YOURSELF AS AN ENERGY FIELD

Our six bands of energy are interconnected in a unified field. We are a microcosm of the universe, which is an infinite field of intelligence, information, and energy.

This concept of ourselves as fields of energy is basic to current scientific thought. Quantum physicists, and even certain medical professionals, assert that we humans (along with every thing else that exists) are accumulations of sub-atomic particles of a certain mass, energy, and density.

The view of the human being as a field of energy harkens back several millennia. Twenty-five centuries ago the concept of kundalini emerged from the Hindu culture. Kundalini is the energy that sustains life and produces higher states of consciousness. It flows through a system of seven chakras, subtle power centers arrayed vertically in the center of the body. Ancient Chinese medicine is based on a similar concept, a fundamental energy called chi. This energy sustains health and flows through vertical bands, or meridian's, running throughout the entire body.

When we are healthy, we generate life energy, and our fields expand. When we are ill or "stressed out," we consume energy. We draw down our reserves and may even describe ourselves as "low-energy." Eating, sleeping, and exercising restore our energy.

MANIFESTATIONS OF YOUR HUMAN ENERGY FIELD

Breathing, oxygen intake, carbon dioxide output, muscle usage, singing, dancing, walking, exercise, balance, sleeping, eating, sweating, eliminating, laughing, cheering, crying, sneezing, speaking, listening, seeing, touching, feeling, brain usage, physical contact/connection, hugging, sex, shaking hands, static electricity, fever, chills, 98.6° body temperature.

Living organisms constantly send and receive messages to each other through the invisible airwaves of their bandwidths. Your human systems are in a constant state of activity or transmission. Chances are you're unaware of this, especially when you operate at a narrow bandwidth. When you are able to detect, distinguish, and utilize your various capacities, you increase your overall bandwidth.

Some of our bandwidth is invisible to the human eye. Most of us are not aware of these bands and experience them only on a limited basis. I like the term bandwidth because it points to the existence of unseen capabilities, much like the word airwaves conjures images of radio or television signals vibrating through space.

Because our bodies are what we see first in our interactions with each other, they become the basis of our identities. In Western cultures we focus heavily on physical appearance: height, weight, skin color, attire, and other external or surface impressions—the tip of the iceberg to our total bandwidth. (And, much of the time, we don't get past bodily form to connect with each other in substance.)

Our senses are visible and serve as our antennae or radar. Senses enable human communication, coordination, mobility, safety, and survival. Senses are natural transmitters and receivers of energy. They also invariably trigger our minds.

Emotions are both visible and invisible. Often a non-verbal form of communication, emotion is energy in motion—e-motion. Linking our thoughts with our feelings, emotions can be expressed through the body or suppressed in the body. We connect to emotions, whether we like the particular emotion of the moment or not.

The mind is our database, and contains all of our life's experiences. The mind is faster and has more capacity than any computer yet invented. Used consciously, the mind is a valuable ally. When we are unaware, our minds tend to use us. There will be more on this later.

The brain is the master coordinator and the receptor of conscious thought from the mind. Much of what the brain does is invisible—regulating hormone levels, digestion, heart rate, blood pressure, body temperature, and other autonomic functions.

Spirit is the animating force in our lives, connecting us to each other and to everything in the universe.

VISIBLE BANDS OF ENERGY	INVISIBLE BANDS OF ENERGY
Outer Body	Inner Body
Senses	Emotions
Emotions	Brain
	Mind
	Spirit

Most of us consistently transmit and receive on only two or three channels, or bands. The rest of our bandwidth is effectively shut down. **Unaware of our full bandwidth, we unconsciously limit our capacities—the convergence and connection of six infinite bands of energy.**

Stop reading for thirty seconds and visualize yourself as a field of energy. Can you feel energy in the various parts of your body?

WAKE UP TO YOUR FULL BANDWIDTH

Genetically speaking, we each have a different bandwidth makeup, just as we have different fingerprints. The human bandwidth of Galileo differed from that of Mozart, Winston Churchill, or Susan B. Anthony. They lived in different eras and had distinctive bandwidths. It is probable, however, that each of them regularly accessed their full human bandwidth.

Exceptional people are often typecast for one bandwidth in which they happen to be masterful. A more in-depth look will often reveal that their other bands of energy are significantly developed and work in concert to elevate their overall capacity and performance. Intellectual achievements occur in the bands of the mind and brain. Keen powers of observation occur in the band of the senses. Artistic or musical expression relates to the bands of emotion and spirit, as well as brain, body, and mind. And the ability to see infinite possibilities

and the interconnection of all human beings primarily comes from the band of spirit.

While Einstein is most remembered for his brain and mind, he was incredibly curious, emotionally sensitive, and captivated by the interconnection of everything in the universe. Interestingly, he often credited his childlike curiosity as the primary source of his work. Ghandi was a spiritual icon, yet he was a lawyer by training and practice.

More light is shed on the notion of human bandwidth by people who are born blind, deaf, missing a body part, or with some type of brain dysfunction. This "missing bandwidth" seems to force such people (as well as those who lose a capacity later in life) to expand their remaining bands. Helen Keller was blind, deaf, and mute. Yet through the loving care of her teacher, Anne Sullivan, she greatly expanded her remaining senses, her emotions, and her body to reveal her brilliant mind, brain, and spirit.

EVERYONE CAN BE EXTRAORDINARY

As a general rule, we take life for granted until we either lose something or somehow wake up to who we really are. Life is a gift, an opportunity. Health is a gift. Breath is a gift. Most people are unaware that to be alive in itself is extraordinary. You won the sperm contest against millions of also-rans. You are here, thanks to the miracle of human birth. You have the innate capacity to be extraordinary.

Everyone has basic human capacities to be exceptional. Everyone! All of us have our extraordinary moments and experiences of expanding bandwidth. You don't have to be rich or famous to be extraordinary. You have only to discover your already exceptional nature.

Why are so few people tapping into their entire bandwidth? I suspect it has to do with the invisible nature of bandwidth and a lack of awareness of the access point. Europeans and North Americans often rely exclusively on rational thought—the domain of the mind. Because many of our most profound experiences occur at the intuitive, or spiritual level, those experiences are not seen for what they really are—portals to our infinite human bandwidth. We can access our bandwidth at any moment, simply by being aware of it.

Exercise

Partial Bandwidth

How many people do you know who have some type of "disability" or congenital defect? Imagine being in their shoes. Visualize reaching into your "inner reserves" to compensate or create the energy necessary to perform everyday tasks.

Visit a children's' or veterans' hospital. Talk to an AIDS patient or someone in an oncology ward of a hospital. Touch base with a recovering drug addict or alcoholic. Talk with a homeless person or an impoverished child. In most cases, you will learn volumes about courage, adaptability, tenacity, and grace.

Most "disadvantaged" people expand their bandwidth in order to attain some semblance of normalcy. While this may seem depressing to contemplate if you are living a "comfortable life," these are examples of being extraordinary in the face of challenging situations.

ACCESS TO HIGH BANDWIDTH— PRESENT MOMENT

Electronics has put the world at our fingertips. Press a button. Flip a switch. Lift a receiver. Move a mouse. Voila! Screens appear. Dark rooms light up. Dial tones sound. Every conceivable kind of information is almost instantly available. Access to human bandwidth is equally simple and convenient. But that access goes generally unrecognized or misunderstood.

Higher human bandwidth is accessed in the PRESENT MOMENT. The PRESENT MOMENT is the source of five-sixths of human bandwidth. In reading the biographies of exceptional people (perhaps you know such a person?), it is apparent that they share the ability to access high bandwidth. They do (or did) this by fully experiencing the PRESENT MOMENT. They lived at different times and followed different pathways, but they accomplished extraordinary results— *through being present to the here and now.*

Many of these people practiced some form of meditation or quiet sitting, perhaps with a cup of tea, for the purpose of generating new ideas. Others regularly walked and communed with nature. Some worked with intense focus, sleeping in studios or laboratories as they experimented with their art or science. Keen powers of observation and the ability to feel very deeply made it possible for extraordinary caregivers, teachers, social workers, and mothers to transform the quality of human life.

Exceptional athletes and artists often say:
   "I was present to the sound, the feeling."
   "I was in the moment."
   "I became one with the audience."
   "The idea came to me as I was waking up."
   "I was in the zone."

Instead of using their minds to analyze what they already knew, they let everything go, giving up any thought of past or future, to venture into the unknown potential and possibility that exists in the infinite present moment.

The present moment is the here and now . . . now, now, now, and now . . . Feeling wind on your face . . . Smelling grass and flowers . . . Feeling emotion — fear, anger, laughter or joy . . . Feeling your heart beating . . . Noticing your breath moving in and out of your body . . . Discovering a new insight or idea popping "out of the blue" as you are driving . . . Feeling the emotions and spirit behind the words as someone speaks to you . . . Speaking with passion from deep within yourself . . . Sensing that someone is in trouble and rushing to his or her assistance . . . Moving fluidly (without thinking) to the sound of music . . . Laughing, crying, screaming, or being completely still.

THE PRESENT MOMENT LIES IN THE GAP BETWEEN THOUGHTS

The unconscious mind generates one random thought after another like a ticker tape of stock quotes. There is a brief gap, interval, or pause between each thought, as illustrated on the next page.

The gap or pause between thoughts is significant. This gap is the PRESENT MOMENT. **When you move into the gap through focus, conscious breathing, meditation, and other practices that quiet the mind, you open a door to wider bandwidth.**

When your mind is still, you can view and feel the world in an entirely new way. There is an unmistakable peace, a detachment from the frenzied pace of life and your mind. It may feel like a space of "nothing." Insights and ideas effortlessly surface from a place beyond thought. You glimpse new possibilities for action and find your behavior changing spontaneously. Instead of seeing people as isolated bodies, they become elements within a single unified field—as waves are to the ocean. Such tranquility may be experienced after a long run or work out, or deep meditation. In the pause of "no mind," you are relaxed. There is no thinking. You're in the GAP.

Clarity, focus, and possibility all occur in the stillness between thoughts. All possibilities exist in the GAP. The key is entering the PRESENT MOMENT. Asking questions in the PRESENT MOMENT brings you into touch with the intelligence of the universe or your "higher intelligence."

This gap is the break in the past-to-future time continuum. It is the space where everything new enters our lives. "Breakthrough" is a break between the historical mind (thoughts about the past) and the future mind (thoughts about the future). The gap is a space of "no mind."

Life occurs in the PRESENT MOMENT or beyond the mind. Spirit is in the spaces around the thoughts of the mind. It is why new ideas or insights so often "pop in" or "breakthrough" as you shower, shave, drive, or just sit with your mind in neutral.

The wider the gap or interval, as illustrated, the more choices and possibilities will be available to you, and the more you can increase your bandwidth.

Actors, artists, and performers access the **PRESENT MOMENT** when they become their characters or allow a paintbrush to flow across the canvas. The same happens in business, as we solve problems, create new products, and serve our customers. In the PRESENT MOMENT, we have access to all of our capacities and therefore the potential to generate, create, or initiate anything. Insights, ideas, possibility, choices, infinity, and eternity occur in the GAP.

THE GAP IS THE PRESENT MOMENT

1. Typical thought pattern of the human mind.

Thought **Thought** **Thought** **Thought** **Thought** **Thought** **Thought**

gap   gap   gap   gap   gap   gap

2. Increased awareness widens the gap between thoughts.

Thought   GAP   **Thought**   GAP   **Thought**

This graphic illustrates the GAP between thoughts. The mind (or thoughts) can only dwell in the past or future. The PRESENT MOMENT is found in the GAP.

A thought can be a word, phrase, or sentence. Examples include:

I don't like that . . . I'm so dumb . . . I forgot . . .
I don't understand . . . It's warm in here . . .
What are you saying . . . This tastes good . . .
That's bad . . . What? . . . Oh no! . . . Great . . .
I'm tired . . . He's mean . . . I forgot my purse . . .
I like him . . . That's interesting . . . She's nice . . .
That's funny . . . This is fun . . . Loosen up . . .
Huh? . . . He's a jerk . . . This is boring . . .
She's pretty . . . I'm late . . . My back hurts . . .
I'm hungry . . . Here we go again

Thoughts like these occur to us dozens or hundreds of times every day. At night, these patterns may change and include conversations and visualizations like those in dreams. In any case, thoughts have structure, each with a specific beginning and end.

PRESENT MOMENT AWARENESS TRANSCENDS THE MIND

The mind is not a portal to full bandwidth (attempting to gain higher awareness through the mind is a common misdirection.) Yes, it's true that additional schooling, training, or advanced degrees can elevate one to expert status, but breakthroughs (unpredictable or unknown outcomes, quantum leaps) don't result from focusing on facts and histories. New thoughts and connections occur from a place of pure potential.

There is only one place we can go to access the pure potential of the unknown and that is the PRESENT MOMENT. The PRESENT MOMENT is a "break" in the past-future time continuum. The PRESENT MOMENT is "beyond the nine dots" or "outside the box" of the mind.

Five of the six channels of human bandwidth can be accessed through and exist in the PRESENT MOMENT. Only one channel—the mind —operates outside the present moment. The human mind is made up only of records, or memories, of the past and projections of those past memories into the future. "Past" and "future" are actually abstractions of the mind. You cannot be both fully in your mind and fully in the PRESENT MOMENT at the same time; they are mutually exclusive. North Americans, Europeans, Japanese, Australians, and other peoples of the developed world are mostly tuned into one channel—the mind—which effectively removes them from the PRESENT MOMENT.

Understanding the mechanism of the mind and getting beyond it opens the door to greater human bandwidth. Access to our pure potential and unlimited possibility happens through emptying the mind, not filling it. Exceptional or extraordinary people transcend their minds to access creativity.

They don't create from the mind's historical perspective, refashioning insights from the past, but rather see beyond known information and create directly from the unknown.

Training and education increase our stores of information, memories of experiences, and data in the mind. Unfortunately, what we do to increase intellectual capacity often serves to block our opportunities for exceptional performance. Locked into our minds, we are effectively locked out of our other capacities.

The mind isn't a bad thing—it truly is an incredible creation, with more speed and capacity than a supercomputer. The problem lies in its overuse. The mind has evolved into such an incredibly deep and complex field that human beings can and do live almost entirely within the mind band. At the expense of exploring possibilities and opportunities with our other bandwidths, we spend a huge majority of our time analyzing, comparing, judging, interpreting, and evaluating our minds' "files" of historical data.

The great news is we have the inherent ability to bypass the mind. We can awaken and make conscious use of all of our capacities, or bandwidth. Knowing that we have six channels and an instinctive ability to naturally select the appropriate channels for any situation gives us access to our entire bandwidth and infinite possibilities.

I am not suggesting that you be in the PRESENT MOMENT twenty four hours a day, seven days a week. That would be impractical. The nature of our civilization requires us to use our minds in much of our daily living. However, the PRESENT MOMENT is available to all of us all the time. Knowing there is an INFINITE PRESENT MOMENT and knowing that you have access to it, will provide you with infinite choice and ultimately alter your life.

Five channels of human bandwidth which can only be accessed through the PRESENT MOMENT:

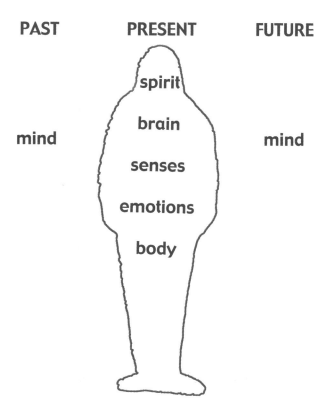

PAST   **PRESENT**   **FUTURE**

spirit

brain

mind   senses   mind

emotions

body

HUMAN BANDWIDTH CONVERGES IN CONVERSATION AND ACTION

In the twenty-first century, we are moving through a technological revolution at breakneck speed. Convergence is a principal feature of the high-tech revolution, illuminating an important aspect of human bandwidth.

Television, radio, telecommunications, and computing converged to create the World Wide Web. Now, the push is on to get higher speed Internet bandwidth into offices and homes of users worldwide. Who would have thought that only 100 years after Guglielmo Marconi's first transatlantic radio transmission we would transact business and entertain ourselves in cyberspace, fusing many technologies into a worldwide network of computers and wireless communication? This is convergence at the level of technology.

Human beings represent a type of convergence that goes far beyond any technology. **In human beings, the energies of the universe converge.** We exist on the material plane as senses, brain, and body. Our existence on the mental plane is manifested in thought, and on the emotional plane in feeling states such as love and fear. On the spiritual plane, we experience our infinite capacities for wisdom, compassion, joy, healing, and peace. It is here that we can know freedom, universal connection, and endless possibility.

All these planes of energy intersect in language. We live in language. We dream, think, feel, see, hear, and act through language. We convert our energy into specific words, allowing us to communicate with others and ourselves. Typically, we perform this conversion in our native tongue, which represents only one of perhaps thousands of ways of encoding our expressions—a fact that's revealed to us when we meet someone who speaks a foreign language.

Conversation is a dance of the elements of bandwidth. It is the substance of human interaction. North American and European cultures emphasize words, written or spoken. However, the verbal portion of a conversation is often less than 50% of the communication, with the rest conveyed through body language, voice tone and inflection, mood, attitude, gestures, and energy level.

ACTIONS: ANOTHER FORM OF COMMUNICATION

Through action, whether carefully chosen or spontaneous, we convert ideas into reality, plans into finished projects, and feelings into behaviors.

Each band of energy (body, mind, brain, emotions, senses, and spirit) can contribute to our conversations and actions, though it is unusual for people to draw from their full bandwidth in this way.

Just as technology converges in ways that connect us through electronics, our human capacities converging at high bandwidth, can connect us through mind and spirit. Is it possible that in technology we have created a mirror of human nature? It is curious that we might derive from the study of electronic technology a deeper perspective of who we are, and who we could become.

BANDWIDTH FLOWS

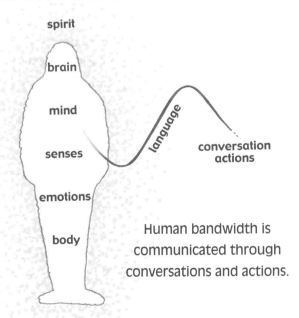

Human bandwidth is communicated through conversations and actions.

EXCEPTIONAL PEOPLE CREATE EXCEPTIONAL ORGANIZATIONS

When we are able to discover and develop our human bandwidth, we increase our human capacities in all areas of our lives. We become more creative, expand and deepen relationships, speak more clearly, listen actively, have more fun, become more productive and efficient, feel more satisfaction, and have higher self-esteem. We also have access to the source of service, productivity, creativity, and transformation for organizations, since organizations of all types have a bandwidth of capacities that parallel the six human capacities.

The basic nature of an organization is human interconnection. An organization is a network of relationships that transcends the organizational structure. Yet the reality of most organizations is that they are functionalized disconnections of people who spend over 90% of their time in the mind or focused on the body—only two channels of human bandwidth. Most business interaction is mind-based and draws upon only a fraction of our capacities.

Tapping into the other channels of bandwidth, individually and collectively, could foster dramatic shifts in creativity, productivity, relationships, service, and results produced by organizations. For example, customer focus begins with an awareness of the customer. Exceptional business leaders and employees notice what channels their customers operate on and then connect with them on as many channels as possible.

Customer connection occurs naturally and effortlessly when those who serve them transcend their minds and access emotion and spirit. Through present-moment awareness, we can listen to our customers (beyond their words) and get a sense of what they want or need. Communication and feedback are offered and received. Requests and suggestions are integrated, resulting in better service. Employees and suppliers are acknowledged more frequently for their contributions. An empathetic spirit emerges, creating satisfaction for everyone involved.

My intention in writing this book is to offer you access to your full human bandwidth — on a moment-to-moment basis—and to the transformation that comes with this discovery.

Language is the house of being. The being of anything that is resides in the world.   —Martin Heidegger

Exercise

A journey of extraordinary moments

Review the extraordinary moments and experiences of your life decade-by-decade, up to your current chronological age. Please use your own definition of the term extraordinary or exceptional to be as comprehensive as possible. Record your observations and reflections using the prompts with each decade. (You will likely notice that the prompts generate negative and positive energy. Keep in mind that problems and negative situations often change our lives in powerful, positive ways by creating the opportunities for us to be exceptional.)

YOUR TEEN YEARS Thirteen to nineteen are years of significant and rapid physical, psychological, emotional, and intellectual change. Bandwidth is developing on all bands. Education, socialization, and independence are major aspects of these years. Recall turning thirteen and inheriting the label "teenager." Record your extraordinary or exceptional experiences of those teenage years. Attempt to visualize yourself as you grew and developed through this phase of your life. At this point don't analyze your writing, just record the moments and experiences.

YOUR TWENTIES These years often include major life events: Continued growth and development. Completion of your education. Developing relation-ships, possibly marriage and children. Entry into the job market, or entrepreneurship and career are primary challenges and adventures. Financial responsibility and dreaming collide. Travel, new experiences, exploration, and discovery are common. How are or were you handling risk? What are or were you committed to or passionate about? What do or did you do for fun? Record your extraordinary or exceptional experiences of this decade.

YOUR THIRTIES Accumulation of material posses-sions begins in earnest for many. Transitions are common as people establish families, travel, or change jobs. Hobbies, volunteering, investing, parenting, and new uses of time are common. The divorce rate increases. How is or was your spiritual life? What brings or brought you the greatest joy? What are or were your most valuable learnings? Record your extraordinary or exceptional experiences of this decade.

YOUR FORTIES Halfway through the perceived work life, people often become more fixed and repetitive. Men often go into a state of resignation if they have not achieved their dreams. Women may question their purpose. High-achievers move forward at a faster pace. Children move

Exercise

A journey continued . . .

on to college or establish their own households. Health issues may begin to arise. Have you made enough money to live the way you want? What was your best financial investment? What great relationships do or did you have? What are you doing to continue your growth and development? What are or were your finest moments as a parent? Record your extraordinary or exceptional experiences of this decade

YOUR FIFTIES Something happens to many people when they turn fifty. It could be termed "age shock." Their minds say that they are old. "I don't feel like I am fifty, but I am and that is old. When I was twenty, fifty was really old and now I am fifty." Our mortality is tested as people begin to die at a faster clip. Men face an increasing identity crisis as they lose jobs or make plans to retire. Women's physical aging speeds up. Do you have any grandchildren? Have you given back to society? Have you been acknowledged for your contributions? Record your extraordinary or exceptional experiences of this decade.

YOUR SIXTIES The big "R" (retirement) dominates the mind band. This requires creating a new identity. What to do and where to live in retirement? Are you aware of the origin of sixty-five as a retirement age?

In 1875, when Bismarck was Chancellor of Germany, he established a pension program for people over sixty-five. At that time, life expectancy was approximately forty-five. Retire is defined as "to withdraw from action or danger: retreat; to move back; recede; withdraw from one's position or occupation." Retirement in this sense is not an empowering framework, though people who plan ahead enjoy this decade as they take advantage of their newfound freedom and good health. What has been your experience with retirement? How is it to live your day exactly as you choose? What is it like to be a grandparent? What are you really proud of? Record your extraordinary or exceptional experiences of this decade.

YOUR SEVENTIES These are reflective years. Grandparents are often expected to offer their wisdom and support to the younger generations. What is your life time accomplishment to date? What have you done to stay healthy? What do you choose to do with the rest of your life? Record your extraordinary or exceptional experiences of this decade.

YOUR EIGHTIES & NINETIES What is it that you appreciate about your life? Will you continue to contribute? How will you continue to grow?

Profile: Albert Einstein

Albert Einstein is probably best known for his papers on the nature of light, a proof of atoms, the special theory of relativity and the famous equation of atomic energy: $E=mc2$, which were written and published at the young age of twenty six. This young man was the same child who scarcely talked until the age of three.

A story Einstein liked to tell about his childhood was of a "wonder" he saw when he was four or five years old—a magnetic compass. The needle's invariable northward swing, guided by an invisible force, profoundly impressed him. The compass convinced him that there had to be "something behind things, something deeply hidden."

Even as a small boy, Einstein was thoughtful and self-sufficient. His sister remembers the concentration and perseverance with which he would build multi-storied houses of cards. It's been said Einstein's uncle, an engineer, stimulated his thoughts. Einstein said of himself, "I have no particular talent. I am merely inquisitive. It's not that I'm so smart, it's just I stay with problems longer," and, "I am enough of an artist to draw freely upon my imagination. Knowledge is limited. Imagination encircles the world."

Although he generally earned good grades (and was outstanding in mathematics), Einstein hated the high school he attended in Munich, where success depended on memorization and obedience to arbitrary authority. Much later, he would comment, "It is almost a miracle that modern teaching methods have not yet entirely strangled the holy curiosity of inquiry; for what this delicate plant needs more than anything, besides stimulation, is freedom."

Fortunately for Einstein, his family moved to Italy and he continued his education at a public school in Aarau, Switzerland, where his teachers were humane and his ideas were set free. He graduated and then enrolled in the Swiss Polytechnic Institute in Zurich. Here he recognized that physics was his true passion where he could "seek out the paths that led to the depths." After graduation, he worked as an examiner in the Swiss Patent Office in Zurich, a job that allowed him free time to spend in scientific investigation.

Einstein's persistence and curiosity took him beyond where most people exist. He had a great understanding of human beings and their interconnection in the universe. Einstein said, "A human being is a part of a whole, called by us—universe—a part limited in time and space. He experiences himself, his thoughts and feelings, as something separated from the rest...a kind of optical delusion of his consciousness. This delusion is a kind of prison for us, restricting us to our personal desires and to affection for a few persons nearest to us. Our task must be to free ourselves from this prison by widening our circle of compassion to embrace all living creatures and the whole of nature in its beauty."

Albert Einstein, a theoretical physicist and author of the theory of relativity, received a Nobel Prize in 1921.

This profile was written by Jan Nilsson.

CHAPTER II:
More about the Six Bands of Energy

All feelings are a variation of love or the absence of it.   —Anthony De Mello

Boyle • David Bramson • Ray Brandt • Carl Bretko • Barbara Bretko • Mark Brew • Mike Brillhart • Lynne Brillhart • Betsey Brodahl • Glen Brolander • Eric Brolin • Martha Brolin • June Brolin • Sherwin Brook • John Brooke Jr. • Sam Bross • Bill Broussard • Bob Brown • Helen Brown • Jane Brown • Jeff Brown • Nancy Brown • Tom Brown • Tony Brown • Anne Browne • Jeff Browne • Amy Browne • Bill Bru • Debbie Brewer • Charles Bruning • Bruce Brunsvold • Sven Bryngelsson • Carin Nilsdotter Bryngelson • Jan Buck • Norm Buck • Angelo Bufalino • Henry Bullen • Ed Burke • Leo Burke • Curt Burnett • Paula Burnett • Rita Huss Burns • Ron Busbee • Gus Busing • Don Buse • Sharon Busse • Ross Bushnell • Martha Burmaster • Dick Butkus • Jay Butterbrodt • Bob Byman • Jane Byman • Jane Byrnes • John Byrnes • George Callantine • Don Caldwell • Denny Calderone • Bruce Cameron • Ken Camp • Betty Campbell • Carole Capritta • Barry Cardenal • Hugo Cardona • Ray Carlin • Gerald Carruthers • David Carlson • Evie Caprel • Tom Caprel • Len Carter • Bob Carlson Jr. • Gordie Carlson • Dennis Carlson • Henry Carlson • Ron Carlson • Stanley Carlson • Tilden Carlson • Rollie Carlson • Ronnie Carlson • Lorraine Carlson • Swan Carlson • Ann Carlson • Ruth Carol • Carol Carpenter • Rico Carr • Raymond Carty • Martin Carver • Ruth Carver • Carl Casale • Kathy Cashatt Roberts • Paul Castro • Ted Chabraja • Nick Chabraja • Harry Chaddick • Bill Chandler • Betsy Chandler • Dorothy Chantler • Art Chantler • Alan Chapman • Rick Chapman • Linda Chase • Raymond Chattwell • Vijay Chauhan • Chip Chesemore • Anetta Chester • Robert Chester • Carl Chevedden • Gloria Childs • Larry Chlum • Dohyum Choe • Mark Chona • Teresa Chona • Depak Chopra • Lori Christ • Tom Christ • Donna Christensen • Michael Clark • Paul Clarkson • Connie Clay • Nancy Clemens • Peter Clemens • Margaret Clemmons • Tom Coates • Jim Cocke • Nancy Cocke • Carol Codemo • Rick Coffin • Becky Coffman • Al Cohen • Jerry Cohen • Mike Cohen • Jody Smith-Cohen • Bill Colaric • Cindy Colaric • Bud Cole • Jody Colemen • Tom Coles • Cindy Collins • Lois Conner • Susan Conrad • Bob Connell • Cathy Connell • James Connelly • Mike Connery • Jack Connor • Ralph Conwill • Barbara Cook • Curt Cook • Jan Cook • Mike Cook • Dan Coogan • John Coolidge • Guy Cooper • Marc Cooper • Walter Cordin • Len Costopoulous • Jack Coy • Carey Cotey • Rick Cotey • James Couch • Judy Couch • Michael Cox • Tom Crawford • Martin Creager • Lesley Crews • Mick Crews • Pater Crist • Lee Crittenden • John Crotty • Karen Crotty • Kevin Crowley • Nancy Crowley • Bob Crowley • Jack Cull • Cece Currie • Jim Currie • Ellwood Curtis • John Dahl • Algot Dahlstrand • Harold Dahlstrand • Sigrid Dahlstrand • James Dailey • Richard M. Daley • Richard J. Daley • Cam Danielson • Curtis Danekas • Anderea Danekas • Sally Danielson

THE BANDWIDTH METAPHOR

The sun shines 365 days a year, constantly bathing the earth in energy and light. Yet in most geographic zones, the sun is obscured by clouds a part of the year. The source of energy is still there, but its influence is weakened.

Similarly, there is a source of human energy that shines 365 days a year. Yet people aren't always energetic and creative; their source of vitality is often clouded over.

What is this source of human energy, and what gets in its way, obscuring it from view? What is it that illuminates or diminishes our awareness, vitality, contribution, productivity, and satisfaction?

In Chapter One, I referred to this source of aliveness as expanded bandwidth and listed six bands of human energy. The first step to accessing this source is to recognize that these bands exist, and then to learn something about the nature of each.

When you read the piece about Einstein in Chapter One, what insights did you have about Einstein's bandwidth and his use of it? Curiosity, observation, and simplicity are practices that access and utilize human bandwidth.

The metaphor of bandwidth is used to convey a simple perspective of a complex subject. The six bands of energy are inextricably linked and not easily separated, because in reality they are not separate. Each is an interdependent and subordinate element of the energy field of a human being.

I choose bandwidth since wavelengths, frequencies, or energies are not observable by the unaided human eye, just as the essence of a human being is not clearly observable. Certainly, the bands could be expanded or contracted, but for purposes of this metaphor, I chose to delineate six. To be technically rigorous, energy exists in varying concentrations in sub-fields or patterns. But bands are easier to visualize. The bands are not equal in energy and have distinctive applications depending on the needs of the moment. Each is explored from several perspectives, to help you distinguish, understand, and access your full human bandwidth.

OUR HOLOGRAM OF MATTER AND ENERGY: THE BODY BAND

First and foremost, we are part of the universe, of a cosmic whole, distinguished by a physical body. We are an accumulation and concentration of subatomic particles with a certain mass and density. We are matter, intelligence, and energy.

Structurally, the body is composed of cells. The simplest organisms consist of only one cell, but complex living beings like humans have billions of cells. Our bodies have many extremely specialized groupings of cells. Tissue is a collection of cells that are similar in structure and function. At a higher level, an organ consists of several types of tissues. For example, the heart consists of muscle tissue, nerve tissue and connective tissue. Each life sustaining function is carried out by a group of organs working together as a system. Major organ systems include the circulatory system, digestive system, and reproductive system.

On the cellular level, the body constantly regenerates. The human body can defend itself against hundreds of diseases and can often repair itself after injuries. The inner lining of the stomach is replaced every three to five days, and the entire skeletal structure replaces itself every sixty to ninety days.

At another level, our bodies are a molecular soup—with elements of carbon, hydrogen, nitrogen, oxygen, phosphorous, and sulfur with lesser amounts of calcium, iron, magnesium, potassium, and sodium. Water is our simplest chemical compound, making up approximately 70% of our bodies. Excepting water, all the principal compounds in living beings contain carbon, which forms thousands of small molecules. Most living matter consists of fifty types of carbon molecules and the macromolecules formed by them. These macromolecules are carbohydrates, lipids, proteins, and nucleic acids.

Our bodies are composed of atoms, each of which is composed of a nucleus of protons and neutrons, around which one or more electrons orbit. Imagine a golf ball lying at midfield in a stadium with grains of sand orbiting the golf ball at the outer reaches of the bleachers. This visual image puts into perspective the relative sizes of the nucleus and electrons and the space that makes up an atom. 99.999999% of an atom is empty space. It is the energy of the electron orbiting the nucleus that produces the illusion of matter being solid. Matter is simply vibration. This vibration is detected by our senses, conveyed to the brain, and interpreted by mind.

The human body is an engineering wonder, as fragile as crystal and as durable as steel. Many body parts, such as the heart and kidneys work uninterrupted for an entire lifetime. The body's constant state of transformation is what makes this wonder possible.

As physical beings, we are finite. The body grows, develops, matures, declines, and dies. Average life expectancy in the world today is sixty-six years, ranging from thirty-four years in Sierra Leone (Africa) to eighty years in Japan.

Seeing ourselves as matter underscores the finite nature of our physical form. It also says something about our unity as a species. DNA analysis reveals that all human beings are 99.9 percent the same—a vivid reminder that we are members of the same family.

Body and mind are unified in ways that we don't fully understand. Each person's body and mind stores information about traumas, injuries, insults, memories, joys, fun, excitement, education, and values learned from parents and society. Emerging research into mind-body connections indicates that this biographical data is stored in our cell tissue, and can create or compromise our health and performance. Our attitudes feed, shape, and influence our behavior and our physiology (a phenomenon explored by Caroline Myss in her book, *Anatomy of the Spirit*).

Myss argues that the average person spends 60-70% of his or her life force to manage and hold on to the negative experiences (trauma, loss, resentment, disappointment) of his or her past. Another 10% is spent worrying about, planning for, and trying to control the future, leaving little energy for the present moment or for healing. (It is important to note that it does not drain our energy to maintain positive memories. Even negative memories will not drain our energy if they have been processed and forgiven.)

Pause for a moment to reflect. What negative experiences from the past continue to drain your energy? Jot down your thoughts in your journal.

The body powerfully exemplifies the difference between form and substance. Think of your outer body (your skin, shape, and appearance) as your form in the world; your internal body (organs and systems) as your substance. We are fascinated, disappointed, and preoccupied with our external form and we constantly evaluate others on the basis of appearance. Television, magazines, and advertising exacerbate this tendency. Whole industries related to food, clothing, cosmetics, health care, diet, exercise, and plastic surgery prosper as people in developed countries spend billions annually to fix, reshape, and implant body parts.

Excessive concern with the outer body may explain such things as why so many heart attacks go undetected, why cancer is often in an advanced stage before it is diagnosed, and why so few people over age forty take an annual physical exam. We tend to take our physical functionality for granted, especially when we are young, assuming that our lungs will provide us with breath and that our hearts will continue to beat indefinitely.

Most of us would do well to balance our body awareness by focusing more on substance—the vitality of our inner body, and less on form. The inner body is much more than an interdependent network of invisible organs; it is a house of miracles that we rarely honor.

> **On a daily basis, the average American**
>
> ingests 1.4 kilograms of food and 2 liters of liquid.
>
> pumps 7,200 liters of blood.
>
> consumes 3,600 liters of oxygen.

OUR ANTENNAE : THE SENSORY BANDS

Senses are the antennae of the brain and our emotions. Consider the speed, efficiency, and variety of the senses. Hearing takes place considerably faster than speaking, seeing is faster than hearing. Although most scientists would tell us there are five senses, others would argue there are twenty-five or more.

The olfactory gland, responsible for our sense of smell, is the most used and least developed sense. Through this gland, the brain receives messages about odors in the environment. Scents have been used throughout history to warn, please, manipulate, and seduce. Smells can also generate intuitive insights. For example, your olfactory gland plays a part in your experience of tension or excitement in a room or when you can "smell trouble."

Close your eyes for five seconds and envision the place in which you're sitting. Then open your eyes and look around. Notice all of the additional information your opened eyes are passing to the brain. Become aware of how adding more stimuli requires more energy.

The Information Age has inundated us with data to analyze, leading us to spend more time thinking than sensing. Culturally, we are predisposed to favor analytical skills over sensory skills. So, when we do notice what we see, hear, taste, smell, or touch (how many times have you been oblivious to the flowers blooming or the food you were eating?), we spend our time interpreting our impressions and creating abstract ideas.

We under-use our senses. Most people see and hear indirectly—through their minds, not their senses. This invisible phenomenon significantly impedes communication. Perceptions are generated by the mind/sense connection, and stored in the mind. Perception then becomes "reality" when, in fact, it is only an interpretation of one moment in time. "Reality" is purely an extension of the mind.

As a way to gain insight into the blending of the mind and senses, imagine you're walking down a crowded city street at lunchtime. What is your first form of connecting with people who pass you? For most of us, it is our eyes.

Physiologically, a simultaneous flow of activities occurs in a fraction of a second. The visual cortex is stimulated; neuropeptides activate the central nervous system; the carotid artery expands to provide additional blood and oxygenation for the brain; and that is just the beginning of a visual experience.

What occurs in the next nanosecond? Without any effort or conscious action, we automatically evaluate, judge, and generate an opinion of the person we just saw. Our visual impression is immediately overlaid with an interpretation.

In that moment, we unconsciously blur our senses and our mind. Our minds categorize people, reducing them to a single sentence or simple description. Our view is almost instantly limited by our mind's conclusions, which are at best woefully incomplete and at worst grossly inaccurate.

After generating our opinions, we choose to either acknowledge or ignore the other person. If we know him or her, we may stop and talk. If we don't, we go on our way. In a few seconds, we move thorough a process that begins with our senses, moves quickly into our minds, and results in bodily action. Imagine how many times in a day this pattern is repeated!

When we learn to distinguish the senses from the mind, we can intervene in this process. We can go beyond the mind's stereotypes. We can stop putting limits on people. We can generate more complete and accurate mental files about others. How? Simply by staying in the sensory phase longer, observing what we are doing.

When we are in the PRESENT MOMENT—whether it be with a stranger or a loved one—we can focus on what we see them doing and what we hear them saying right here, right now. Their actions and words in this moment may contradict all our opinions about them! We can stop reacting to our historical opinions and interpretations. We can leave our comfort zones, and release our desire to avoid embarrassment, to be right, and to be in control. We can allow others to become real, three-dimensional, energetic, creative, and to change and grow. In these moments, we increase our bandwidth.

Close your eyes, insert your index fingers into your ears, and walk around your house or apartment. Then sit down for several minutes and appreciate your senses.

OUR FEELING GUIDE: THE EMOTION BAND

Emotions are energy in motion—e-motion—to which we attach labels like joy, sorrow, fear, and anger. In general, they are our bodies' reaction to our minds. The mind produces thoughts and memories which in turn produce fluctuations in the body's energy field in the form of physical sensations. Pressure, pulse and respiratory changes, pain, and relaxation are examples. Occasionally, emotions trigger the brain and mind. During emergencies, for example, the emotional response releases chemicals in the brain which direct the body's appropriate response.

Dr. Candace Pert, a noted neurobiologist, confirmed the mind-emotions-body connection in her research. She stated that, "Your mind is in every cell of your body . . . **The chemicals that mediate emotion and the receptors for those chemicals are found in almost every cell of the body.**" Neuropeptides, which are triggered and released from the brain by emotions, become part of our cellular structure. Therefore, emotions are images and thoughts occurring in the mind which are converted into matter and stored in the body.

As infants, emotions were our initial form of communication. They precede language and are authentic expressions of sensations. When infants and small children express their emotions, parents often don't understand what's being communicated. They may respond with, "tell me where it hurts," "stop crying," or "that's enough now." This gap, between the emotional expression of a child and the intellectual response of an adult, is usually created by the adult. Adults rarely communicate on the emotions channel while it is the primary channel of infants and small children.

Children are often disciplined for acting out their feelings. Over time, they learn to control themselves (read: shut down their emotional expression.) The programming for girls is different from that of boys, but both get clear messages about what is and isn't appropriate.

Girls are taught to be "nice." Consequently, many find it difficult to stand up for themselves or to pursue what they want without being labeled as difficult or overbearing. While society grants women permission to more freely express certain emotions, "emotional" women are considered to be illogical, incoherent, irrational, and less capable than men. This "emotionalism" is construed as a detriment.

Young boys are taught to be tough, and in particular, to "stop crying." Emotional displays are perceived as a crack in the armor. This remains true even though great speeches are often memorable solely because a man's voice was cracking or he was visibly and valiantly holding back tears.

Suppressed emotions are stored in the body, as Dr. Pert's research demonstrated, shedding light on the term "emotional baggage." Health and relationship problems often result. Suppressed and negative emotions are correlated with obesity, stress, heart attacks, cancer, and other illnesses, and they also frequently generate misunderstandings between people.

When emotions are not acknowledged and addressed, real communication suffers. Situations like performance evaluations, tests, sudden changes, or unexpected layoffs can cause emotions (especially fear) to run high. Disregarding customers' emotions can be disastrous. Merely handling a complaint may not address the real issue. Listening for the emotional message beneath the complaint makes it more likely that the true problem will be solved.

No emotion needs to be destructive. We can learn to experience, express, manage, and even constructively use our full band of emotion. Our emotions often contain the seeds of intuition or valuable insight. *"My gut was telling me to get a second opinion about the roof repair." "I knew your father was the man for me the moment I saw him thirty-two years ago."*

Emotions can tell us when we are in sync with our values and integrity, the extent to which we agree or disagree with others, whether we are likely to enjoy a prospective activity or outing. Our conscience often makes itself felt through our emotions.

The goods news is we can reconnect with our emotions. We have the capacity to experience sensations in our bodies and express them appropriately. Meditation and other spiritual practices are valuable in part for their ability to cultivate "feeling states" such as empathy and compassion. These practices also help us respond skillfully to emotions such as grief, fear, and anger.

When I feel a rush of emotion, I think of it as my spirit peeking through. Recently, my youngest daughter graduated from high school. As I watched her and her friends walk across the stage to get their diplomas, a wellspring of emotion rose within me. These were the kids I had coached in sports when they were six years old. The impulse to cry on such occasions is, to me, a spiritual impulse.

OUR COORDINATION CENTER: THE BRAIN BAND

The brain is the master coordination center of the body, the synthesizer of human bandwidth. In the PRESENT MOMENT, the brain receives sensory information regarding conditions inside and outside of the body. It processes these inputs and returns messages to all effected areas of the body, stimulating appropriate responses.

Human brain activity is incredibly swift and complex, involving between ten and one hundred billion neurons. Each neuron consists of a cell body and a number of tube-like fibers. Electrical signals are transmitted by chemical reactions from cell to cell along neurological pathways. These pathways receive, process, store, and retrieve the information that makes it possible for us to live—to see, hear, think, feel, move, and breathe.

The brain is the coordinator and integrator of all six bands of human energy and intelligence. For example, the emotional band is located in the cerebral cortex. Emotions are provoked or produced by a message from sense organs or from the neocortex, which is the seat of our intellectual capacities.

The main control centers for body processes are in the brain stem, regulating functions such as breathing, heartbeat, blood flow, swallowing, and the movement of the stomach and intestines.

The cerebellum coordinates muscle movements. When motor activity is called for, for instance moving spoon to mouth, impulses inform the cerebellum of how the action is being carried out. The cerebellum compares the movement with the intended movement and signals back necessary corrections. In this way, the cerebellum ensures that the body moves smoothly and efficiently.

There may also be an area in the cerebral cortex that serves as a connection to one's inner world and to the band of spirit. In 1983, Howard Gardner, a Harvard psychologist, proposed a model of multiple intelligences, with one kind of intelligence defined as the ability to know one's inner world.

Finally, there is the mind-brain connection. I have intentionally separated mind and brain, though future medical research may disprove this separation. However, today scientists know little about the mind and its principal capabilities of thought production, memory, analysis, organization, and planning. What is known is the substantial conjoint functioning between mind and brain. The mind and the brain often act in concert in processes such as analysis or thinking. Research by Sir John Eccles, a Nobel Laureate, showed that the brain acts as a receptor for energy patterns housed in the mind, which exist as awareness expressed as thoughts or insights.

A few additional points of interest:
- A newborn infant's brain weighs less than one pound and reaches its full weight of three pounds at age six.
- The vast majority of brain cells are present at birth and grow and develop during these six years. During this period, a human being learns and develops at its fastest rate.
- The human brain represents less than 2% of total body weight of an average adult, yet it consumes approximately 20% of the oxygen used by the entire body when at rest.

Based on my own experiences and the teachings of dozens of people from various disciplines, a powerful distinction is established when mind and brain are viewed as separate bands. The brain is the coordinator of conscious and unconscious activity, while the mind is the center of memory, problem solving, and analysis. **The brain always functions in the PRESENT MOMENT, while the mind almost always exists in thoughts about the past or future.**

If you should argue that the mind is a function of the brain, or parts of it, I will concede the point. What's important is to experience, examine, and investigate the various elements of your bandwidth. Intellectual understanding is a distant second to this experiential knowing.

Take a break from your reading to turn on some music. Get up and dance for at least thirty seconds. Dancing involves the brain, the emotions, and the body—a wonderful example of integrated bandwidth. Strenuous exercise is similar, integrating bandwidth simply and effectively.

OUR INTERNAL MONOLOGUE: THE MIND BAND

A continuing mystery to most scientists, physicians, and psychologists, the mind defies a single definition that is acceptable to all authorities. Medical research has yielded limited information on the chemical basis of the mind. Neurologists commonly hold to the view that the mind is on a plane above the brain and below spirit, given its higher reasoning and functioning capacities. Dr. Candace Pert, mentioned above, describes the mind as "some kind of enlivening energy in the information realm, throughout the brain and body, that enables the cells to talk to each other, and the outside to talk to the whole organism."

According to *Webster's Collegiate Dictionary*, **mind** equates with "recollection; memory; opinion; view; remind; remember; mood." The *American Heritage Dictionary* lists synonyms like intellect, intelligence, wit, reasoning, thinking, acquiring and applying knowledge, perception, memory, and decision.

These synonyms provide a starting point for our consideration of mind. **The human mind is first and foremost a "thought factory"**—producing up to 40,000 thoughts in a twenty-four-hour period. **This involuntary flow of thoughts is the noise or "little voice" endlessly speaking in the background of our minds.** This background chatter increases as we get older. Some neurologists estimate that 80% of thoughts are repetitive, random, historical, and—useless.

We spend a huge amount of time reacting to "our internal monologue." This monologue continues day and night, periodically interrupted and triggered by external stimuli. Our minds constantly conjure up stories, memories, judgments, comparisons, opinions, fears, and desires in response to our thoughts themselves or what is going on outside of us. (It also has a tendency to "cut and paste," selectively focusing on thoughts and experiences that reinforce our world views, leaving us with memories that are only partially accurate.)

When conversing with others, our internal monologues will often, but not always, shift to the content of those conversations and may slow down temporarily. More often than not, though, our mind chatter gets in the way of listening fully and being present. Our little voices either argue with what is being said or rehearse our responses. We spend a lot of time "listening with our answers running."

When we are in difficult, stressful, or uncomfortable situations, like getting ready for a trip, preparing for a test, or planning a presentation, our internal monologues kick into overdrive. They create or exacerbate anxiety, tension, and stress.

Sometimes the mind will replay a piece of history, triggering emotions in the body. Thoughts actually create disturbances in our physical bodies, demonstrating the interdependency between bands of energy. A phone call from a former spouse, for instance, can cause a tremendous mood swing. Returning to the scene of an accident or crime can do the same. So can seeing someone you don't like. These chain reactions all begin with the mind but quickly move through other bands of energy.

We unconsciously give most of our attention to, and are heavily influenced by, our internal voices, to the exclusion of almost everything else. The mind's perpetual "stream of consciousness" chatter

and the way we unconsciously listen to it, seem to be fundamental to human nature. Much mental energy is directed to our unconscious minds (our little voices or mind chatter or internal monologue) and particularly to past traumatic events.

The unconscious mind creates ongoing interference and distraction, constantly taking us away from the PRESENT MOMENT. It can drain our energy and prevent us from taking action. Even so, few people are aware of their inner monologues.

Don't jump to the conclusion that the mind is bad; it is not. Though the mind can be wasteful or even destructive (How many healthy risks have you talked yourself out of taking? How many unhealthy risks have you talked yourself into?), the mind has tremendous value and capacity when properly used.

It is possible to gain a measure of freedom from this internal monologue by learning to consciously observe it. This is what the Buddhists call "mindfulness." It is possible, even, to harness the internal voice in service of one's goals.

Start noticing your thoughts. For instance, when you first meet someone, notice how your internal voice immediately begins generating labels. *"Short." "Too much make-up." "Nice." "Preppy." "Stuffy." "Scratchy voice—probably a smoker." "Great smile." "Big diamond—money." "Suit," "Jeans,"* etc., etc., etc. Watch your mind compare and contrast, agree or disagree, adopt or dismiss, virtually everything someone else has to say. *"I know that." "He's out to lunch." "That can't be right." "Who made her princess for the day?"*

Also notice your high-volume thoughts, those images and words that tend to occur over and over again. *"I'm late," " I don't like...," "There's not enough...,"* are common high-volume thoughts. Be aware of your first thought of the day. When do you have it and what is it? These observations will bring your internal monologue into your consciousness.

As you become more intimate with your internal monologue, you can start making choices about how you want to use your mind. For example, you can become aware of where your thoughts exist in time: in memories of the past; in predictions of or planning for the future; or in events taking place in the PRESENT MOMENT. Once you've raised your awareness about this, you can choose where to place your attention. You can be more deliberate about focusing on the past or the future. And, you can choose to dwell more in the PRESENT MOMENT.

Conscious use of your mind is the key. You are either using your mind or it is using you. Conscious repetitive thoughts such as *"I can and I will"* will make a positive difference in your life. Unconscious thoughts such *"I can't"* or *"I am not worthy"* are destructive over time.

Close your eyes and sit quietly. Start to notice your in-breath and out-breath. Then notice the thoughts which come into and leave your mind. This goes on 24/7 and is your internal monologue.

OUR INFINITE CAPACITY: THE SPIRIT BAND

Spirit: an "animating or vital principle held to give life to physical organisms." Spirit is synonymous with being, energy, essence, heart, and soul. Human beings vary dramatically in physical appearance, personality, roles, problems, goals, and accomplishments. Yet people do share a common denominator, one that lies in their ability to naturally connect and align with all other human beings. The common denominator is spirit, and we can learn to access it.

If you were ever in a car accident, you may have noticed something occurring in your consciousness right before and during the crash. In the second or two before impact, time slows down or even stops. Everything in the environment becomes clear and distinct—the other car, the people in the car, details of the location, the moment of impact, and the noise, flying objects, bending metal, smells, and physical sensations.

Life-threatening events as well as "peak experiences"—arriving at the summit of a mountain, completing a marathon, having a baby—generate intense awareness of everything in and around us. Such experiences are essentially spiritual, lying beyond time and comprehension.

Spirit continually manifests in the form of love, caring, sharing, deep connection, insight, trust, clarity, and courage. It is both mystical and practical. It is the space of our connection to God, Buddha, or whatever name you give to the Divine. It is transparent one moment, visible the next. Spirit is only and always in the PRESENT MOMENT, waiting to be unleashed as the substance of life.

We need to make a key distinction at this point between spirituality and religion. As used in this book, the word spirit does not refer to any system of beliefs or practice of worship. Instead, spirit refers to our essence—who we are as distinct from our mind, body, senses, brain, and emotions. Spirit is essence or being. It is the ability to rise above ordinary limits and experiences.

Sports, performing arts, painting, writing, and creativity offer us opportunities for peak awareness, times that we can be "in the zone." On these occasions, when time disappears, we experience the infinite nature of the PRESENT MOMENT.

Spirit is accessed through awareness. Awareness is defined as "having or showing realization, perception, or knowledge; cognizant; conscious; sensible; alive; vigilance in observing."

Awareness is a phenomenon. It is an internal impression of what is actually occurring in the PRESENT MOMENT. It cannot be thought, analyzed, or intuited. Spirit is a very high state of awareness. The unconscious mind is a low state of awareness.

Awareness can only occur in the PRESENT MOMENT, and the act of being aware is a means of distinguishing mind from spirit. Spirit exists in the infinite PRESENT MOMENT, whereas mind exists mainly in past memory and future projection.

Conscious breathing, silence, meditation, attention, and focus are practices that reveal and enhance awareness. Whenever we are able to silence our minds and be in the moment, we increase our awareness of and gain access to the core of our beings. Living from awareness, from spirit, allows us to engage in experiences that may promote our growth and creativity. Living from spirit often takes courage and practice because it requires suspension of the old and familiar— the mind—which is limited by experience and can only modify ideas from the past.

Go outside and look up at the sky. Feel the wind and sun and smell the odors in the air. Notice your heartbeat and breath and let your whole body become still. Continue breathing and let go of thoughts as they come in your head. Just be in the silence.

THE PHYSICS OF AWARENESS

Based on my readings of Einstein and Niels Bohr, various lectures, and discussions with other physicists, there is a common belief that the Universe is infinite and eternal. There is no known beginning and no predictable end. There is consensus that the Universe is constantly expanding.

The Universe exists in the PRESENT MOMENT, as does our connection to it. Access to our infinite and eternal capacity of spirit is also in the PRESENT MOMENT, where we are connected to all that is. "I am one with everything" expresses that connection.

Being present to pure potential and possibility is a state in which ordinary people become extraordinary. Here is where people can instantly expand into their basic human capacities.

The following paragraphs provide further insight into awareness. I have combined the scientific perspectives of physicists, my own experiences, and the practical input of Thaddeus Golas, author of *The Lazy Man's Guide to Enlightenment.*

Human beings constantly expand and contract their awareness of thoughts, feelings, sensations, and experiences, usually unconsciously. When we choose to consciously respond, we can access a broader range of possibilities. A certain willingness is called for here, to overcome our automatic avoidance of things we may construe as negative or scary. (This is not to say that we should act on every idea or emotion that enters our consciousness.)

The state of expansion or higher awareness has taken on various names throughout human history: enlightenment, liberation, salvation, and many more. Spirit is the ultimate state of expansion.

Words that evoke expansion include:

Share	In the moment	Joyful
Give	In the flow	Peaceful
Connect	In the groove	Happy
Contribute	Experiential	Imaginative
Feel	Open-hearted	Grow
Empathic	Wise	Create
Releasing	Clear	Learn
Productive	Compassionate	Listen
Free	Tuned in	Trust
Healthy	Generous	Care
Expressive	Patient	Reach
Aware		

AWARENESS vs. INTELLECTUAL DEVELOPMENT

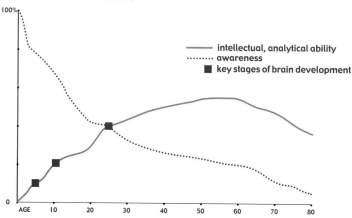

----- intellectual, analytical ability
.... awareness
■ key stages of brain development

The previous graphic compares human awareness to key stages of brain development and growth of intellect. It demonstrates how our intellect often develops at the expense of our capacity to be aware. As we age, we dwell more in the mind and less in the PRESENT MOMENT.

Another term for expanded awareness is love, a state of oneness with all people and creation. In this state of oneness, we naturally love others and ourselves. We feel no need to be loved because we know that we are love. Imagine that!

In contrast, when we contract, we resist certain thoughts and feelings. Suppressing these internal experiences drains our energy and limits our possibilities to create new insights and actions. Unconscious use of the mind, or being used by your mind, is the principal context for contraction.

Words that embody contraction include:

Tuned out	Ill	Disinterested
Isolated	Arrogant	Trapped in the mind
Unwilling	Disengaged	Compromised
Repetitive	Rejecting	Cynical
Habitual	Resisting	Prejudiced
Historical	Avoiding	Deceitful
Regretful	Uncaring	Vindictive
Needy	Distrustful	Dogmatic
Angry	Depressed	Resigned
Hateful	Stuck	Distant
Afraid	Addicted	Closed
Shallow	Impatient	Selfish

Space, mass, and energy

Depending on our relative levels of expansion or contraction, we fluctuate between states of space, mass, or energy.

In our fully expanded state of awareness, we are space. This is the highest level of human existence, where we release all our thoughts about the past and the future. We release our interpretations and opinions. We release our attachments and fixed ideas about who we are—our personal and professional identities. In essence, we are nothing. Ironically the source of creativity is the willingness to dwell in nothingness. Here we are free from all self-limiting thoughts, free to think or feel anything. Exceptional people have frequent access to this state of being.

Now take a few minutes to dwell on the notion of awareness expanded to space—to a state of nothingness. Open yourself to the possible benefits of this strange—sounding idea.

When our awareness contracts, we become mass. Awareness ebbs and flows. At its lowest, it congeals into a near solid. We are shut down, tuned out, disengaged. Our consciousness may shrink back if we are attacked, chastised, judged, or disempowered. When we feel embarrassed or criticized, when we fail or give up, our energy can be zapped. We feel heavy, literally weighed down—a state of increased mass.

Most traumatized, victimized, or abused people will contract their awareness to some extent in reaction to events. Most illness is ultimately a state of contraction, sometimes exacerbated by fear of the illness itself. Life force often flows at a very low level in people who are fearful, physically sick, or mentally ill. In this state, it is difficult to release unpleasant thoughts and feelings. Bandwidth is constricted.

Between pure space and pure mass are infinite levels of being. We are dynamic. We can be anywhere on the spectrum at any time, and we may shift levels from moment to moment. **When shifting between states of expansion and contraction, we are energy.**

Energy has an obvious range of high to low and, not so obvious, multiple dimensions. During the course of a day, we naturally move through different levels of energy. Sleeping restores energy. Physical activity uses it. Passion and excitement give us energy. Loving or supporting another gives him energy. Discouraging or disempowering people zaps our energy. Pep rallies generate positive collective energy. Angry protests or strikes generate negative collective energy. Fear is negative energy. Caring is positive energy.

A visual summary of the notions of space, mass and energy.

EXPANSION
space (spirit)

energy
(senses • brain
emotions • body)

Contraction
mass (mind)

EXPANSION OR CONTRACTION?

As children, we had unlimited energy to expand our awareness. Infants are not taught to cry, to crawl, or to use their senses. They naturally, effortlessly, and spontaneously experience these capacities.

As we age, contraction sets in. We begin to go inward, to dwell in our mind, and perhaps even to become trapped there. But at any time we can choose to expand again, to reawaken to what is occurring inside and outside of us. We can connect more often and more deeply with everyone and everything, expanding our energy to the level of space. **This shift from** contraction to expansion is transformational, occurring in a second.

We are not mechanical human "doings"—we are human "beings." We can selectively and purposefully create our world. We can stop reacting to the thoughts that dominate our historical mind. We can spontaneously choose to let our energy flow on all levels. And we can make these choices instantly, outside of time—before thinking or taking any visible action.

How we choose to use our energy determines our day-to-day living. Most people divert their energy to the past, managing or even feeding unresolved issues, regrets, problems, and traumas. Since 9/11/01, much energy has been diverted into the future in the form of anxiety, fear, and worry about additional terrorists acts. Thus, little energy is left for the PRESENT MOMENT. Diverting our energy to past or future often results in contraction.

As we become aware of the simultaneous, interconnected existence of our mind, body, brain, senses, emotion, and spirit, we access our full bandwidth. Each band may be expanded or contracted in accordance with our intentions. To be awake is all that is required.

Exercise

Observe your states of space, mass, and energy

Start to notice your energy fluctuations. Then observe other people's energy. Jot down the names of people who give you energy and how they do so. Note the names of those who drain your energy and how they do that. (The same names may be on both lists!) Write about how you give or absorb other people's energy. Recall thoughts and physical sensations associated with your experience of the states of space, mass, and energy.

BANDWIDTH IS THE
SYNTHESIS OF ALL THE BANDS

Several examples will illustrate the interdependency and interaction of the bands during some experience. Each experience could occur in less than one second, simultaneously rather than sequentially.

You notice a geographic landmark which sparks a memory.

You hear a familiar voice on the phone.

You see a stranger.

Driving through an intersection, you notice the traffic light turn red.

A brick falls from a building, almost hitting you.

You get an insight.

You pray.

41

# Exercise

Take a Bandwidth Inventory

These questions are designed to offer a taste of each band of energy. Please record your responses to this exercise in a separate journal.

For the next fifteen minutes, reflect on your use of your body, brain, mind, senses, emotions, and spirit bands by answering the following groups of questions. Then, estimate how much of each day you spend focused on each band, and what percentage of each band's capacity you use in a typical day.

BODY BANDWIDTH: *Have you noticed any changes in your overall health and energy level over the last year? The last month? The last week? If so, what are these changes? Is your immune system strong? Is your stamina high or low? Are your muscles strong or weak? Do your bodily systems (i.e. respiration, digestion, blood pressure, etc.) function well?*

BRAIN BANDWIDTH: *Do you ever notice or observe yourself walking, running, peeling an orange, or threading a needle? Notice the perfect coordination of the neuromuscular and central nervous systems acting in concert to make each action and movement fluid by doing these movements in slow motion. Observe your breathing, swallowing, and eating.*

MIND BANDWIDTH: *Sit quietly for one minute and observe the parade of thoughts flowing through your mind. Notice the judgments, evaluations, opinions, and interpretations of your mind. Try writing them down. Watch yourself planning. Notice the thoughts that stimulate anxiety. Notice the thoughts that bring you peace.*

SENSORY BANDWIDTH: *What were the first sights and sounds you noticed as you awakened today? Do you feel your body sitting in a chair? Do you notice your feet touching the ground? What's your favorite smell? When do you notice the arrival of Spring?*

EMOTIONAL BANDWIDTH: *Are you able to experience strong emotions such as fear or anger without trying to repress them or act on them automatically? Describe the physical sensations and mental images that you typically experience with strong emotions. Name a time when you were moved by a piece of music or art or a scene.*

SPIRITUAL BANDWIDTH: *Have you ever had experiences where time stopped or disappeared? Where your attention focused on the present moment without any reference to past or future? Have you ever experienced a sense of joy or completeness that seemed independent of your current circumstances? Have you ever felt inexplicably connected to another or nature or music or . . . ? Describe any such experiences in detail.*

NOTICE: *This exercise is for your benefit. It is intended to give you direct experience of your six bands of energy—your full human bandwidth. Distinguishing and experiencing each band is the first step in discovering your basic human capacities. Please complete this exercise before reading Chapter Three.*

Exercise

Take a look in the mirror

This exercise will allow you to become aware of yourself—specifically, your self-judgments. (For a more detailed version of this practice, see the section on self-reflection in Chapter 11.)

STEP 1: To begin, simply look at yourself in a mirror. What are the first thoughts that come in to your mind? Speak these thoughts out loud, no matter what they are. Keep speaking your thoughts for at least two minutes as you continue looking in the mirror. Observe the activity of your mind band. Many people who do this exercise find that they've plugged into a stream of thought that offers constant self-criticism (I'm too fat. . . . I look old. . . . I can't stand to look at myself. . . .)

STEP 2: This time, as you look in the mirror, con-sciously choose about how to use your mind. State out loud what you like about yourself. It's ok if you need to think between statements. Most of us are not accustomed to speaking our positive self-judgments. Do this for at least two minutes.

STEP 3: Finally, look into mirror and just be silent for a minute or two. Notice your breathing, and release any thoughts that arise. See if you can get in touch with bands of energy other than your mind, such as your senses, spirit, emotions, and body. Take a few moments to simply embrace the human being you see.

VARIATION: You can also experiment with putting other people "in the mirror." Create a vivid mental image of a key person in your life (or tape a picture to the mirror.) Then, speak or write the first thoughts that come to mind about this person. Notice the role of these thoughts in connecting or disconnecting with the person. Then repeat steps 2 and 3. Notice your sense of the person after you've completed the exercise.

Profile: Caroline Myss

Imagine that you have a hundred circuits of life-force energy coming into the top of your head. This life force is the pulsating energy behind cell mutation and division, behind the heartbeat, behind the functioning of the body. This electromagnetic energy is also the energy that you invest into memories, thoughts, and attitudes — into your history.

When I do a reading on somebody, I go after where you've invested those circuits; I go after every investment you have that is not in present time. I begin to pull your traumatic memories, your negative attitudes and self-image. So I'm looking at your biography. These are the biographical events that leave biological debt factors.

Imagine that, when you get up in the morning, you have a hundred dollars' worth of energy coming in. And you have a memory that's costing you sixty dollars a day to finance, and an attitude that's costing you twenty-five dollars a day. By the time you're done, you've got three bucks left over to manage your biography today!

What I recognized is that your biography becomes your biology--you are one and the same with your life and your history. Events that you have not yet reconciled, haven't forgiven, and haven't let go of, are carried as that debt in your cell tissue.

Does that mean we create our own illnesses? No Instead, it's much better to say that we influence our health. That is certainly true. Do we create it? No, we haven't got that kind of power. But we certainly do have an influential factor.

Another way to say it is that we're learning how incredibly empowered we are, how powerful every one of our thoughts is, how powerful every one of our attitudes is.

The language we're familiar with says, 'We have to become more responsible.' That's true, but that word doesn't hold it completely enough; it's not a big enough word to embrace the fact that we're becoming conscious of how multi-dimensional we are, how much power we are managing right through our system, and that we are actively participating in the health of every single one of our cell tissues by the thought forms that we hold in our head.

I tell this to people who are at a choice point. This is probably the most difficult thing for people to get, because they think there is such a thing as a right or a wrong choice. In truth, what the gods are really looking at is the energy with which we make the decision we do.

That's the determining factor. So whether or not I choose the right or the left door is, quite frankly, in the Buddhist l anguage, illusion. What matters is what motivated me to choose, and that's what will end up (being important). Then I'll discover what is behind the door. So I tell all my students, "Take the riskiest path that you can find." What looks like the safe path is illusion. What looks like a risk is illusion.

Take the riskiest path you can find; keep your attention in the present time; carry no extraneous baggage; forgive everybody you can possibly think of; pray daily; just manage your spirit with integrity, and keep your honor code between you and God.

Caroline Myss worked as a journalist and book publisher before becoming a medical intuitive. She is a popular international/workshop leader/lecturer and author of several books, including Anatomy of the Spirit. and Why People Don't Heal and How They Can. This passage is excerpted from a radio interview by Michael Toms, aired on the nationally syndicated public radio series, "New Dimensions". It is enti-tled Healing with Spirit and is program # H411. The program in its entirety may be ordered from the website, www.newdimensions.org and is published in full at www.myss.com.

CHAPTER III:
Influences on Bandwidth

It is good to have an end to journey toward; but it is the journey that matters in the end.
~Ursula Le Guin

• Tony Danielson • Tait Danielson • Monica Davenport • Carole David • Larry David • Rob Davis • Brooke Davis • Ailen Davis • Kenny Davis • Marsha Dawson • Susan Debolt • Yvonne Decker • Pat DeBonnet • Betsi DeFrates • Troy DeFrates • Kim Dennis • Al DeSimone • Ed Detgen • Jane Detgen • Betsy Detgen • Molly Detgen • Charlie Deull • Mildred Deutschmann • Jane Deutschmann • Rudy Deutschmann • Rudy Deutschmann, Sr. • Rick Devleeshower • Linda DeVries • Chuck Di Francesca • Ann Di Francesca • Cliff Di Lorenzo • John Dickey • Terri Dickey • Amy Dickinson • Sherry Dickholtz • Jo Ann Digman • Leo Dignan • Ingrid Dilley • Tom Dinwiddie • Agnes Dister • Justine Ditch • Bruce Dittman • Patti Dittman • Char Dittman • Ben Dittman • Diane Divall • Bill Dixon • Harry Dixon • Peter Dolan • Arnold Donald • Hazel Donald • Pat Donegan • Agnes Donohue • Barbara Donohue • Brendan Donovan • Dr. Bop • John Dragon • Bill Drevant • Beth Drost • George Drost • Tom Drucker • James Drury • John Duax • Phil Duke • Skip Duhlstine • Bruce Duncan • Michael Duncan • Judy Durham • Steve Durien • Andrew Durot • Mary Ann Duffy • Michael Durot • Jennifer Durot • George Durot • Rob Durot • Ann Durot • Brian Dupuis • Carol Dupuis • Chris Dwyer • Bud Dykstra • Sue Ebert • Tom Ebert • Buddy Ebsen • Dale Eck • Mark Eck • Scott Edelstein • Gary Egger • John Eggert • Ellen Eisner • Tom Eisner • Peter Ekblad • Jack Ekstrom • Gordon Ellingsworth • Dave Ellis • Jill Elsdon • Enarsson Anders • Rangella Andersdotter Anders • Stu Edwards • Sue Edwards • Paul Ellis • Marylin Ellis • Sue Eisenbarth • John Enneking • Michelle Erdman • Werner Erhard • Diana Epstein • Ed Erickson • Fred Erler • Ellana Erler • George Ewasko • Julie Eyres • Harry Faust • Herb Feldman • Shelia Feldman • Maureen Ferg • Bill Ferguson • John Ferguson • Sue Ferguson • Mary Ann Ferry • Marvin Field • Ron Field • Elliott Fiedler • Harry Fink • Barb Fischer • Burney Fischer • Terry Fischer • Sarah Fischer • Art Fitzgerald • Art Flanagan • Fred Floberg • Fernando Flores • Ed Flowers • John Fogleman • Jeff Ford • Laurie Ford • Jeannie Forloine • Donna Fortney • Fred Fortney • Don Fortunato • Lynne Fortunato • Don Fortunato Jr. • Joe Fortunato • Maggie Fox • Nancy Fox • Gary Francis • Evelyn Francis • Dennis Francis • Roya Francis • Bud Franklin • Bob Franson • Ragnar Franson • Alain Frecon • Leslie Frecon • Bill Freistat • Steve Frels • Tom Frey • Shelly Friedstein • Art Firgo • Judy Frigo • Fred Frish • Ron Friske • Bill Fritz • Alan Fry • Nancy Fry • Robert Fuqua • Jane Fuqua • Anne Fuqua • Jon Gabrielsson • Elsa Jakobsdotter Gabrielsson • Doug Gage • Nancy Gahl • Tom Gahl • Nick Gahl • Chris Gahl • James Galley • Ted Gamble • Carol Gard • John Gard • Mark Garfien • Bob Garman • Dick Garrigan • Joe Gorski • Chuck Gately • Barbara Gately • John Gault • Willie Gault • Barbara Gazzolo • Francis Gazzolo • Bob Gbur • Olga Gbur • Andy Gbur

BANDWIDTH IS PRESENT BEFORE BIRTH

The body is the dominant band during the nine months of gestation. While brain, mind, emotions, senses, and spirit are not visible through an ultrasound examination, their development begins as well. People become curious about size, length, weight, and gender. ("That looks like a big baby!") Little, if any, conversation is about the baby's other basic human capacities.

Birth, from the child's perspective, is almost certainly traumatic. After spending one's whole life in the warmth and comfort of the womb, imagine the shock of being thrust into the bright lights and loud noises of a delivery room. Imagine those first few stinging breaths of air, as the lungs are forced to expand. The doctor cuts the umbilical cord and the old life support system is gone.

Yet, a child's capacities are highly developed and engaged in the moments following birth. A baby only hours old can distinguish the scent of his mother's breast milk from that of another woman's. The new baby readily communicates her feelings of contentment or distress, demonstrating broad emotional bandwidth. The brain supports the baby immediately, initiating and regulating breathing, eating, digestion, elimination, and other bodily functions formerly carried out by the placenta.

The newborn's brain (12 to 15% of total body weight compared to less than 2% in adults) and central nervous system develop rapidly. They quickly move from rolling to sitting to crawling to standing to walking, typically by the twelfth or thirteenth month. The concurrent development of body, brain, senses, and emotions is striking.

BANDWIDTH DEVELOPS RAPIDLY

From birth to age five, children experience their most rapid development and learning. They begin to sense danger, explore, listen, and speak. There is a purity to their explorations, speaking, and listening.

The energy of a two year old is renowned. Their unbridled exuberance is witnessed, if not appreciated, by everyone who comes in contact with them. Rapid neuromuscular and motor skill development allows them to use their bodies in many new ways. Children naturally and fully bring forth their capacities. Development, usage, and learning are occurring simultaneously.

The mind is the last element to begin development but it too develops rapidly. Initially a child's mind does not interfere with its being present. Children absorb everything and can feed it back in great detail. Between ages two and five, memory increases significantly. Cognitive skills such as association and relationship, coupled with memory, are the basis for the rapid acceleration in a child's vocabulary.

Parents, older siblings, preschool, and kindergarten teachers begin to put a governor on the rapid pace of balanced bandwidth development with rules invoked in the name of safety. Words such as *"no," "don't," "you can't," "you shouldn't," and "you will not"*, are early phases of programming the child's mind.

While each band develops in unique stages, when viewed from a human bandwidth perspective, childhood development follows concurrent, coordinated patterns. For example, imagine a six-foot tall, eighth grade boy with chin hair. His body band development may be three to four years ahead of the norm, yet his emotional, mind, and brain development may be slower than the norm. Typically, these disparities between young adolescents balance out in their late teens and early twenties.

SHIFT IN BANDWIDTH USAGE OVER TIME

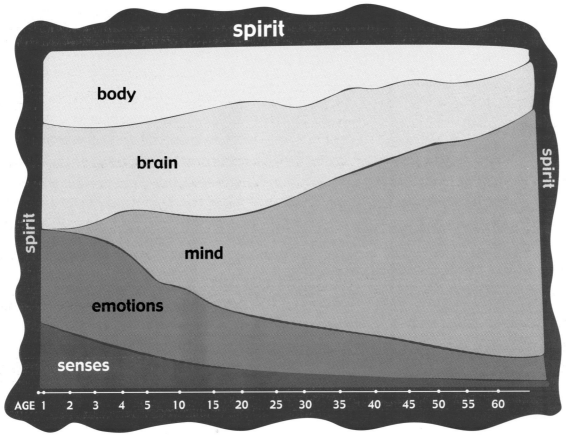

HUMAN BANDWIDTH GETS COMPARTMENTALIZED

As civilization has evolved, we have chosen to dismantle the unified field of human bandwidth. Instead of viewing bandwidth as an interconnected whole, we create specialized or individual methods to partially and ineffectively develop portions of our bandwidth. Parents and specialists participate in this fragmenting and disconnecting process.

For example, since the focus is on the body, brain, and senses during the first few years of life, young children make many visits to pediatricians. Once they have satisfactorily completed vision, hearing, and other tests, children's senses are taken for granted. We assume everything is working unless something leads us to believe otherwise.

The emotional center of the brain is on a parallel growth path with the body. Tending to emotional development is considered the primary responsibility of parents. Unless there are problems. Then counselors, psychologists, or therapists get involved, and their focus is rehabilitation, not development.

Spiritual development is typically influenced by parents, but often takes on the added pressure of other authority figures and peers.

Educators are the primary caretakers of the brain and mind bands. Most children begin formal schooling around age five when their cognitive skills have sufficiently developed to enable reading, writing, simple reasoning, and memory. From age five to the early twenties, brain and mind continue to develop, corresponding with the timing of thirteen- to eighteen-year educational processes (kindergarten through master's degree).

During the early twenties, the mind band expands, eventually dominating an individual's capacities for most of adulthood. This goes unrecognized because most people do not have a distinction for bandwidth and they have become accustomed to dwelling in their minds. It is difficult to tell the trees from the forest when you are standing in the middle of it. Given the choice, most would not accelerate their minds at the cost of disconnecting from their other capacities.

As a result of this compartmentalization, few people experience the power and capacity of their bandwidth as a unified force field. A person may have to rise to the level of an Olympic caliber athlete, concert pianist, prima ballerina, or Rhodes scholar before experiencing the convergence of basic human capacities.

Many exceptional people were not in the cultural mainstream during their lifetimes. The phrase, "she marches to the beat of a different drum," tends to be interpreted negatively. Maybe marching to her own beat really means she has discovered her unified bandwidth.

PARENTS UNCONSCIOUSLY LIMIT BANDWIDTH

As mentioned in the previous section, parents play a key role in the "development committee" for human bandwidth. That role deserves more discussion. As you read this section, reflect on your childhood and/or look at your experience with your own children.

The fact is **few adults have any formal training in parenting. In addition, most adults in the developed world operate on narrow bandwidth**, most of the time. If those adults happen to be parents, they will unconsciously raise their child in an environment of narrow bandwidth. (Parents, in this book, are defined as the adults primarily responsible for raising a child.)

Primary care givers (usually mothers) are typically at their highest level of awareness from pregnancy through the first six to nine months of a baby's life. Body, emotional, and sensory awareness are significantly increased by the growing fetus within. From birth through the first several months of a baby's life, there is shared high bandwidth between mother and baby. During this fifteen to eighteen month period, a nurturing and natural connection occurs. The baby's entire bandwidth continues to expand and develop, nourished by the mother's feedings, talking, singing, hugging, kissing, and caressing. All of these natural actions are a form of language, expressing emotions, spirit, senses, and body. Mother-baby interactions involve little of the mind band during the first few months of life. (These comments assume there are no birth defects, illness, or complications).

Then something happens to Mom, Dad, and baby's bandwidth: **mobility and independence. Mobility is the initial disconnection.** At some point, the baby starts to roll and crawl. This very simple action creates a shift in bandwidth. Almost immediately, parents begin to worry that the baby may be hurt. Imagining what could happen in the future, usually imagining the worst, the adult's bandwidth shifts away from the emotion, spirit, sensory, and body channels of the PRESENT MOMENT toward mind-based projections about the future safety of the child. In most cases, the relationship becomes more mind- (and language-) dominated.

So, the development of the child's central nervous system, which produces the impulses for increased mobility, induces a shift away from the emotion, spirit, sensory and body channels in adults. The mind re-emerges, becoming the primary band of interaction with the baby.

If the parent is operating on high bandwidth, the transition to verbal communication will be more gradual and include more sensory input. Attachment parenting, including breast-feeding and other sustained nurturing contact, along with attentive responsiveness to the baby's cues, typifies higher bandwidth parenting.

My parents were first-generation immigrants who had me late in life. They attempted to raise me in their native Swedish traditions, including speaking Swedish at home. As I grew, many conflicts arose from the clash of American and European lifestyles. While I perceived my parents to be old-fashioned and naive and treated them disrespectfully on occasion, I still received steadfast and unconditional love from them. Unknown to me, their "parenting style" emphasized spirit, emotion, sensory, mind, and body development. in that order.

Exercise

Reflect on how you were parented

Our parents, or their surrogates, have the strongest influence—genetic, environmental, and experiential—on how we develop. Reflect on your parents' style of parenting. How has it shaped you? How has it shaped your parenting?

Are we programming our children for low bandwidth? Yes. Is this a conscious act or process? No. The operative word is conscious. To be conscious, you have to be in the PRESENT MOMENT. To be conscious is to be awake, aware, and present. Most parents are not conscious enough to guide their children into high bandwidth.

EDUCATION OVER-EMPHASIZES THE MIND BAND

Traditional education targets the mind almost exclusively. We teach primarily through lecture and repetition, and reward those best able to memorize and accurately repeat information. Analysis, evaluation, and the development of higher reasoning skills are increasingly emphasized as students progress. **Adult and professional education and business training follow similar formats.**

The mind is a repository of past and future, incapable of full-bandwidth learning. Every other element of bandwidth is a PRESENT-MOMENT phenomenon.

Many schools have mission statements, logos, and symbols that advertise "mind, body and spirit" development, but they generally do not deliver on their promises. **"Body and spirit" are mostly missing from our educational system.**

Learning is a multi-layered phenomenon that takes place on many bands. Yet the western world educates almost exclusively with a "fill-the-mind" approach. The more information we can cram into our minds and the faster we can retrieve that data, the smarter we claim to be. Valuing content of the mind over everything else is a one-dimensional approach to learning that dims our awareness of our other capacities.

While music, art, and PE are included in most school curricula, they are often elective rather than required. These "fluff" subjects are generally isolated from, rather than integrated into, academic courses as they could be for full-bandwidth development. Courses such as physical education and health are wonderful opportunities to create body awareness and develop healthy living habits, but they often fall short of their desired impact. Consider how physical fitness, weight loss, and stress reduction have become major industries for adults!

There are promising exceptions to this view of Western educational practice. Efforts are underway to make primary grades more experiential and less intellectual. If this expands into the entire spectrum of public education, students will maintain their "child-like" awareness of the full spectrum of their bandwidth. Awareness of and access to broad bandwidth enhances creativity and contribution. Students thus educated will be better equipped to make their contribution to society.

Some private schools have designed their curricula to reach, nourish, and expand all the basic human capacities. The Waldorf School and Montessori-based education are examples.

Waldorf education has its roots in the work of an Austrian scientist and thinker Rudolph Steiner. Waldorf education views children as multi-dimensional: beings with hearts and limbs, will and feelings, as well as intellect. To ensure that education does not produce one-sided individuals, crippled in emotional health and violating the less conscious aspects of our human nature, these aspects must correctly be exercised, nourished and guided. When the Waldorf curriculum is **carried through successfully**, the whole human being—head, heart, and hands—is truly educated.

The Montessori method sees children as competent, creative, and committed learners. Dr. Maria Montessori, guided by her discovery that children teach themselves, designed a "prepared environment" in which children could freely choose from a number of developmentally appropriate activities. That environment is intended to foster the fulfillment of a child's highest spiritual, emotional, physical and intellectual potentials.

A growing niche of schools offers programs to full-time workers based on a practical approach to upgrading the capacities and experience of workers. They emphasize hands-on practice vs. theory. Many colleges and universities offer internships, work-study experiences, international studies programs, and collaborative efforts with businesses. These provide opportunities for students to learn by engaging their senses, emotions, body, and spirit as well their brain and mind.

Increasing numbers of schools provide "Outward Bound" kinds of experiences, emphasizing the realm of the senses and bringing focus to the interconnectedness of life. Unfortunately, these are usually "cameo" programs, lasting only a few days or weeks.

This is not intended as a criticism of educators. In today's society, teachers wear many "hats," serving as role models, mentors, and often, surrogate parents. Thousands of high-bandwidth teachers share their gifts of sensory, emotional, and spiritual development, along with content expertise, with their students. These teachers love to teach, love their students, and that way of being transforms the educational experience for children.

I can look back at my own education in the Chicago Public School system, college, and graduate school, and name a dozen teachers who greatly influenced me. They cared about me, were passionate about their subjects, and shared their knowledge and experiences with me. In spite of the system, they created classroom environments and experiences that prepared me for my opportunity in the world. In their own ways, they were getting me to access more of my bandwidth.

Until the foundation for education is the PRESENT MOMENT (i.e., based on the full spectrum of bandwidth), countless more generations of children will be deprived of the opportunity to be exceptional or extraordinary. Traditional education misses the foundation. Life cannot be learned; it has to be experienced. Crying, laughing, seeing, touching, talking, listening, thinking, walking, running, jumping, balance, and breathing are not theoretical. They are the nature of being human, and unless people are rooted or grounded in their basic nature, education is disconnected, cerebral, and illusory.

Exercise
Teachers who contributed

Reflect on your schooling. Recall the teachers who influenced you. How did they contribute to the growth and development of your full bandwidth? What did they have in common? Did any discourage you?

Scientific observation has established that education is not what a teacher gives; education is a natural process spontaneously carried out by the human individual, and is acquired not by listening to words but by experiences upon the environment. The task of the teacher becomes that of preparing a series of motives of cultural activity, spread over a specially prepared environment, and then refraining from obstructive interference. Human teachers can only help the great work that is being done, as servants help the master. Doing so, they will be witnesses to the unfolding of the human soul and to the rising of a New Man who will not be a victim of events, but will have the clarity of vision to direct and shape the future of human society.

Maria Montessori, Education for a New World

GENDER INFLUENCES BANDWIDTH

Gender is another significant influence on bandwidth. Genders are highly stereotyped, and often fairly so, because there is truth in the generalizations. I am not saying, "All men are competitive," or "All women are nurturing." But, I am pointing to strong tendencies which have evolved over centuries from either biology or acculturation.

Also, bear in mind that no human being is genetically all male or all female. It is more exact to say that we are male-dominant or female-dominant; every human being has both male and female genetic characteristics.

Male bandwidth is body- and mind-dominated. For thousands of years, men have used their bodies to protect and provide for their families. Men dominate the realms of strength, power, culture, politics, business, and religion. More often than not, men held the role of chief, king, emperor, warrior, cleric, explorer, or inventor.

As the industrial revolution took hold and the service economy evolved, men began working away from home, transitioning into factories and offices, which required less body and more mind. At the beginning of the 21st century, males are still the primary workers in construction, manufacturing, and other physical-labor jobs. They also dominate the more mind-based jobs such as engineering, accounting, and information technology.

Male bandwidth is exemplified in the interplay of mind and body, particularly in competition and rivalry. Male warrior energy is at the heart of competition. Tested on battlefields for thousands of years, men have faced death for the sake of freedom, plunder, power, and glory— for themselves, their families, communities, and countries. While the warrior of old was mainly interested in acquiring or defending land and protecting his family, today's warrior competes for position and wealth ("Whoever dies with the most toys, wins!"), and freedom from the constraints of work. The goal to retire at a young age is simply an evolution of the mind/body-dominated bandwidth of men.

Nothing exemplifies the bandwidth of mind more than a man on a mission. Men enjoy the challenge of achieving goals. Thus, many men plan and focus on the future of their career, finances, and other steps on the way to independence, which gives them feelings of accomplishment.

Men also crave recognition, manifesting in the quest for money, power, and status. Look at the typical office, library, or den, and you may see mounted trophy heads, pictures with dignitaries, plaques, awards, and medals. All are symbols of accomplishment, conquest, and the desire for acknowledgement.

For much of history, women personified the object of desire, the possession, the servant, or the helpmate to man. In most cultures today, men continue to dominate. In the developed world however, women increasingly compete for and win positions in politics, business, education, and government. The advantage of female bandwidth is making itself felt.

In general, women's bandwidth is more evenly developed and better balanced than men's. Day-to-day, women utilize more of their cumulative capabilities than do men. **Characterized by higher levels of sensory and emotional development, both**

of which are access points to spirit, the band of mind is not as dominant in most women. Thus, they tend to be in the PRESENT MOMENT more than men.

A woman's expanded bandwidth creates one of her principal capabilities, to love and be loved. Women are generally perceived as more empathetic caregivers, more nurturing, more emotionally expansive, more sensitive, and more compassionate. Just watch a mother with small children. Words such as flexible, free flowing, multi-tasking, and attentive will often describe her. Women head most single-parent households. This is likely because of the natural emotional dependency stemming from women's life-giving and nurturing capacities.

As a father of three women and through my work with female leaders and executives, I can say that women are better listeners, more open and self expressive. They also develop faster and deeper relationships, the fabric basic to any organization. And in spite of the odds of succeeding in the corporate world, women are more in touch with the needs, feelings, and desires of their various constituencies—employees, customers, suppliers, and investors. I suspect women's broader bandwidth, more freely exercised around the world, will ultimately have a mitigating effect on the global pattern of strife and conflict.

While brain anatomy is different, function and capacity appear to be very similar in men and women. Standard testing of intellectual capacity reveals no measurable difference. **In the realm of spirit, there is no difference between men and women.** Whenever we are present to our band of spirit, we experience the interconnection of everything and everyone. We see beyond separateness and differences, focusing instead on our commonalities and relatedness.

CULTURE LIMITS BANDWIDTH

As this chapter points out, our bandwidth development faces both parental and educational hurdles. Add to these the obstacles raised by culture. Virtually every facet of nearly every country's social, political, and economic infrastructure is characterized by male-dominated, mind-dominated, hierarchical organizational structures.

There are hundreds, maybe thousands, of subtle and not so subtle cultural and societal blind spots that prevent us from recognizing and utilizing our basic human capacities. If these structures, norms, and behaviors are not altered at a conscious level, the possibility for human bandwidth development is directly and significantly decreased. Consider the following questions in this light.

Does the typical immigrant of the Twenty-first Century have the same opportunities as the millions of immigrants who passed through Ellis Island in the beginning of the Twentieth Century? Do women in business have the same opportunity to progress as their male counterparts? Does a person of color get the same respect and trust as a white person? How many corporate diversity programs are really committed to diversity? Is accessibility to opportunity a reality for people with handicaps? How many people alter their behavior to conform to the implied standards of a social or business organization?

Stereotyping, racial profiling, cultural biases, societal traditions, subtle and blatant prejudice, and hatred have seriously compromised, even obliterated, the ability (on individual and societal levels) to access the full capacities of those affected. Perhaps less obvious is the consequence to the bandwidth of those who hold such attitudes, consciously or not.

In spite of the efforts to date, human bandwidth remains stunted by historical infrastructures and the individual (and collective) mind's store of judgments, opinions, and preconceived notions. This is likely to be perpetuated because most human beings have no clue that their basic capacities are unlimited. Thus, billions of children grow up with grossly inadequate development of their bandwidth.

During an interview on the Oprah Winfrey Show, Tiger Wood's dad was asked "What race is Tiger?" Tiger Woods is multiracial. His father responded, "He is a member of the human race."

TECHNOLOGY LIMITS OUR PERCEPTION OF BANDWIDTH

Scientists and demographers are telling us that the post World War II era is unique in the history of the world. We have experienced more technological change in the last fifty-five years than in the previous 3,000, and the pace of change is accelerating. In fact, the last decade of the Twentieth Century produced more change than the entire period from 1945 to 1990. Thanks to technology, change is almost instantaneous.

Yet this change is taking place with significant imbalances. A surge in stock market value that creates affluence for several million people in the United States does not necessarily benefit a billion others who are living in poverty or slowly dying of hunger. The speed of technological change creates human disconnection, alienating families, workplaces, communities, and nations from each other. People in the undeveloped world are being left behind, as are pockets of people in the developed world.

Bill Joy, CEO of Sun Microsystems, one of the United State's most successful high-tech companies, maintains that we must aggressively build a different brand of conscious, morally committed leaders. Without such leaders, he writes, the current pace of technology will overwhelm us and we will face extinction as a human species by the end of the 21st Century. Whether you believe his prediction is secondary to the fact that we have a widening gap between technological interconnection and human disconnection.

Speed, information access, efficient communication, and entertainment are only a click or two away. Computer technology is mind-dominant, exacerbating the imbalance of our bands. Designed to replicate the human mind, computers, in some respects, are actually an improvement. They are incredibly accurate, providing volumes of organized data where a human being might only recall isolated facts. But we often forget the human mind is much faster than even a super computer: A computer can produce stacks of printouts, but only a human being can write a novel. While a computer can sequence sounds, only a human being can compose a symphony.

Technology is meant to enable human endeavors, not to disable them. We must never lose sight of the fact that we are human beings, not merely human "doings" (technicians who process information and perform tasks).

THE GOOD NEWS

Much as genetics may predispose one to certain health issues, or to longevity, early influences on bandwidth tend to program and push people down particular pathways in life. Life-long passions and scars can accumulate at each level of bandwidth.

Powerful as they are in their effects on growth and development, these early influences do not rob people of their basic human capacities. People are resilient.

Accumulated damage, as well as positive effects picked up along the way, is not irreversible. We can consciously alter the course of our lives at any moment. We have choices, whether we consciously exercise them or not. Often, the choices we make are external, such as moving, getting married or divorced, changing jobs, or making new friends and leaving old ones. Examining our inner beings can provide clues about the kinds of choices that will enable us to create and sustain happier, more fulfilling lives.

As people evolve, so do their bandwidths. We have the capacity to go beyond the circumstances of our birth, the parenting we received, our childhood experiences, education, and gender. We can shift from survival into growth, from fear into love. Human beings are capable of adapting, responding, growing, and creating their lives from the inside-out, based on awareness and choice.

We also possess a capacity which transcends life on the physical plane. Whether we believe we are spiritual beings having human experiences, or human beings confined to a life span, we are co-authors of our lives on earth. While we live, we are all interconnected through spirit in the infinite and eternal present moment.

Life is the intersection where the plane of the finite, visible, material world meets the plane of the endless, timeless universe. Human bandwidth extends to both planes, but this realization has to be individually discovered and developed. When we reach this higher level of awareness, we are capable of redesigning our lives and living from choice instead of heredity or habit.

Exercise

What overrides our capacities?

Read the following questions and jot down your thoughts, intuitions, feelings or senses. There are no "right" answers.

- *Why is bandwidth or human capacity missing from our everyday language and conversation?*

- *Has anyone spoken to you about your basic human capacities?*

- *Are you aware of the access points to your capacities or bands of energy?*

- *Are your dreams, relationships, education, career, and life's purpose utilizing or overlooking your inherent capacities?*

- *Are you uncertain, unclear, struggling, resigned or "faking it"?*

- *Have you created a life based on a shaky or unknown foundation?*

- *Are you aware that a male and female's dominant bandwidth energy is distinctly different?*

- *How are these differences manifested in you?*

- *What, if anything, prevents you from visualizing and acting on your goals in life?*

- *What occurs when problems arise?*

- *Is there a correlation between your self-esteem, health, and performance in the classroom or at work?*

- *What is your life's purpose?*

- *What will you die for?*

- *What promises will you make to yourself and others about fully participating in life?*

- *What difference will you make in the world?*

The overriding question is: What occurs in the cycle of human development and in our lives that blurs or overrides our basic human capacities?

Profile: Katie Byrnes

An ultrasound during pregnancy revealed that Katie had hydrocephaly as a result of a stroke. This created an abnormal increase in the amount and a partial blockage of spinal fluid, causing an enlarged skull and compression of the brain. John and Jayne Byrnes, her parents, were told that she had a five percent of surviving birth. Born deaf and with other physical disorders such as scoliosis and Goldenhar syndrome, Katie spent her first fifty five days in a childrens' hospital having surgery for a brain shunt and a stomach feeding tube.

At four months, Katie began communicating with Jayne and John by wiggling her eyebrows. When she was nine months old, she began using American Sign Language. To emphasize a point or when she was really excited, Katie would wiggle her entire body. Speech, physical and occupational therapists, deaf educators, and early intervention teachers supported her growth and worked with her family. She attended a Cincinnati area Early Childhood Center for three years; was featured in a video that was part of the Greater Cincinnati Inclusion Network's recognition of outstanding education for the disabled; and participated in the "Shared Reading Program" developed by Galludet University which taught Katie how to read childrens' books.

Katie inspired countless doctors, caregivers and patients at Childrens' Hospital and General Electric ELFUNS. Jayne said "Katie absorbed energy and love, and then radiated it back in a human glow." While some of Katie's bandwidth was physiologically constricted, her senses, emotions, and spirit engaged and energized people. She was fully alive and her energy was a wake-up call to everyone who met her. She exhibited the purest of human capacities, love.

Katie died unexpectedly at 5 1/2 when her brain shunt acutely malfunctioned. Her "human glow" touched thousands of people in their hearts and spirits. "She gave back double to those who gave to her, with her gifts of loving enthusiasm and uplifting spirit." Over 1500 people attended her wake and celebration of life service. She had beaten the statistical odds and her mere presence contributed to others. She was extraordinary!

Born November 9, 1995

Awakened March 1996

Died April 24, 2001

CHAPTER IV:
Bandwidth is in a Constant State of Change

Life is known only by those who have found a way to be comfortable with change and the unknown. Given the nature of life, there may be no security, but only adventure . . . —Rachel Naomi Remen

• Mike Gbur • Sue Gbur • Karen Gbur • Dan Gbur • Amy Gbur • Paula Gbur • Garry Gbur • Barb Gbur • Greg Gbur • Anita Gbur • Myron Gbur • Harriet Gbur • Alex Gbur • Ann Gerdom • Jackie Gerval • Michael Gesas • Gary Gesme • Arlene Gesme • Kevin Getz • Bud Getchell • Mark Giesting • Margie Gipson • Paul Gipson • Bob Glass • David Glick • Scott Glespie • Sue Gnospelius • Dick Gnospelius • Larry Gold • Susie Golderg • John Goldberg • Howard Goldman • Lisa Goldman • Joan Goldstein • Gene Golub • David Gomberg • Dennis Goode • Dick Goodin • Steve Goodman • Bob Gottschall • Bruce Gottschall • Sue Gottschall • David Gottschall • Hannah Gottschall • Rebecca Gottschall • Katie Gottschall • Margaret Gottschall • Deborah Gouge • Doug Gouge • Dan Gould • Don Graff • Katy Graff • David Graf • Nancy Graf • Ty Graf • Alison Graf • Elaine Grauer • Jim Gram • Mary Gram • Dennis Grant • Barbara Graver • Jeff Gredwig • James Green • Ruth Green • Patty Greene • John Grieve • Margaret Grieve • Al Griever • Bill Groebe • Chuck Gudbrandsen • Mike Gudbrandsen • Peggy Gudbrandsen • Tom Guild • Andrew Gustafson • Brent Gustafson • David Gustafson • Dick Gustafson • Margo Gustafson • Elaine Gustavson • Gary Gustavson • Ralph Guthrie • Eddie Gutman • Twila Habegger • David Hackman • Marvin Hackman • Kim Oslund Hadd • Doug Hager • Jim Haig • Roger Hains • Bob Hall • Larry Hall • Theresa Hall • Katie Hall • Kelley Hall • Christine Hall • Ken Hall • Bruce Hamming • Edward Hamming • Mary Hamming • Nancy Hamming • Tich Nacht Hanh • Bonnie Hansen • Paul Hansen • Diane Hansen • Rich Hanson • Bob Hanson • Fred Harburg • Susie Harburg • Tom Harney • Laura Harney • Valerie Harper • John Harper • Pam Harper • Brian Harper • Jeff Harper • Lauren Harper • Bill Harris • Diantha Harris • Andy Harris • Billy Harris • John Harris • Coco Harris • Peonita Harris • Sandy Hartman • Chris Hashioka • Tim Haskett • Nils Hasselmo • Pat Hasselmo • Tom Hau • Richard Haugen • Edward Havlik • Ray Hawrylak • Bill Hayes • Charles Hayes • Jane Hayes • Marty Hayden • Buddy Heckler • Marcia Heckler • Val Heeren • Nate Heeren • Karie Heeren • Daryle Heeren • Jack Heeren • Tom Hefner • Rich Hegg • Linda Hegg • Daniel Heiman • Jineen Heiman • Denny Heitzman • Marcia Heitzman • Lissa Hektor • Christine Hektor • Otto Hektor Jr. • Otto Hektor • Frank Helle • Bill Heller • Jim Hemphill • Eric Hengst • Gail Hengst • Dave Henkel • Pam Henkel • Andrew Henkel • Emily Henkel • Leo Hennessy • Mike Hennessy • Allen Henning • John Henning • Rami Henrich • Tom Henrich • Bob Henry • Donna Henry • Sharol Henry • Darlene Herb • Elaine Herb • Jerry Herb • Jeanne Herman • Steve Herman • Richard Hermann • Rich Hergert • Dan Herrington • Missy Herrington • Michael Herrick • Barbara Herzog • Beth Hess • Denny Hetler • Barbara Hetler • Jack Higgins • Earl Hildebrandt • Lisa Hilgenberg • Dan Hill • David Hill

CHANGE OCCURS NATURALLY

The laws of physics tell us that there is no such thing as a static state. **The nature of life is change. Everything cycles through phases of expansion and contraction, inhalation and exhalation, birth and death, creation and destruction.**

Our capacities (bandwidth) are fields of energy, ebbing and flowing, 86,400 seconds a day. Our bandwidth transforms moment-to-moment, adapting and responding to all our activity and every thing around us—breathing, eating, digesting, eliminating, speaking, seeing, thinking, listening. Our pulse, emotions, and neurological impulses fluctuate constantly.

We are intimately familiar with cycles of change throughout all life and the broader universe. We see cycles in the movement of the stars and planets, seasons, phases of the moon, passage of time, and growing of crops. Our human bodies experience the cycles of maturation and decline, and bodily functions like digestion and reproduction. The movement from the parent-infant bond to the parent-adult child relationship or from the anxiety of falling in love to the comfort of a trusting and committed partnership illustrate cycles in relationship. Businesses also have production, inventory, product life, and other cycles.

Extraordinary people are change agents, living at high bandwidth (in an expanded state). They connect, create, invent, explore, and discover. They view problems, the unknown, and the uncertain, as fertile fields of possibility. Extraordinary people are more often in an expansive state because they spend more time in the PRESENT MOMENT. The rest of us spend more time in our minds, a state of contraction and narrower bandwidth.

Rather than expand the discussion on change, I would like to focus on change from the perspective of human bandwidth—within and beyond the mind.

THE FAMILY PHOTO ALBUM

We are often asleep to the changes constantly taking place in our lives, and our family photo albums document them. Photographs generally capture special or significant moments in time, such as births, birthdays, weddings, anniversaries, family gatherings, outings, events, and vacations.

Photos show the life cycle—birth, growth, aging, and dying—for each member of our family. The interconnection of the generations and the dynamics of expansion and contraction are also recorded. Many events, often not included in family albums, impact families for years, such as an accident, illness, arguments, job loss, death, divorce, addiction, embarrassment, child leaving home, bankruptcy, or inheritance.

MIND-DRIVEN HABITS OBSCURE CHANGE AND CONSTRICT BANDWIDTH

Change is constant and inextricably linked to creating new possibilities. Yet our habits and patterns create the illusion of a stable state. The masses seek comfort and security while the passion for exploration and adventure is relished by a relative few. Change threatens our perception of stability. Thus, the mind's habitual operation holds great appeal for most people.

Repetitive routines stifle creativity. Throughout the day, each of us repeats hundreds of habits, often unconsciously. Our facial expressions, posture, handshake, walk, choice of words, gestures, motions, greeting, focus or lack thereof, listening, voice tone and speed, mood, constructive comments, putdowns, opinions, judgements, evaluations, energy level, and intensity are typically habitual and unconscious. Day after day, these routines permeate our lives.

Historically-based, survival-oriented, habitual, and repetitive, our minds reinforce unconscious habits and resist change. Perhaps as much as 80% of our thoughts are repetitive. These repetitive thoughts are primarily responsible for program-ming our behavior and actions. The voice inside of our head keeps us in our habits and patterns. Our minds serve as tour guides throughout the day. This repetitive programming robs each of us of the creativity, spontaneity, awareness, and human spirit inherent in our bandwidth because it takes us out of the PRESENT MOMENT.

Granted it doesn't require much creativity to accomplish the routine tasks of the day—brushing our teeth, putting out the garbage, etc. But the progression of routines and mechanical behaviors that accompany aging can erode the energy or spirit of a human being. We devolve into mind-driven, routinized, predictable, and often dissatisfied people. And we are supported in these tendencies by automation of electronic products and technology, activated through our fingertips. We unwittingly sacrifice awareness, consciousness, aliveness, creativity, and energy in the name of "efficiency."

In addition to its habitual tendencies, the mind is the only band of human energy that perceives change as a threat to its existence. Change can threaten the mind's identity (its beliefs, judgments, opinions, etc.) With the (perceived) survival of the identity at stake, our minds attempt to create a static state to assuage our fear of change. Faced with the prospect of change, the mind defends itself with questions such as:

How will this change affect me?

What will happen to my friends and associates if this change takes place?

Why are we changing?

What is my new role after the change?

Will I be able to do my new job or take on my new role?

How long will the change take?

How much will this change cost me?

Where are we going now and how do we get there?

Though these questions could possibly lead to useful answers, more often than not they produce a litany of reasons for resisting the change.

To live peacefully with the universal reality of change, be willing to go beyond your mind and its various traps. You can willfully choose to expand or contract your capacities in the PRESENT MOMENT. You can learn to access bands of energy other than your mind that have no perceived identity and consequently, are not threatened by change. In fact, the other five bands of energy are in a constant state of change, meaning that change is compatible with all bands except your mind. We can accurately say that you don't resist change—only your mind resists change.

Not all habits and patterns are bad, nor should they all be discarded. What is important is to become aware of your daily routine, ingrained habits, and patterns. Some are practical and useful, while others hinder the development of your capacities. As the final exercise in this chapter suggests, keeping a log of your observable habits and patterns for a few weeks can reveal how many you have and give insights into their value or waste. Asking co-workers, family, and friends to give you feedback on habits and patterns will create further insights.

To the mind, the most basic danger posed by change is the threat to your perceived identity. This identity is illusory, simply based on repetitive thoughts about who you believe yourself to be. To test this idea, just ask yourself "Who am I?" Then observe the source of the response. Chances are good that you will respond to that question from your mind. You have created your identity from a habitual, ongoing, internal monologue.

I prefer a life of surprises.   —Marc Chagall

CHANGE IS EASIER FOR CHILDREN AND YOUNGER WOMEN

As babies become toddlers and toddlers become young children, change is anticipated, accepted, and rapid. For the parent, the pace can be overwhelming. For the child, who is much more often in the PRESENT MOMENT, life, and all it's changes, is just a natural unfolding.

Teenagers are wont to question everything, experiment with limits, and explore the edges. These behaviors, also natural unfoldings, often overwhelm parents. All aspects of teens' bandwidth are expanding. They can easily resent the mind-dominated bandwidth of adults. Adults value predictability and certainty. Teenagers thrive on exploring the unknown. Their mind bands are still flexible, and they often consider themselves "bullet-proof." The adult habits of conforming, seeking comfort and safety, and resisting change have not yet solidified.

Adults often want to "routinize" these unfoldings. Getting children into day care or school introduces them to more structure and rules, allowing parents to escape the chaos. Encouraging teenagers to be totally scheduled with school, jobs, activities, and homework can be a coping mechanism for stressed-out parents.

This focus on structure and rules continues throughout the two-decade-long process of schooling and societal conditioning. The result is supposed to be the creation of responsible, rules-obedient adults. Structure is necessary in a civilized world, however it is also valuable to foster skills for creatively negotiating change.

As people progress through life, the vast majority become more rigid and narrow in their thinking, rarely venturing beyond their minds' parameters of comfort or survival. Fortunately, there are change agents in every facet of society. Both respected and suspected, they challenge the status quo.

Many of the last century's change agents were women. Physically, emotionally, and psychologically, women are generally better than men at adapting to change. Ancient Chinese philosophy used the principle of yin and yang to illustrate the duality of life. Yin is the female energy and is always changing. Yang is the masculine energy and is much more structured. Natural multi-taskers, women are more effective at simultaneously managing their households, raising children, and holding down jobs in the workforce.

Historically, women's bandwidth capabilities have been narrowly prescribed. Full expression of broad bandwidth was "unladylike" and discouraged. Even today, in most male-dominated fields such as business, government, and the military, women are forced to conform. Such conformance has come to mean "to think like men and behave like ladies."

As a result, women are increasingly entering the business world as entrepreneurs. According to the Department of Commerce, of all new businesses in 2000, 40% were formed by women.

The ability to flow with change creatively and flexibly is greatly enhanced when we broaden our bandwidths. While women, particularly younger women, and children may naturally demonstrate greater bandwidth range and adaptability, anyone can adapt better to change when they have access to broad bandwidth.

TRANSFORMATION MEANS INSTANT CHANGE

How long does it take to click a mouse or to change channels using a TV remote? Shifting between bands of energy occurs just as quickly. While a click is mechanical, deliberately surfing our bandwidth is merely the act of becoming conscious of the PRESENT MOMENT.

Human beings are equipped with basic capacities that act in concert as a unified field of energy. We have the ability to change instantly, adapting to new circumstances in the PRESENT MOMENT. That is the nature of consciousness or awareness.

Change occurs in response to negative stressors (such as an accident, injury, or illness) and to positive stressors (such as sexual ecstasy, success, or beauty). Our emotions and bodies are activated. Our senses are heightened. Our brains engage in immediate, coordinated activity and movement. All of our bands of energy synchronize and become more acute, reacting on a moment-to-moment basis to changes in the environment. Even the mind undergoes instantaneous changes in thought patterns.

Most mental and physical activities are coordinated oscillations between several bands of energy. Problem solving involves oscillation between mind and brain. Filtering conversations occurs between the senses and the mind. Physical activity requires oscillation between senses, brain, body, and sometimes mind and/or emotions. This high speed, coordinated movement between bands is barely detectable, even as we consciously observe our inner beings. The word which best describes this high-speed change is transformation.

Children are transformed when they first experience balance on a "two wheeler." A similar thing happens when someone who fears public speaking makes a powerful presentation. Transformation occurs whenever someone takes a risk and succeeds. In these moments people step out of their mind's identity. They go beyond their embarrassment, fear, low self-esteem, historical patterns, and self-imposed limits. In the moment of transformation, they experience a shift from the past or future into the present. Insights, emotions, and/or body sensations are irrefutable.

Transformation is a shift from our historical perspective to a new vantage point. **It is a shift in** context—seeing, hearing, or feeling something from a different or new perspective. We find ourselves to be expanding, opening to new possibilities. Experiencing ourselves as creative beings, capable of new possibilities, spurs the desire for more self-discovery.

Continuous, moment-to-moment transformation is possible. At any time our anger can transform into neutrality, our sadness into joy. We can transform resistance into cooperation or resignation into participation. These changes can happen whenever we 1) become aware of our present state, 2) are willing to release that state, and 3) are willing to see other possible ways of being.

Transformation is an individual phenomenon. A transformative experience offers a glimpse of our true being—of who we are and who we can become. Experiential, rather than intellectual or conceptual, transformation defies analysis. (We "understand" in our minds, but we "experience" through the other bands). The experience is usually abrupt, like switching on a light.

Through transformational experiences, we are awakened to our potential. We expand into our capacities. The knowledge that we are capable of transforming our lives is a powerful and exciting— the reward of accessing our full bandwidth. There is a saying that "life is a work of art designed by the one who lives it". This possibility is always waiting for us in the PRESENT MOMENT.

It is in this realm, beyond the mind, that we can create ourselves as we choose to be. It is here that we can take negative, historical patterns and convert them into new ways of being. Selfishness can be converted into the satisfaction of serving others. The anxiety and fear that accompany low self-esteem can be converted into calm self-assuredness. Resentfulness can be converted into acknowledgement. Rather than resisting change, we can become agents of change. This is transformation.

Transformation happens not through struggling to change our existing habits, but through seeing them fully, in the PRESENT MOMENT, without judgment or blame. We have the opportunity to just accept what we are experiencing. When we focus our attention and confront who we are, we go beyond our minds and all the intellectual strategies intended to produce, or resist, change. We come to clearly see the current situation, we then can choose to simply release thoughts and habits that no longer serve us.

Your insight is the key that unlocks a door beyond your mind. Through non-judgmental awareness you push open the door and see the potential and possibility that exists for you, free from the limits of the past. There are no boundaries on who you can be. The eternal PRESENT MOMENT is always and forever infinite.

INDIVIDUALS TRANSFORM ORGANIZATIONS

Just as every human being has a personality, every organization has a culture. This culture consists of the prevailing customs, habits, patterns, and traditions that formally and informally govern behavior and actions. Usually these customs and traditions are rooted in organizational history and are preserved through conversations as well as rituals, both formal and informal.

If the possibility exists to transform any situation, can it be done at the level of an organization?

Stories are passed on about adventures, mishaps, successes, and failures within the context of the organizational culture. Organizational habits and patterns become ingrained just as quickly as personal habits and patterns. Many company cultures achieve almost mythical status. (Often stories about the company have been changed and are myths really).

Leaders intent upon preserving culture will take steps to maintain these historical customs and traditions. Tenure generally increases compliance and pride in the culture. New people are expected to adapt; and conformity is like a badge of honor. Nonconformists don't usually last.

Organizational transformation occurs as:

1) an unacceptable situation is recognized, such as declining revenue, customer dissatisfaction, or inefficiency relative to competitors;

2) new possibilities are seen for improving the situation (new or different products or services, changing production lines, redesigning processes);

3) a team commits to the new possibility, forming a nucleus of support for the change and enrolling others in the transformation;

4) a critical mass is formed and the business transforms, one person at a time, from one way of being to another.

For example, an airline had a notorious reputation for being late—the on-time arrival rate was only 65%. Its pilots, flight attendants, gate agents, baggage handlers, and schedulers saw another possibility. They collectively decided to shift their focus to the needs of their customers. Through new processes and committed action, these people increased their on-time arrival rate to 90%. With a similar cultural commitment, Federal Express transformed the small package shipping industry— delivering packages by 10:30 a.m. the next day.

When people experience themselves making a difference individually, actions and behaviors change. When a factory worker realizes that his performance impacts customers as well as the company, his relationship to the work is transformed. Resignation and low self-esteem are replaced by feelings of contribution and self-respect.

By seeing, hearing, and feeling the needs of customers, suppliers, vendors, managers, and fellow workers, each member of an organization can act to satisfy those needs. Knowing "I make a difference" generates increased value to customers and rewards each team member with a sense of satisfaction and pride. The collective bandwidth of the organization shifts from predominantly "mind" or internal focus to a broader and more externally-focused bandwidth.

Exercise

Become conscious of your habits

People are creatures of habit, which are products of the mind. Consider that you may have established repetitive and mechanical ways of living many aspects of your life.

- *How many habits and patterns can you identify in your life?*

- *Can you observe personal habits that lead you to waste time or sabotage your enjoyment of life?*

- *Is your mind robbing you of your freedom? Are you a slave to the habits and patterns of your mind?*

To make this idea come alive, practice some self-observation. (Pick a slow month!)

On a separate piece of paper, create three columns with these labels:
Column 1: Habits
Column 2: What precipitated the habit
Column 3: Origin of the habits (date)

Notice what you do from the time you awaken until you fall asleep. Record your daily routine in a journal. Keep track by day and week. Look at the repetition cycle. How many daily habits can you spot?

Once you've made a comprehensive list, ponder the inception of the habit. When did you first start the habit? What was the origin of the pattern? Are the circumstances that precipitated the habit or pattern still valid today? Why or why not? It may take a while to discover the origin of the behavior, but stick with the search. Knowing how a habit began is one path to releasing or changing it.

Note: In doing this exercise, you may discover issues or problems that require professional help. If so, take the leap and consult a qualified mental health or medical professional.

Profile: Buckminster Fuller

Buckminster Fuller, the discoverer/inventor of the geodesic dome, at age thirty-two contemplated suicide for a few hours one night at the edge of Lake Michigan. As the story goes, a series of business failures left him feeling he made such a mess of his life that the best move would be for him to remove himself from the scene and make things simpler for his wife and daughter. Apparently everything he had touched or undertaken had turned to dust in spite of his incredible creativity and imagination, which were only recognized later. However, instead of ending his life, Fuller decided (perhaps because of his deep conviction in the underlying unity and order of the universe, of which he knew himself to be an integral part) to live from then on as if he had died that night.

Being dead, he wouldn't have to worry about how things worked out any longer for himself personally and would be free to devote himself to living as a representative of the universe. The rest of his life would be a gift. Instead of living for himself, he would devote himself to asking: What is it on this planet [which he referred to as Spaceship Earth] that needs doing that I know something about, that probably won't happen unless I take responsibility for it?" He decided he would just ask this question continuously and do what came to him, following his nose.

Buckminster Fuller was an engineer, architect, poet, and philosopher. He devoted his life to designing structures that would conserve the world's energy resources. This passage about Fuller appears in Jon Kabat-Zinn's book *Wherever You Go There You Are* © 1994, New York: Hyperion.

CHAPTER V:
Living on Narrow Bandwidth

YOUR NAME

Born:

FELL ASLEEP:

Awakened:

Died:

"Life's but a walking shadow, a poor player that struts and frets his hour upon the stage, and then is heard no more. It is a tale told by an idiot, full of sound and fury, signifying nothing." —Macbeth, by William Shakespeare

• Larry Hill • Lynne Hill • Rich Hill • Gus Hillenbrand • Sue Ann Hillman • Hannah Hilton • John Hidenburg • Gina Hinrichs • Dave Hirt • Irene Hnatusko • Mike Hnatusko • Morrie Hnatusko • Dorothy Ho • John Hobart • Walter Hobgood • Tom Hodgson • Sue Hodgson • Linda Hoey • Peter Hoey • George Hoey • Ronald Hoff • David Hoffman • Mike Hoffman • Steve Hoffmann • Steven Hofstetter • John Hoglund • James Hollensteiner • Ann Hollis • Joe Hollis • Dean Holm • Faye Holm • Ben Holmes • Joan Holmes • Shelly Holmstrom • Skip Holmstrom • Vicki Holt • Fred Holzl • Dick Homer • Mert Hornbuckle • Donna Hornbuckle • Asayo Horibe • Yetta Horn • Carol Horstmann • James Horstmann • Pete Horos • Kathy Horos • Jen Horos • Laura Horos • Peter Horos • Bill Hotz • Bonnie Houdek • Jim Howard • Ted Howard • Robert Howey • Eric Hovde • Steve Hovde • Bill Hubbard • Don Hughes • Jack Huck • Jack Hullett • Greg Hunter • John Hunter • Tom Huyer • Mary Maisey-Ireland • Caroel Ingeson • Bryngel Ingewaldsson • Kierstin Ingewaldsson • Bob Irsay • Carl Ivey • Barry Jackson • Denise Jackson • Darold Jackson • Mimi Jackson • Hannah Jacobson • Gary Janko • Roger Jansson • Donna Jarvi • Mike Jarvi • Karen Jenkins • Lou Jenn • Baker Jenner • Ginny Jenner • Bibbi Jensen • Ingvar Jensen • Jens Jensen • Jim Jensen • Nisse Jensen • Tova Jensen • Jack Jester • Nils Johansson • Maglena Larsdotter Johansson • Carol Juhlin • Al Johns • April Johnson • Ed Johnson • Edwin Johnson • Eric Johnson • Fred Johnson • Gary Johnson • Gary Johnson • Gwen Johnson • James Johnson • Linda Johnson • Marcia Johnson • Pat Johnson • Carl Johnson • Tracey Johnson • Kip Johnson • Ted Johnson • Viola Johnson • Linnnea Johnson • Linda Johnson • Wesley Johnson • William Johnson • Bill Jones • Ken Jones • Anders Jonsson • Margareta Olofsdotter Jonsson • Jon Jonsson • Sofia Andersotter Jonsson • Nils Jonsson • Sue Ann Jinbo • Erika Lindfors Jonsson • Barb Jones • Rod Joslin • Kathy Jowers • Marshall Jowers • Bob Judelson • Thomas Juedes • Margie Juedes • Merel Julia • Raul Julia • Greg Junkin • Michelle Junkin • Ben Kadish • Mitch Kahn • Helen Kane • Jim Kanki • Koji Kakizawa • Linda Kanning • Myron Kanning • Mindy Kaplan • Karol Karlblom • Robert Karlblom • Greg Karr • John Kasper • Sam Katz • Sue Kaufman • Kristy Keefe • Rick Keenan • Kath Keenan • Patrick Keenan • Norman Kerr • Carol Keddie • David Keddie • John Kehoe • Mary Jo Keith • Kevin Keith • Ed Keley • Dennis Keller • Connie Keller • Bernard Kelly • Peter Kelly • Bob Ketchum • Terry Kennedy • Donna Kindl • Priscilla Kim • Young Kim • Beth Kim • Sarah Kim • Vicky Kim • Brendon Kim • John Kindschuh • Bill Kirkwood • Dan Klaus • Arnie Klein • David Klein • David Klein • Eric Klein • Shelia Klenia • Dan Kletnick • Terry Klocke • Martin Knanishu • Sally Knanishu • Sonja Koenig • Tom Koenig • Lida Koerner • Ron Kok-Alblas • Linda Kok-

WE ARE ASLEEP

Good morning, guten morgen, bon jour, dzien dobry, buenas dias. In any language—this is your wake-up call.

Sleep is defined as the natural periodic suspension of consciousness during which the powers of the body are restored. Focusing on the first part of the definition, **I assert that we are asleep more than 90% of an average day. We are robotic and mechanical, unconsciously living our lives in and through our minds.** We cruise along on autopilot, stressed out, spaced out, preoccupied, and internally focused. We confuse busyness and the accumulation of material wealth with well-being. We confuse "showing up" with being present. We are not actively, consciously participating with ourselves, our families, our communities, our nations, or the world.

These descriptions don't apply to you? Perhaps you don't know that you are sleeping. Try playing around with some new distinctions and watch where they lead.

People who are fully awake:

feel pain, suffering, or stress as it occurs and take appropriate action.

sense a friend's turmoil and respond accordingly

absorb the sights, sounds, and smells when they're outside

connect during conversations with a spouse or best friend

back off when they tailgate someone

notice if they smoke, eat, or drink too much

recognize when they "tune out" in a conversation

notice when they're in the "Huh" state (as in "Huh, what did you say?")

observe themselves daydreaming or feeling bored

notice when they are blaming/acting to please others, or feeling guilty or obligated

can identify lack of passion in their lives

vote, volunteer, recycle, and otherwise contribute to their community

get to know their neighbors

feel comfortable when meeting new people

have a vision for their lives

routinely tell the truth

schedule time based on priorities

make and keep commitments

take actions based on their promises and desires

acknowledge themselves and express appreciation of others

If this list does not describe your typical behavior, you may be asleep—your consciousness suspended, out of touch with yourself and the world—even during your waking hours.

Chapters Five and Six are intended to support you in observing your inner world. As you read each article, put yourself into the text and observe yourself, rereading as necessary to gain clarity. Keeping a journal will aid your self-discovery.

Exercise

Observer Consciousness

Observer consciousness, the act of noticing our state of being in the moment, is a process by which we can discover when we are wakeful and aware and when we are on "autopilot."

You can observe the difference between awareness and an unconscious, rote, reflexive, habitual way of being. Self-observation allows you to get in touch with your attitudes, behaviors, and thoughts at a deeper level.

Ponder the following questions and write your responses in your journal.

How many hours do you typically sleep each day?

How often do you catch yourself daydreaming?

How often do you have an internal conversation with yourself?

How often do you forget who you are calling or what you want to say?

How often do you forget to do something?

How often do you misplace or lose something?

THE JUDGE—THE INNER CRITIC

Typically, our most frequent thoughts are self-critical. A steady dose of self-criticism is like an anesthetic, progressively deadening, closing down our bandwidth, putting us to sleep. To make matters worse, we fortify the inner critic with fear and self-loathing.

This tendency toward destructive self-criticism develops over a period of many years, beginning when we are small children. Insatiably curious, we wanted to touch, grab, bite, and taste everything around us. Our parents, sitters, and siblings, ever concerned for our safety, told us hundreds of times, *"No," "Don't touch," "Watch out," "You'll hurt yourself!"* While some of this guidance was necessary, the negative tone constituted a dramatic shift away from pure love.

At age two, fascinated with wheels, buttons, levers, switches, elevators, escalators, and fire, we were safety risks. The "terrible two's" moniker was slapped on, and exploration was termed "misbehaving." In this time of tremendously creative growth, nearly everyone around us was unconsciously squashing our developing bandwidth. Thus began our conditioning to negativity; "Something's wrong," "I'm messing up," "I'm failing." This training continued as we grew.

As children beginning school, our bandwidth was expanding with unbridled energy and enthusiasm.

We were pure potential and possibility "in progress." Our capacities to learn and process new experiences were fully engaged.

Simultaneously, we were also experiencing the hurtful behavior of others—as we were ignored, ridiculed, embarrassed, and criticized. Ill-equipped to cope with these insults from adults and other children, we naturally developed our defenses and internal survival mechanisms.

Soon we began criticizing ourselves, in an unconscious pattern, which, for most of us, will continue until death. We started thinking, "Something's wrong with me." **Controlled by fear, we learned to question our desires and to distrust our instincts.**

Flash back to a traumatic or embarrassing memory from elementary school. Maybe you had to read a passage aloud, or you didn't get to the bathroom in time, or you were picked last for dodge ball. Perhaps your stomach ached, your throat felt constricted, or your hands became clammy. Overwhelmed by the experience, you simply didn't know an appropriate response to the confusion, upset, and fear.

These incidents (and others like them) stimulated significant contraction of bandwidth, leaving a trail of emotional debris in your mind and often in the cells of your body. The conclusions drawn from these childhood experiences became the basis for most of your negative, high-volume thoughts. And, your high-volume and repetitive thoughts are the constraining parameters of your bandwidth.

The internal monologue of the mind becomes more and more self-critical during the teen years. Mounting peer pressure and criticism from siblings, parents, teachers, and other adults add to teens' struggles. They begin to seek ways, often inappropriate, such as alcohol, drugs, and unsafe sexual behavior—to escape this network of negativity.

Most parents are well-intentioned and truly love their children. But, they are blind to the impact of their self-critics on both themselves and their children. Compounding matters, parents often "beat themselves up" for not doing a better job of parenting, and sometimes blame teachers or other adults who have their own self-critics operating. No wonder there is such friction and frustration in relationships between teens and adults!

Nearly everyone in our self-criticizing culture ultimately succumbs to the norms of society and, to differing degrees, become mature self-critics. This programming is reinforced through news, magazines, movies, soap operas, and sitcoms. Most of what is presented as comedy is heavily salted with criticism, antagonism, or put-downs. Stinging one-liners, one-upsmanship, and sarcastic references, and all forms of external criticism work to reinforce our inner critics.

BANDWIDTH CONTRACTION SPIRAL

INNER CRITIC
UNSURE PERFORMANCE
LACK OF CONFIDENCE
SELF DOUBT
UPSET
POOR RESULTS
LACK OF TRUST
struggle, effort, tension, pressure
fearful, contracted, overwhelmed

This graphic illustrates the contraction that occurs with self-criticism.

Some people are able to break out of this cycle. To them, self-doubt is perceived as a challenge to be overcome. **A low volume of self-critical thoughts is conducive to bandwidth expansion.** For most of us, however, our inner critics are high volume—loud and frequent—constricting bandwidth at every turn and lowering self-esteem.

THE OTHER JUDGE—THE OUTER CRITIC

Because what we see outside of ourselves tends to be a reflection of our inner world (view/orientation/ experience), a natural extension of the inner critic is the outer critic. Harsh judgments and hurtful opinions leveled at us by others can be just as incapacitating as the voices of our inner critics.

People who criticize others are inclined to be very self-critical as well. My own mother was more critical than my father. He tended to be very accepting. But, I spent considerably more time with my mother, and guess whose trait I picked up!

Honest feedback or straight talk from the "heart" (or spirit) is not the same as criticism. Consider the source of the words and how you feel when you hear them. Criticism will generally trigger a negative or defensive reaction in your mind. Straight talk or constructive feedback feels different. It is not reflexive, vindictive, or malicious. Frank, constructive feedback serves no ulterior motive and carries no hidden agenda. It is an authentic, genuine, and clean, observation, and it's easier to listen to.

Our inner and outer critics drain the energy of those around us and form the basis of disempowering relationships. Collectively, criticism is the source of low- or negative-energy in organizations.

EXTERNAL CONTRACTION SPIRAL

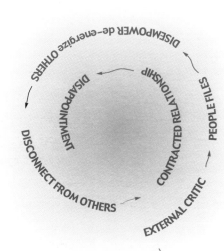

Note how the External Critic Contraction spiral is connected to the Bandwidth Contraction Spiral, and how they feed each other.

THE VICTIM

Another high volume thought is that of the "victim." *"I'm getting shafted." "Why does this always happen to me?" "Nobody likes me." "If it weren't for bad luck, I wouldn't have any luck at all." "I'm a walking example of Murphy's Law." "I can never win." "Woe is me!"*

Hundreds of millions of people in the developed world abdicate responsibility, blaming and complaining about the quality of their lives. All their problems are the result of circumstance, timing, and fate. Family, schools, spouses, governments, bosses, corporations, religions, politicians, and interest rates are to blame for their predicaments.

Resenting, seeking sympathy, manipulating, whining, and passive-aggressive behavior are common manifestations of victim mentality. Health problems can spring directly from the victim mindset. Such a mindset can speed the progression of an illness or prevent healing, especially if attention, sympathy, and freedom from responsibility are included in the victim package.

Low self-esteem and victimhood often fly below the radar screen. We have all played the victim role, and we all have, at times, experienced low self-esteem. These insidious killers of human spirit impact our energy levels and those of everyone we touch.

WE INTERACT WITH "PEOPLE FILES"—NOT PEOPLE

Waking up one morning in Bombay, India, I looked out of the hotel window to the street below and wondered: Why was I born in Chicago? I looked at the carts, mopeds, and miniature taxis making their way into the center of the city. For a fleeting moment, I mentally traded places with a man riding on an ox cart. What would it really be like to be that man?

What if we adopted such questions during every conversation? "If I were the other person, what would be occurring in this conversation for me?" Our sense of each other could only be improved as a result.

We North Americans are very quick to judge (a common manifestation of the external critic), and judgments are seldom accurate. **A judgment results from a particular point of view at a particular point in time. The point of view could change an instant later, invalidating the judgment. Judgments, by their very nature, are incomplete, yet our minds fix on them as if they are matters of fact, the whole story.**

Our minds interpret (categorize, classify, judge) our impressions of other people based on what we can perceive—physical characteristics, temperament, personality, dress, speech, accent, role, status, reputation, how they remind us of someone else, etc.

We store these judgments and interpretations in our mental filing systems. Then, we interact with our "people files," instead of the actual people. This process of profiling and stereotyping disconnects us from others.

Most of us have thousands of people files catalogued in our minds. Each new person we meet is instantly compared with our stored mental files. Drawing on these comparisons, we fill this stranger's file with our own historical data! Cheerful, poor, bright, funny, uneducated, chauvinistic, ingratiating -these are labels we apply to others within moments of our first meeting them.

At around age four or five we begin passing our people files to others, often unsolicited. As adults, we constantly exchange people files in social, business, and family conversations, sometimes deliberately (i.e. networking), but often unconsciously (gossiping).

Once we create a file to describe someone, we tend to resist or overlook his growth. We operate as if he will always match what is in our file on him. The longer our history, the more this tendency is true. Consider how difficult it is to throw off childhood labels with family or old friends. *"Oh, she's been a ditz ever since I've known her." "You never could spell / cook / be on time / keep your clothes clean." "He's a control freak—always was. Remember how he used to decide which game we would play?"*

One of my former clients, a human-resources executive, often described his coworkers as if they were their resumes. For him, someone's work history automatically predicted her future behavior. (His predictions were pretty accurate, which certainly reinforced his pattern.) Such characterizations, however, tend to blind us to the complexities and potentials of our colleagues.

People files are not just in our minds. Real files exist, too. There are files about you at the schools you attended and the jobs you've worked. Hospitals, clinics, insurance companies, banks, brokerage firms, and credit card companies have documented your health and financial histories. Airlines, hotels, and car rental firms have your travel habits on file. From an institutional perspective, we are our files, and decisions are regularly made about us based on those snapshots.

In addition to people files, we create files on everything we experience—from foods to cities to almost any kind of thing or event in our lives. Name it and you will immediately access a corresponding file for it, containing your opinions, interpretations, and conclusions gathered since early childhood.

But who are we, really? Does the most exhaustive list of characteristics, roles, experiences, and stereotypes come even close to defining us? Does being categorized, slotted, and labeled serve a useful purpose?

Obviously, we are more than a collection of conclusions, opinions, and interpretations. Each of us participates in this life journey in our own unique way. **No set of files, however comprehensive, can totally capture our human spirit and essence.**

None of our people files contain current (up to the PRESENT MOMENT) information. Even fewer are future-oriented. Our files, whether stored in our mind, in a computer, or on paper, are historically based. People files (and every other kind of file) are only records of the past. The moment we create a file, both the file itself and its contents are outdated.

HIGH-VOLUME THOUGHTS PROGRAM OUR WORLD

High-volume thoughts are those that recur frequently. The volume and content of a person's daily thoughts are a function of that person's age, gender, occupation, and level of awareness. A young child's thoughts are fewer and less repetitive than a sixty-year-old's. Men typically have a greater volume of thoughts than women, because men tend to live more in their minds and less in other dimensions of their bandwidth. Women working in male-dominated environments may experience growth in their volume of thoughts as a response to that culture. Mothers, on the other hand, are generally predisposed to action, emotion, and sensory activity, and they will have correspondingly fewer thoughts.

Accountants, lawyers, or systems analysts might easily have more thoughts than people working at counter sales or giving care to the elderly. As awareness grows, however, one is likely to spend more time in the PRESENT MOMENT and less time in the mind with his or her thoughts.

High volume thoughts typically have their genesis in early childhood experiences and may often be of a traumatic nature. Such thoughts can repeat thousands of times a year. For example, when I was ten years old, my family was awakened by the screams of our neighbors, whose house had caught fire. Fortunately, everyone was evacuated safely, including my friend. The fire started at a stove burner, causing a towel to ignite. Afterwards, I began checking the stove burners every night before I went to bed. Not a bad thing, but it started in response to trauma, which gave rise to a repetitive thought, which resulted in years of daily ritual behavior!

Some say that each person has five or six high-volume thoughts repeating hundreds of times every day. If true, then adults over age forty have repeated those thoughts over a million times. This repetitive thought process programs the way we view the world, other people, and ourselves. These thoughts shape our behavior and influence our preferences, expectations, and opinions. To a large extent, they determine our habits and patterns.

The same phenomenon occurs in organizations. When a group of people share the same thoughts, those thoughts become part of the corporate culture. This culture shapes behavior, which produces either valuable or detrimental results for the company.

While the majority of high-volume thoughts are problem- or fear-based, **some high-volume thoughts are constructive. They enable perform-ance.** Thoughts of compassion, courage, achieve-ment, accomplishment, and contribution often provide inner strength or inspiration to take on challenges. Early childhood successes in school, arts, or sports provide a platform for adult accomplishment. Such experiences produce an internal monologue with thoughts such as, *I can do this ... Almost there...I have done this before...This really gets my adrenaline going... I love a challenge.*

Self-observation will reveal your high-volume thoughts. Once identified, examination of each high-volume thought can provide deeper insights and learning. Examination may involve questioning, investigating, or testing a thought to find its core or source. I suggest making notes of your thoughts. Then, when you are alone, quiet, and able to focus, examine your thoughts to discover what is behind your habits and patterns.

Notice the stream of thoughts you experience as you wake up on a workday. This flow continues through the day and even as you dream in sleep.

ARE YOU USING YOUR MIND OR IS YOUR MIND USING YOU?

One of the most powerful choices we can make is to use our minds, rather than be used by our minds. When we are unconscious, our minds "use us." We can only use our minds when we are awake. Being awake provides us the opportunity to choose.

When solving a problem, analyzing information, or deliberately remembering an experience, I am directing my mind to a purpose. I consciously use my mind to retrieve information, recognize, associate, analyze, synthesize thoughts, compare, and evaluate.

Retrieving a phone number, remembering someone's name, recognizing a physical landmark, giving directions, remembering a list of groceries, or analyzing a financial statement are practical examples of conscious use of mind. Likewise, offering an opinion, answering or asking a question, making reservations, remembering appointments, and creating to-do lists are useful, PRESENT MOMENT, mental actions.

When you are preoccupied with the chatter of your inner monologue, your mind is using you. You are in an unconscious state, an involuntary mode,

listening to your thoughts like you listen to background music in a restaurant. You do not consciously tune in. Your thoughts are just broadcasting and you get hooked. Unconscious mental activity may include tuning out, daydreaming while someone is speaking to you, interrupting, eating without tasting, over-reacting, responding automatically or habitually, indulging a habit, worrying, or fearing the unknown.

Your mind can be accessed through many portals. It is something like an attic, a repository of all your history, the warehouse of your paradigms. Triggered hundreds of times every day by thoughts, comments, or visual cues, you move into your history so quickly that you may not even realize that you've left the PRESENT MOMENT.

Thoughts about the past or future—states that exist only in the mind—pull us out of the PRESENT MOMENT. People often ask, "How do I get into the PRESENT MOMENT?" In reality, we never leave it. We exist only in the PRESENT MOMENT. It is home base. But, our habit of overlaying the PRESENT MOMENT with steady streams of thoughts obscures this fact.

Dwelling in the world of our thoughts, our minds deprive us of access to the universe—the pure potential of the PRESENT MOMENT. Most of our time is taken up by our unconscious, internal monologues.

Observation and examination are keys to distinguishing between consciously using the mind versus being unconsciously used by it. Observe your thoughts as you would clouds drifting across the sky, or floats passing by in a parade. Simply notice them and let go of any attachment you have to them. When you're able to distinguish conscious use of your mind from unconscious use, you take the next step to full bandwidth.

Following are some conscious uses of the mind:

Analyze	Calculate	Think
Identify	Plan	Visualize
Read	Associate	Question
Write	Remember	Answer
Recognize	Follow instructions	

These are some common, but not absolute, manifestations of unconscious use of the mind:

On Autopilot	Tuned out	Interpretations
Judgments	Habits	Stereotyping
Patterns	Nervousness	Preoccupation
Comparison	Worry	Reaction
Opinions	Daydreaming	Repetition
Stressed out		

COMMUNICATION

Our practice of communicating (listening and speaking) predominantly from our mind bands is severely limiting, leading to disconnection and ineffectiveness. Opening to our emotional, sensory, and spirit bands will often provide greater opportunities and insights into people's needs, wants, and possibilities, leading to deeper and more satisfying connections.

Filtering our listening narrows bandwidth

Listening is an incredible human capacity, one that most of us will sabotage to one extent or another. When listening, we tend to shift, imperceptibly, from the sensory activity of hearing to the mental activity of "processing the communication," which then interferes with our listening!

How often, in meetings, do you sense people are busy, preparing what they will say, rather than truly listening to the speaker? How many times in a day do you tune out other people? Have you ever said to yourself, "Here we go again!" when someone brings up a subject? Are you able to interrupt your internal monologue long enough to really hear another? How long can you listen before you drift away? How often do you retreat into your mind to judge and evaluate what others are saying instead of staying with them and really listening?

Most of us filter our listening through our minds, triggering history, attitudes, biases, opinions, judgments, memories, etc., all the while formulating our responses. This process effectively tunes out much of what is being communicated, as well as the other channels or bands. A conversation between minds is inauthentic because it is not grounded in the PRESENT MOMENT. Consequently, mind-to-mind is the weakest of all potential connections.

Listening beyond the words

How many times have you spoken to someone only to realize they are not listening? When we really listen to someone, we listen beyond the words. We feel for the emotional undertones. We check out the unspoken messages. *"You sound frustrated."* We make certain we have heard the whole message before launching into our response. *"You are angry that I forgot to pick up milk. You asked me three times. You think I wasn't listening. You think I don't listen to you a lot. You feel like you aren't important to me."*

If we have listened carefully, the speaker will often respond with *"Yes, and not only that, but,"* continuing to send more of the message. If we have misunderstood, he will clarify, *"No, I'm don't think I'm unimportant. I just think talking to you is a waste of time."*

When you tune into what is happening with the speaker on all levels, you become a vessel waiting to be filled, encouraging the speaker to express himself fully and without censor. You dwell in the PRESENT MOMENT, expanding your awareness to include whatever you see, hear, and feel. You move beyond your mind's filters, connecting through your eyes, ears, emotions, and the rest of your being. As a result, the speaker is empowered by your listening. (Another possible outcome is that others may listen to you in the same way when it is your turn to speak.)

Speaking

The flip side of unconscious listening is unconscious speaking. Most people speak as unconsciously as they breathe. Words come out of their mouths, without regard to who is listening, how what they are saying is being received, or if their verbal message is consistent with their non-verbal signals.

How often do you speak over others to "get the floor?" How often do you attempt to influence or project your point of view on someone? When you speak, do you know if you are connecting with your listener(s)? If you aren't connecting, do you stop? Or talk more loudly? How often do you allow your emotions to become a part of your message? Speaking with passion or emotion can create connection, depending on the emotion and where it's being directed. Do you communicate appreciation?

Dialogue is much more effective than monologue. Talking *with* people rather than *at* people produces substantially different communication. People want and need to participate. Give and take is crucial. Questions and answers (or debriefing sessions, in work environments) allow people to speak and listen.

Learning to communicate from broader bandwidth enables us to speak or respond appropriately in each situation. **Authentic communication involves being fully present with one another, speaking and listening, transmitting and receiving.** Sometimes the message is wordless and mindless. It is a touch, a smile, a shout, a silent walk together, or tears. Words are important, but not always mandatory.

When we are listened to, it creates us, makes us unfold and expand. Ideas actually begin to grow within us and come to life. You know how if a person laughs at your jokes you become funnier and funnier, and if he does not, every tiny little joke in you weakens up and dies. Well, that is the principle of it. It makes people happy and free when they are listened to . . .

When we listen to people there is an alternating current, and this recharges us so we never get tired of each other. We are constantly being recreated . . .

In order to learn to listen, here are some suggestions: Try to learn tranquility, to live in the present a part of the time every day. Sometimes say to yourself: "Now. What is happening now? This friend is talking. I am quiet. There is endless time. I hear it, every word." Then suddenly you begin to hear not only what people are saying, but also what they are trying to say, and you sense the whole truth about them. And you sense existence, not piecemeal, not this object and that, but as a translucent whole.

A passage from *If You Want to Write: A Book about Art, Independence and Spirit* by Brenda Ueland.

OUR MINDS BECOME OUR PERCEIVED IDENTITIES

The cumulative effect of self-criticism, judgment, people profiling, high-volume thoughts, and speaking and listening from the mind is contracted bandwidth. Poor performance, low initiative, lack of creativity, deteriorating relationships, ego problems, disconnection, low self-esteem, introversion, and aggression are all indicators of low-bandwidth. Whenever we experience such states, we are unconsciously allowing our minds to be our masters. Our minds are using us.

After a lifetime of conditioning, most of us come to believe that our internal voices are who we are. This false identity, forged in the mind, constantly asserts itself to remind us of who (we think) we are. High-volume thoughts and years of judging and criticizing ourselves have programmed us.

If we cannot get beyond our minds, we'll always operate on low bandwidth, limited by the boundaries of our perceived identities. If I call myself a worrier, then what else can I become? If I say I am a conservative, what will I be? If I label myself "nice," or "not good enough," or "lazy," or "shy," then how will I behave?

It is critical to understand that we are not the ones labeling ourselves in such ways. It is our minds—only one of our six bands of energy—that are labeling, stereotyping, judging, evaluating, and opinionating. As we discussed earlier, the process of internal judgment, criticism, and labeling begins early in life and later manifests in behaviors consistent with those labels.

This internal labeling is hard on any kind of relationship. We project our minds' historical identities on to our partners, children, bosses, friends, and then we expect conformance to those projected patterns. Giving up this habitual way of being may be required for success in relationship, but such a radical change constitutes a serious threat to our survival-oriented minds. People living at low bandwidth will always resist or avoid change, artfully or otherwise.

As a result of our attachment to our mind's perceived identity, we cling to beliefs that no longer serve us and to opinions that no longer reflect reality. We repeat techniques, strategies, and habits that may have worked in the past but are only marginally effective now. In these ways, we inhibit

our aliveness, our natural curiosity, learning, and growth. We no longer yearn for change, and instead seek comfort. We reside with a fixed stock of attitudes and actions, bound to the past and asleep to the PRESENT MOMENT.

We can see this process in people who seem to be perpetually caught up in fear or pain. Unwilling to let go of their habitual beliefs and behaviors or to trust their senses, feelings, and spirits, they misidentify their ability to tolerate the status quo as security, the comfort of their routines as happiness. The old hurts are too painful to confront. The status quo, as miserable as it may be, is preferable to the unknown. Fear keeps them in that "safe" place, where they have adjusted to their problems, inhibiting them from leaping into the unknown for real solutions to their problems.

Stilling our minds to the PRESENT MOMENT is only possible when we overcome our fear and directly confront our pain. It is in that moment of courage, releasing our attachment to the past, that we are able to free up the energy we have spent on maintaining the past. It is then that we get our first glimpses of new possibilities for the future.

YOU CAN GO BEYOND YOUR MIND IN ANY MOMENT

You do not have to be a slave to your mind. At any moment, access to the creative power of full bandwidth is available—through awareness of spirit. As you become aware of the distinction between mind and spirit, you can let go of your mind's thoughts, habits, and patterns. You can calm your mind, turn down your internal monologue, and access your higher intelligence.

Accessing our human spirit effectively is only possible when we have discovered and confronted our attachment to our minds. (North Americans, as a group, have notoriously full minds. Our culture reflects the extent to which we are mind-dominated. Witness the complexity, confusion, and chronically short attention spans of most adults).

When we are able to observe and examine the mechanisms of our minds, we can go beyond them. The goal is not to harm our minds or to make them disappear. They are far too useful and entertaining for that.

The real enemy is not the mind but our attachment to the mind. Thinking, analysis, and judgment are indispensable skills, when used consciously and appropriately. The problems arise when our minds take over as our sole source of guidance, using us for their own survival (the survival of all the opinions, stories, beliefs, judgements, and labels that constitute the identity of the mind). The ability to clear or bypass our minds whenever we choose will give us access to the energy and possibility of the PRESENT MOMENT.

# Exercise

Observe the impact of your mind

Waking up is essential to being present, and being present is the access point to higher bandwidth. You can begin by waking up to your "mindfield"—your stream of thoughts. Begin to observe the mechanics of your mind and the impact your mind has on you. Record your observations and insights in your journal.

Reflect on the beginning of your day. What is your pre-work routine? What is your attitude and mood as you awaken? As you begin work? How much of the first two hours of your day are you present? What are the repetitive thoughts you have every morning?

Be aware of your repetitive thoughts throughout the day. Are you present when you greet your co-workers? Does your mind automatically pick up where you left off yesterday? Do you approach your day with dread, upset, irritation, annoyance, or resignation? Doing so will produce a different set of thoughts then when you like what you do and the people you do it with.

Next, consider what happens to your mind band as you leave work. What thoughts occur as you leave work? Do you drive home in a "veg out" state? If you commute, do you sleep on the train?

Now reflect on mind activity during your time away from work. What do you do after work? Do you shift into higher bandwidth, being present with friends or family? Do you use alcohol or other drugs to numb your mind or emotions? What kinds of activities help you "empty" your mind? What kinds of activities get your mind "buzzing?"

Observe your mind activity during the transition to sleep. How many and what kind of thoughts do you have right before bed? Which ones are repetitive thoughts? Do your thoughts keep you awake? Can you quiet your mind enough to drift into sleep? How active is your mind when you sleep?

Studies have shown that approximately one third of adult sleep time is similar to being awake. During the rapid-eye-movement stage of sleep, heartbeat and respiration become irregular. Electroencephalograms reveal brain activity similar to that which occurs in the waking state. An active mind diminishes the quality of sleep. Combining this with too little sleep leaves people tired and operating on decreased bandwidth. It is very difficult to be aware when you are tired. An over-active mind, during either day or night, perpetuates low bandwidth.

Profile: Jelaluddin Rumi

A simple and eloquent metaphor for thoughts is that they are house guests. Imagine that your mind is a house. Every day, thousands of guests visit this house. Most of the guests are uninvited; nonetheless, they are present. Your job is simply to become aware of them without judging them—an attitude captured in this poem from the 13th century by Rumi.

THE GUEST HOUSE

This being human is a guest house.
Every morning a new arrival.

A joy, a depression, a meanness,
Some momentary awareness comes
As an unexpected visitor.

Welcome and entertain them all!
Even if they're a crowd of sorrows,
Who violently sweep your house
Empty of its furniture,
Still, treat each guest honorably.
He may be clearing you out
For some new delight.
The dark side, the shame, the malice,
Meet them at the door laughing,
And invite them in.

Be grateful for whoever comes,
Because each has been sent
As a guide from beyond.

Jelaluddin Rumi was born in 1207 in Afghanistan and spent his first 37 years as an Islamic teacher and scholar. After meeting a wandering dervish named Shams of Tabriz, Rumi began a new career as an ecstatic mystic and poet.

CHAPTER VI :
Living on Wide Bandwidth

YOUR NAME

Born:

Fell Asleep:

AWAKENED:

Died:

It takes a person who is wide-awake to make his dreams come true.
—Roger Babson

Albas • Pat Kolas • Debbie Kolb • Tom Kolb • Barry Komie • Pam Kopach • Marty Kopach • Frank Koranda • Detlef Koska • Izzy Kosover • Dave Kowalczyk • Hope Kracht • Tom Kracht • Pat Kramer • Richard Kramer • Don Kreag • Joan Krikau • Mark Krikau • Joseph Kruszynski • Mike Kucinic • Nancy Kucinic • Ken Kuehnle • Carolyn Ash Kuhn • James Kuhagen • Judith Kuhagen • Neal Kuhn • Annie Kuhn • Marcia Kurtz • Bob Kunkel • Scott Kuperberg • Marylin Kuypers • Gary LaCroix • Harry Lake • David Lambersten • John Lambert • James Lambert • Jack Lancaster • Jim Lancaster • Rick Landry • Moses Landsman • Bob Lane • Dick Lane • Wendy Lane • Lynn Landers • Bob Lang • Steve Lang • Larry Lannon • Jim Lantz • Sandrine Larsen • Mary Larson • Lars Larson • Bert Larsson • Carol Larsson • Scott Laster • Evelyn Laster • Alan Laster • Barry Laub • Joanne Laub • David Laurine • Al Lavender • Bob Leach • Lisa Leawitt • Gary Leblanc • Gene Lee • Tricia Lee Liberti • Robert Lehman • Pete Lennox • Paula Leonard • Pierre LeRoy • Gary Lester • Donna Lester • Ted LeVander • Harry Levine • Howard Levine • Abby Levinson • Ellen Levitt • Jason Levy • Matt Levy • Bill Levy • Marge Levy • Don Lewis • Sheila Liberman • Tricia Lee Liberti • Chris Liethen • Steve Liethen • Paul Lilek • James Liljegren • Michael Linburn • Ron Lincoln • Wally Lindahl • Ethel Lindahl • Ann Lindahl • Karen Lindahl • Charles Lindberg • Beverly Jean Linden • Viola Linden • Wally Linden • Jonas Lindfors • Elsa Norberg Lindfors • Bob Lindmark • Pat Lindmark • Thorsten Lindmark • Sigrid Lindmark • Gunnar Lindmark • Gary Lindmark • Marcia Lindmark • Jennifer Lindmark • Kyle Lindmark • Rick Lindmark • Susan Lindmark • Carl Fredrick Lindmark • Anna Kajsa Olsson Lindmark • Ingrid Lindmark • Johan Lindmark • Maria Ruderberg Lindmark • Nils Lindmark • Katarina Wennersten Lindmark • Nils Lindmark • Maria Assmundsdotter Lindmark • Bob Linehan • Valerie Linehan • Todd Linehan • Brian Linehan • Kevin Linehan • Tim Linehan • Bob Linehan • Gladys Linehan • Ron Link • Alicia Lipe • Richard Litt • Charles Lo • James Lo • Russell Lockridge • Rollie Loess • Roy Lofquist • Viola Lofquist • Marvin Lofquist • Dale Lofquist • Charlie Logullo • Frank Loll • Dick Loncar • Bob Long • Marilyn Long • Lance Lorentzen • Brian Lonstad • Bucky Lord • Sy Lotsoff • Daniel Lounsberry • John Lounsberry • Jim Lovell • Bud Lowell • Kathy Lowell • Shelly Lubar • Jerry Lucas • Maureen Lucas • Andrew Lumbrazo • Pamela Lundblad • Bryce Lundeen • Charles Lundholm • Marv Ludwig • Dan Lupiani • Dominic Lupo • Gary Lussenhop • Pauline Lussenhop • Ronda Lynch • Eric Lynch • Natalie Lynch • Lloyd Mabbott • Susan MacCoy • Helen Mackie • Del Mackie • John Mackenbach • Lynn Maddox • Cindy Magnuson • Keith Magnuson • Bob Mahoney • Don Maier • Marcia Makepeace • Gosha Malgorzata • Jim Malito • Barb Malito • Jim

WAKING UP!

Whether your awakening is gradual and pleasant like a cat stretching in a sunbeam or abrupt and harsh like being jolted out of a sound sleep, when you become conscious, there is a shift in your energy. From a bandwidth perspective, you regain the use of your senses, emotions, spirit, brain, and body. You move beyond your mind into the PRESENT MOMENT. You begin to see, hear, know, and feel your inner and outer worlds.

As you go about your everyday activities, you judge less, are less critical, feel calmer, more focused, connected, and engaged. You speak with greater clarity, listen more deeply, and think and learn more quickly. You are more creative, compassionate, open, and present.

Self-awareness creates awakening. It is one path to rediscovering and encouraging the inner self to unfold. Self-awareness has a light and a dark side. It is a journey that, when undertaken with commitment and patience, will produce thousands of insights and connections, transitions and trans-formations, upsets and disappointments, choices, actions, and results.

Self-awareness is our innate ability to observe and report what is happening inside our selves. It is one manifestation of activated bandwidth. Generally, we aren't aware of our emotions, senses, bodies, or thoughts. When we are aware, we often mistake these experiences and sensations for our identities, allowing them to define who we are.

Self-awareness allows us to observe ourselves with detachment. In this detached state of disidentification, we know that we are not our sensations, emotions and thoughts. Rather, we have these capacities which produce emotions, sensory inputs, thoughts, and body sensations. In other words, you are not your back pain, anger, poor eye sight, or thoughts of insecurity.

Awareness feeds on itself. As self-awareness increases, overall awareness expands beyond self to others and to the world at large. We can contribute by increasing our own awareness and helping others to increase theirs.

Most people are born healthy and with their basic human capacities intact. Unfortunately, over two-thirds of the world's population are not provided with opportunities to exercise their capacities because they are unable to meet their most basic needs. But, most of us who are not starving, sick, malnourished, or at war, still do not access the breadth of our bandwidth. We spend the majority of our lives in our minds (i.e. on narrow bandwidth).

As we discussed in prior chapters, our parents, mainstream society, and most educational systems do not question, study, or seek to engage all of our human capacities. There are, however, institutes, organizations, and communities which offer forums for learning, practicing, and living on wider bandwidth (although it is not termed bandwidth.) And, of course, there are thousands of books and tapes exploring every aspect of human potential.

The possibility for being exceptional or extraordinary is within each of us. Like a muscle weakened or atrophied through disuse, our capacities remain intact, dormant, waiting to be exercised and developed. Ultimately the discovery, development, and utilization of one's capacities is an individual journey, taken from the inside out. The launching pad for this journey is the PRESENT MOMENT.

One of the great human mysteries is that the source of our creativity, power, and aliveness is invisible and intangible. Saints and sages throughout the ages were in agreement: life occurs in the PRESENT MOMENT. Examine the philosophies of India and the Far East, the works of Socrates and Plato, the teachings of Buddha, and the life of Jesus. Behold the creative genius of Michelangelo and Beethoven, the persistence of Madame Curie or Thomas Edison, the courage of Martin Luther King, Jr., Nelson Mandela, and Mother Teresa, and the loving care of mothers. One thread unites them all—their strength, wisdom, clarity, or genius illustrated their being in the PRESENT MOMENT.

LIVING IN THE PRESENT MOMENT INCREASES BANDWIDTH

Those who live on wider bandwidth experience higher levels of consciousness or awareness, and are in the PRESENT MOMENT with greater frequency. They channel their energies away from what drains them toward more productive, present moment endeavors.

The PRESENT MOMENT is the realm of energy, creativity, true awareness, talent, potential, and possibility, the gateway for anyone who chooses to be truly alive. Being in the PRESENT MOMENT gives rise to peace, love, vibrancy, productivity, and satisfaction.

After his team's sixth NBA Championship victory, Michael Jordan was asked, "What happened during those last minutes of the game?" Jordan responded, "I was in the moment. I was totally focused. On the last shot, I saw the rim so clearly. I just elevated and shot the ball." In sports, this is known as being in the "zone."

Such experiences are not confined to athletes. In the PRESENT MOMENT, we tap into an individual and collective energy that enables us to be creative in any context — sports, the arts, healing, public speaking, listening, a sales call, or a school assembly. Through the PRESENT MOMENT, we connect to a reality beyond our bodies and minds.

In the PRESENT MOMENT, we can access and express our whole beings, our full bandwidths and our full ranges of potential. We feel our emotions. We come alive to sensory inputs. Our minds no longer interfere with the spontaneous creation of our lives (remaining quiet until the moment we choose to think actively). With expanded awareness, our human spirits are expressed. The integration of all our bands and their dimensions occur naturally and spontaneously, moment after moment after moment.

LIFE: TIME & ETERNITY MEET IN THE PRESENT MOMENT

Awareness unfolds in the PRESENT MOMENT, where there is no mind to interfere with the direct link-up to our potential, power, energy, or possibilities. While the mind is limited to its historical inputs and extrapolations of those inputs into the future, awareness is the unlimited and untapped quantum field of all possibility.

THE GAP IS THE PRESENT MOMENT

1. Typical thought pattern of the human mind.

Thought	Thought	Thought	Thought	Thought	Thought	Thought
gap	gap	gap	gap	gap	gap	

2. Increased awareness widens the gap between thoughts.

Thought		Thought		Thought
	GAP		GAP	

Apollo 14 astronaut Edgar Mitchell had a transcendental experience on his return flight from the moon, about which he wrote: "On February 9, 1971, when I went to the moon, I was as pragmatic a test pilot, engineer and scientist as any of my colleagues. But when I saw the planet Earth floating in the vastness of space…the presence of divinity became almost palpable and I knew that life in the universe was not just an accident based on random processes. The knowledge came to me directly, noetically."

If you've ever looked toward the heavens on a clear night and focused on the stars for a little while, you may have felt an inexplicable sense of connection. Your essence, being, or spirit is part of the field of information, intelligence, and energy known as the universe. To paraphrase Einstein: "The universe is this vast quantum field of possibilities with different probability amplitudes. There is an unexplained mystery to all this which is confrontive to the logical mind."

Each of the more than six billion human beings on the planet occurs as a different and distinct possibility in the infinite PRESENT MOMENT. Imagine the variety of human activity occurring at any one point in time. There is no history or predictability in the infinite and eternal PRESENT MOMENT, only billions of possibilities. Accessing this infinite field of possibilities can occur through any of our capacities.

The probability of successfully harvesting this field of potential increases as we more fully use the breadth and depth of our capacities.

The vertical line represents a moment—the PRESENT MOMENT. If we covered the page with a series of parallel vertical lines, each would represent a moment of NOW, NOW, NOW, NOW, NOW. **Each point on the vertical line represents a possibility, anything that could occur in the PRESENT MOMENT.** The vertical line represents the non-observable bands of energy. This is our connection to the collective energy field known as the universe.

The horizontal plane represents time from past, through present, to future. Thoughts, actions, and emotions occur in time. We age from moment to moment. Our historical minds are the primary band on the horizontal plane. Our material possessions, status, roles, successes, and failures exist on this horizontal timeline.

The horizontal line contains our life stories, the progression through all of life's milestones — birthdays, graduations, marriages, anniversaries, deaths. The horizontal plane encompasses our daily schedule of activities, our typically mind-based existence, bouncing between the past and the future. At its worst, Shakespeare called it the "petty pace of life." At its best, it is the opportunity to create the lives of our dreams!

We all live our lives on both planes. Shifting from narrow to wide bandwidth may be very subtle, yet the difference is spectacular. **Those who live a life of narrow bandwidth hold close to the time plane, reacting to the circumstances of their daily lives.** They are watching life go by, perhaps complaining about their situations. Rarely do they generate energy for others.

People on broader bandwidth live more often along the vertical line — the PRESENT MOMENT. They participate more fully in life. Such people lead, create, and take responsibility for their circumstances. They generate energy and share it with others. They seize opportunities and add value. These are the agents of change.

LIFE IS THE INTERSECTION OF TIME AND ETERNITY IN THE PRESENT MOMENT

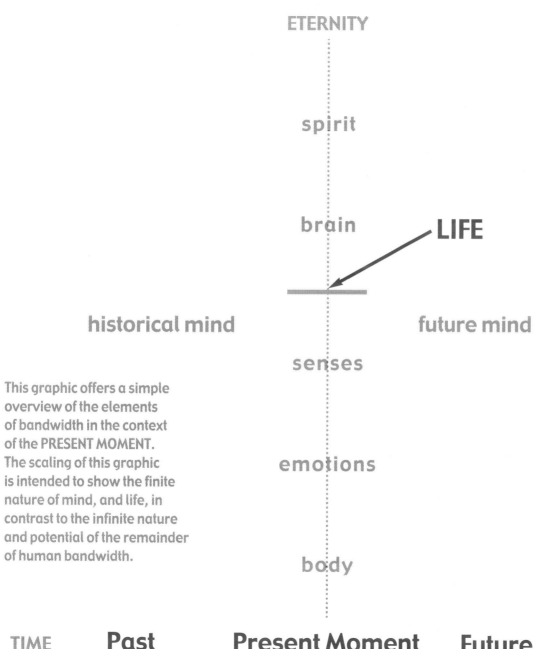

ETERNITY

spirit

brain

LIFE

historical mind   future mind

senses

This graphic offers a simple overview of the elements of bandwidth in the context of the PRESENT MOMENT. The scaling of this graphic is intended to show the finite nature of mind, and life, in contrast to the infinite nature and potential of the remainder of human bandwidth.

emotions

body

TIME   Past   Present Moment   Future

WIDENING BANDWIDTH THROUGH OBSERVATION

By quieting your mind, you can begin to notice yourself, your environment, and other people. You become aware of your body — feeling your hands on the steering wheel and your back pressing against the seat. You feel your feet on the ground when you walk or run. Aches, fatigue, and other sensations are felt in various muscles. You notice the spontaneous neuromuscular coordination occurring naturally in all of your physical activities. You notice the fluctuation in your energy levels during the day. You become more and more conscious of yourself in an active state.

By quieting the mind, you notice your emotions coming up spontaneously. You notice when you are pulled into the internal monologue of your mind. You notice the reaction set in motion by a fearful thought or experience: your hands becoming clammy, your shoulders tightening, your stomach churning, and your thoughts racing.

You hear your own speaking. You become conscious of your tone of voice, your choice of words, and of how others are listening to you. You begin listening to others in such a way that they experience your energy and connection.

Then you go even deeper, noticing your breathing, conscious of the air flowing into and out of your lungs. You may sit for a while and soak up your surroundings. After exercising, you may choose to rest and experience the calm in your body. You observe the never-ending parade of thoughts coming and going, coming and going.

As you sink into a more peaceful state, your powers of self-observation and awareness increase. You can intentionally attain this state through conscious breathing, meditation, or by just being still and focusing in your body.

In the development of self-awareness, your powers of observation grow keener. You may begin to see and feel beyond the physical form to the person's inner spirit. You may connect with a loved one in ways you have never experienced before. You may begin to reach teams of people with all the bands of your energy field. Touching upon the spirits of others, you become aware of the limitless possibilities in relationship. Spirit has no boundaries; it is intertwined with everything and everyone.

The act of quieting your mind, being in the PRESENT MOMENT, creates greater awareness. The result is greater:

Caring	Sharing
Giving	Peacefulness
Focus	Gratitude
Appreciation	Contribution
Expansion	Clarity

Initiative   Satisfaction

Passion   Energy

Spiritual connection Productivity

Fun   Loving

Laughter   Acknowledgment

Acceptance   Joy

Heightened awareness will also reveal how much time you spend daydreaming or lost in your internal monologue. You may find it unpleasant to discover how often you:

Go unconscious   Don't respect others

Don't listen   Are self-centered

Are petty   Daydream

Feel angry   Have low energy

Forget things

Are late for appointments

Tolerate clutter in your surroundings

Forget people's names Are bored

Judge and evaluate people

Indulge habits or addictions

Don't speak what is on your mind

Tell people what they want to hear

Ignore the signals of your body

EXAMINATION AND INVESTIGATION

The initial level of self-awareness occurs through observation — of one's thoughts, body, behaviors, attitudes, and habits. **Recording these observations facilitates examination, which in turn leads to insight and action.** These are powerful steps toward expanding bandwidth.

As you reflect on your observations, do you see patterns or trends? What is their frequency? What are the influencing factors or root causes for those patterns? Is action necessary? What people come to mind as you examine these insights? What more do you want to learn?

Questions of this type help us to stay focused. Answers are not as important as staying in aware-ness. (Answers are typically mind-based explana-tions, justifications, rationalizations, judgments, etc. Awareness transcends the mind.) Bring focus to your insights from as many perspectives as you can. Keeping a journal is useful since insights often occur over a period of time.

You may deepen your inquiry by talking to other people, sharing your insights with them, and get-ting their perspectives and feedback. For example, siblings, parents, or family friends may be able to share details about childhood events or experi-ences. You may discover information that facilitates further breakthroughs, connections, or insights. You may discover that you are genetically predisposed to certain traits. By all means, be the detective. Pursue and investigate. But do so consciously, for the ground you tread upon may be sensitive.

Examining our insights will often reveal "what we don't know that we don't know." Many of our thoughts, patterns, and habits are stored at a subconscious level, and our insights may crack them open. Insight may awaken you to a relationship between your unpredictable and turbulent childhood and how you now play the role of "control freak" or "victim." You may discover that you are on a life long quest for attention or affection. Perhaps you experienced your parents abandoning you emotionally. You may feel the need to constantly "prove yourself," and connect that with being told as a child that you weren't good at something. Ever since then, it's been "I'll show them!"

We all have these patterns. Some people successfully use their patterns to motivate change. Most of us are shackled by our unreconciled histories.

SELF AWARENESS REVEALS CHOICES

Have you ever caught yourself in the middle of an argument, realized you were wrong, admitted it, and apologized? That is an example of powerful self-awareness. **When you catch yourself in the middle of an experience, you can turn up the wattage on the spotlight of your self-awareness.** You recognize what is going on in your body, you notice your emotions, you are aware of your energy. You notice if you are reacting, creating, or avoiding. **This self-awareness gives you choices to act upon: to move more deeply into, revise, or discontinue the experience.**

As our awareness of each band of energy or capacity grows, we naturally expand. When we experience the vastness of our capacities—a sunset truly seen, an unthinkable goal accomplished, a connection deeply made—we often cannot find words to express what we have experienced. Experiencing the indescribable is a sure sign that we have gotten beyond our minds.

Increasing your awareness and experiencing yourself can put you in touch with suppressed emotions. If you feel frightened or upset, it is time to pause, take a few deep breaths, notice the thoughts linked with the emotions, and the powerful effect they have on you. (Professional counseling, during this process of increasing awareness and investigating patterns, can be very beneficial, especially if you feel overwhelmed by your insights and emotions.)

At some point, you will discover the common thread that runs through all of your observations, inquiries, investigations, experiences, and learnings. In that moment, set aside self-blame, shame, or guilt. Set aside self-esteem, pride, and satisfaction. Consider, instead, the possibility that you are the creator of your life.

Naturally, many of these experiences are not created at a conscious level. You are often reacting to influences outside your control. But you are the one who is reacting. You can choose to act instead of react.

Whether we believe it or not, we are at the helms of our human lives. As we progress on the inner and outer journeys of widening bandwidth, we will detect more and more of our own fingerprints on our adventures.

CREATING IN THE MOMENT

In his epic book, *Man's Search for Meaning*, Viktor Frankl wrote that "life holds a potential meaning under any condition, even the most miserable ones." As he described his life in the concentration camps during World War II, he concluded, "What was really needed was a fundamental change in our attitude toward life. We had to learn ourselves and, furthermore, we had to teach the despairing men that **it did not really matter what we expected from life, but rather what life expected from us.**"

This change in attitude allowed Frankl and other prisoners to share food, share memories, share hope, and to help each other survive the conditions of the camps. Frankl and others who survived the concentration camps lived on broader bandwidth than most of those who awaited death. Even in the most harrowing circumstances, they claimed authorship of their lives. They experienced an inner freedom, and they acted with compassion.

Your nature is one of pure possibility. You are capable of creating whatever you choose. In the PRESENT MOMENT, faced with infinite possibilities, you are free to choose the focus both of your attention and your attitude. In the PRESENT MOMENT, you can choose a new way to interpret your current circumstances. In the PRESENT MOMENT, you can declare your commitment. In the PRESENT MOMENT, you can choose the life you are willing to create. In the PRESENT MOMENT, you can choose to live or die. (Think of the people with "terminal" illnesses who beat the odds and survive. Those whose mindsets are *"I am going to die,"* tend to spiral downward quickly.)

True choice happens in a space of consciousness or awareness in the PRESENT MOMENT. Habits, patterns, analysis, and evaluations are the tools of the historical mind. They create biases, not choices. Life doesn't have to be an extrapolation of the past. It can be a creative act occurring NOW, in the PRESENT MOMENT, utilizing all of your basic human capacities.

People are always blaming their circumstances for what they are. I don't believe in circumstances. The people who get on in this world are the people who get up and look for the circumstances they want, and if they can't find them, create them. —George Bernard Shaw

BEING CREATIVE IS OUR RAISON D' ETRE

Our unlimited capacities exist in a state of possibility, waiting to be unleashed. We are in a constant state of readiness, ready to create or generate an action correlated to whatever is occurring in the world.

Our purpose, our raison d'etre, is to create. It is the very nature of our beings. To be creative is to access our capacities and to exercise them through language and action. Since childhood, each one of us has had this fundamental human capacity.

Terms such as competencies, skills, aptitudes, levels of performance, and techniques imply that wide bandwidth can be taught. It cannot; it can only be experienced or expressed. Nor can creativity be taught. Creativity, generation, exploration, inquiry, and discovery are the natural unfolding of wide human bandwidth in the PRESENT MOMENT.

Creativity is to bring into existence, to grow, to bring about a course of action, to make, or to invent something new for the benefit of the creator and others. **Everything generates from the same "source," "possibility," or "pure potential:" the PRESENT MOMENT, activated by human bandwidth.**

People who see their lives as moment-to moment creative acts, for the benefit of themselves and others, lead extraordinary lives. Great teachers may see their purpose as raising students' awareness of their inherent capabilities. Some writers see their purpose as creating benefits for readers, who in turn share those benefits with others. Many doctors and nurses live to care for and facilitate the healing of others. Committed business people live to create products and services that are needed and wanted by others. Entertainers assist people to detach from their minds for a while and literally "re-create" (as in "recreation") themselves.

At this point, you may notice your inner voice talking about your lack of creativity. "I have nothing in common with DaVinci!" OK, you aren't DaVinci, but you have access to infinite possibility to be creative in your own unique way.

During the last 300 years, people have changed little in a physiological sense. Yet, their range of basic human capacities — their bandwidth — has expanded significantly. Increased creativity is the natural result of bandwidth expansion. Look at the breakthroughs in standards of living in the last 100 years: nutrition, medical care, food production, housing, transportation, and communication. In our homes we have electricity, plumbing, automatic furnaces, washing machines, and televisions.

Consider expanding your definition of being creative to include yourself. In some areas of your bandwidth, you are in the early stages of creativity and in others, you are more advanced.

Not everyone who reads this book will move to higher levels of creativity. Yet, everyone I have known who expanded their bandwidth made quantum leaps in their performance in many aspects of their lives. Awareness is the first step, an awakening to who we are and what is possible. Once we become more competent self-observers, we discover we have the choice to utilize our expanded capacities. Expanded capacity (bandwidth) is a natural outcome of creativity, and creativity is enhanced as bandwidth expands. It is a wonderful, self-reinforcing cycle.

Each of us has the choice to be either in our minds or in the PRESENT MOMENT, where we have access to the energy of the universe. When we dwell in our unconscious minds, life is a perpetual process of reaction. When we live in the PRESENT MOMENT, life is an ongoing process of creation.

CREATING BANDWIDTH PAINTINGS

As you begin to get a feel for your capacities or bands of energy, try to see them as an artist sees a palate of watercolors. Each color (or band) can be used directly, or shaded, blended, or thinly brushed on the canvas. Accessing only your mind band is like painting with only one color — intense and arresting, perhaps, but ultimately one-dimensional.

Living according to others' expectations, or being limited by your own belief system and history, is akin to paint-by-number. Instead, you can use your capacities the way an artist uses color, creating light and dark, perspective and connection, depth and meaning.

A painting is an expression or experience of color, style, tone, theme, highlights, brush strokes, sensory perceptions, emotions, and spirit. Similarly, you can choose to consciously blend your words, feelings, thoughts, body movements, sensory perceptions, and energy level. You can modulate the depth and breadth of each capacity, depending on the situation. The wider your bandwidth, the more combinations of colors, styles, and themes you will have to choose from. **Higher awareness allows you to imagine, visualize, and paint rich scenes, evoking emotional or spiritual responses in others.**

CONVERSATIONS AND ACTIONS REVEAL US

Consider that our daily lives consist entirely of conversations and actions, wherein all the elements of our capacities converge. All that we create or do occurs in one of these realms. Dreaming, thinking, speaking, listening, loving, hating, fighting, cooperating, building, writing, cleaning, traveling, playing, gesturing, crying, shouting, laughing, dancing, and breathing all occur in conversation and/or action.

Words often make up only 30 – 40% of a conversation. The other 60 – 70% is nonverbal: emotional mood, tone of voice, eye contact, body language, and energy level. Unfortunately, as mentioned in Chapter Five, most conversations (and actions) occur at the level of intellectual content — one mind speaking to another mind. Even worse, "conversations" are often really parallel monologues. Instead of an exchange, a giving and taking between people, the parties are on autopilot, operating mechanically.

You've probably observed this in its most obvious form: people with a longstanding disagreement, rehashing the main points, neither willing to let go of his ideas long enough to try on a different perspective, neither truly listening to the other, both tenaciously entrenched in their world views.

Conversations that exercise a wide range of capacities are different, and you can feel the difference.

When we begin to connect with others at wider levels of bandwidth, we experience a shift in our attitudes and in our beings. We begin to see others as contributors and collaborators, rather than critics and competitors. Our conversations move from problems and pitfalls to possibilities and solutions.

Through words and motions, we convey our beings. We expand or contract our energy and connect with or disconnect from others through conversation and action.

> Commitment is what transforms a promise into reality. It is the words that speak boldly of your intentions.And the actions which speak louder than the words. It is making the time when there is none. Coming through time after time through time after time after time, year after year after year. Commitment is the stuff character is made of; the power to of; the power to change the face of things. It is the daily triumph of integrity over skepticism.
>
> — Shearson Lehman, American Express

LIVING AT WIDE BANDWIDTH

Commitment

Commitment is being your word. It means giving your word and taking the actions necessary to deliver, regardless of circumstances. Commitment comes from the heart and spirit. It transforms possibilities into action. **Commitment is that which propels you through the circumstances of your life toward your stated goals, values, and outcomes.**

It often exists in conflict with your thoughts and feelings. It is akin to passion.

Expanding bandwidth and developing capacities fuel commitment. Commitment requires the energy embedded in passion. It can rearrange an energy field or create a pathway to the moon.

On May 25, 1961, John F. Kennedy said, "I believe this nation should commit itself to achieving the goal, before this decade is out, of landing a man on the moon and returning him safely to earth." This was at a time when no one had a clear idea of how to accomplish this goal. Yet, by invoking this commitment, President Kennedy created a possibility, aligning the passions of scientific, academic, government, and military personnel to accomplish this utterly extraordinary feat.

Without commitment, the circumstances of life can easily derail you from living on wide bandwidth.

Creative Action

Creative action is the physical manifestation of bandwidth. It is multiple bands of energy in use simultaneously. Creative action may be natural, spontaneous, caring, conscious, appropriate, practical, loving, serving, or passionate. Creative action aligns energies and assists people to deal with the circumstances of life.

Creative action occurs everyday, all around the world, manifested in the technological, medical, and cultural advancements of our society. Yes, it is often a dance of "two steps forward, one step back." But, there is progress.

Did you know that microprocessors and Teflon™ were invented in support of the space program? Microprocessors were needed because booster rockets and landing craft could not carry the weight of existing computer hardware. Teflon was invented to protect spacecraft from the heat of atmospheric reentry.

Many creative actions serve to link or further the interconnection of the universe. Creative action occurs all around us in day-to-day living. Observe the actions of a first-time mother or those of a small child. And what, if not creative, are the actions of people in emergencies, or of almost anyone caught up in a dilemma or crisis?

Action in the PRESENT MOMENT is relaxed. When we are not present, our minds create tension and our actions are tense. Relaxed action generates energy. Tense action contracts energy.

Mechanical, awkward, fearful, reactive, hurtful, or mind-based actions are not creative. Neither are ego-based or identity-protecting actions. These tend to disempower people or generate negative energy.

Staying Awake

Staying awake is synonymous with being present – easy to write about but a bit more difficult to achieve. Being present entails a shift in consciousness. It requires the ability to get beyond the unconscious mind.

You can use your body and your breath to stay awake. Your body and breathing are always in the PRESENT MOMENT. When you are aware of your buttocks touching the seat of a chair, your feet touching the ground, a ring around your finger or air entering or leaving your nose, you are awake. When you feel the wind against your face, the heat of the sun on your neck, or the texture of a cracker in your hand, you are awake.

TOP BENEFITS FOR BEING PRESENT
Being present gives one access to:

Authenticity and truth	Love
Vision	Creativity
Contribution	Connection
Effectiveness	Original thinking
Genuine listening	Feeling
Discovery	Possibility
Responsibility	Choices
Observation of self and others	

* Add your favorites!

BROAD BANDWIDTH PRODUCES THE EXTRAORDINARY

Mind, brain, and body are the minimal bands required for writing poetry. Senses, emotions, and spirit are the bands which infuse poetry with palpable depth and character.

Ballet is fundamentally the body in motion. Expressing emotions, senses, and spirit, a dancer transcends mere motion and becomes music incarnate.

Basketball is legs running and jumping, and hands passing, shooting, and rebounding. When passion, court vision, and neuromuscular coordination are combined, the result is akin to ballet, with high energy flowing from one end of the wooden floor to the other.

Learning to play an instrument requires the senses, brain, and body. When emotions and spirit are woven in, true music is produced. A master musician is at one with the instrument, one with the music, and "out of her mind."

Service people use their brains, minds, and senses to help others and solve problems. Adding energy, spirit, and empathy generates satisfied customers and repeat business.

Your basic human capacities emanate from awareness itself. Waking up and expanding your level of awareness transforms your invisible bands of energy into the visible and audible manifestations of conversation and actions

▬▬〰▬Exercise

Reflections

At this point, I want to reiterate and underscore several points. Please pause for a moment and reflect on each of them.

First, there is no specific formula, right way, or precise methodology to widen bandwidth.

Second, the mind is overused, improperly used, and misunderstood by 99% of the population.

Third, each band or capacity has its unique ways of knowing, creating, doing, and sharing and yet is part of an integrated whole.

Fourth, spirit is the infinite capacity.

▬▬〰▬Exercise

Creativity Demonstrated

Draw a dozen identical circles on a sheet of paper. Are your circles exactly the same? Do you need an instrument to measure them or can you tell just by looking that each circle is unique?

Sign your name a dozen times. Are you able to write it exactly the same each time?

Record yourself speaking a greeting and your name a dozen times. Do any of your recordings sound exactly the same?

I think more than anything it seems there's absolutely no limit to what plain, ordinary working people can accomplish if they're given the opportunity and the encouragement and incentive to do their best. Because that's how Wal-Mart became Wal-Mart: Ordinary people joined together to accomplish extraordinary things. —Sam Walton

Profile: Brenda Ueland

But before I get down to brass tacks and talk about writing itself, I want to say a few more things about the imagination, the creative power in you, how to detect it, and how it works.

I will tell you what I have learned myself. For me, a long five or six mile walk helps. And one must go alone and every day. I have done this for many years. It is at these times I seem to get re-charged . . .

. . . when I walk grimly and calisthentically, just to get exercise and get it over with, to get my walk out of the way, then I find that I have not been recharged with imagination. On the following day, when I try to write, there is more of the meagerness than if I had not walked at all.

But if when I walk, I look at the sky or the lake or the tiny, infinitesimally delicate, bare, young trees, or wherever I want to look, and my neck and jaw are loose and I feel happy and say to myself with my imagination, "I am free," and "There is nothing to hurry about," I find then that thoughts begin to come to me in their quiet way.

My explanation of this is that when I walk in a carefree way, without straining to get to my destination, then I am living in the present. And it is only then that the creative power flourishes.

Brenda Ueland wrote books, articles, and short stories and taught writing. This passage is from *Strength to Your Sword Arm, Selected Writings* by Brenda Ueland (Holy Cow! Press, 1992). Copyright by the Estate of Brenda Ueland and reprinted by permission of the publisher. All rights reserved.

CHAPTER VII :
Organization and Disorganization

Powerful individuals are compassionate and generous because they instinctively realize that power continues to flow through them only when they pass it on. Like electricity [bandwidth], the more energy, inspiration and information they can conduct, the more they can receive.
—R. L. Wing, *The Tao of Power*

Mallnar • Bill Malloy • Tom Maloney • Gene Mandarino • Nelson Mandella • Paul Mangimele • Tony Manno • Diane Manno • Juliet Manno • Johan Mansson • Stina Stockkrisdotter Mansson • Frank Manzeske • Linda Maravich • Mitch Maravich • Rajyo Markman • Toba Marks • Chic Martin • Bill Martin • Ed Martin • Larry Martin • Larry Marshall • Arnold Mason • Bob Massini • Ray Matesevac • Ollie Matson • Ron Marek • Brian Matura • Marlan Matus • Jeffrey Maurus • Joellen Maurus • Robert Maxwell • Kristen Maxwell • Liam Maxwell • Sheila Maxwell • Guthrie May • Bernard Mayle • Jack Mc Cabe • Bob Mc Kinney • Ann McAdory • Bill McAdory • Marti McAllister • Jack McCabe • Becky Mc Cleery • Karen McCollough • Paula McCoy • Donald McCraw • Malcom McClean • Tim McGinley • Mark McGuffie • Bill McKeand • Will McKeand • Marty McKeand • Bill McKenna • Molly McKenna • Will McKenna • Kelly McKenna • Laura McKenna • Michael McKenna • Michael McHugh • Marion McMaster • Mike McMaster • Tom McMillan • Ann McNulty • Dave McNulty • James McNulty III • Marilyn McVicker • Kim Meador • Tom Meador • Don Meek • Bob Mellander • Betty Mellinger • John Mengelt • Joan Menke-Schaenzer • Jim Merkel • Joe Messina • Sue Messing • Richard Metzner • Bob Meyer • Chris Meyer • Dennis Meyer • Pat Meyer • Phyllis Meyer • Tom Meyer • Bob Meyers • Gary Meyers • Jean Meyers • Patty Michalek • Bob Mike • Richard Miles • Arthur Miller • Bert Miller • Diane Miller • Geoffrey Miller • Nancy Miller • Pam Miller • Terry Miller • Larry Miller • Monty Miller • David Mincberg • John Minichiello • Kim Minichiello • Minne Minoso • Steve Minteer • Bob Mitchum • Bernie Mnichowicz • Barb Mnichowicz • Rog Mohr • Janet Moline • Norman Moline • Norman Moline Jr. • Ragnar Moline • John Molburg • Arlene Monahan • Jim Monahan • Phil Montanus • Pierrette Montroy • John Mooney • Susan Mooney • Bill Moorcroft • Doug Moore • Rob Moore • Sarah Moore • Sherry Moore • Jerry Morales • Tom Moran • Harry Moravec • Wayne Moretti • Jack Morphew • Butchie Morphew • Jim Morris • Larry Morris • Don Morton • Doug Morton • Arthur Mueller • Graydon Mumford • George Munno • Edwin Munson • Bruce Murray • Pat Mulhearn • Bill Mullins • Jack Munfield • John Munsell • Don Murphy • David Murray • Ron Mushinsky • Alan Musikantow • Caroline Myss • Bob Naas • Val Nache • Dale Nagelkirk • Ron Nahser • Keith Nakamoto • Susan Nakamura • Glen Nakayama • Jay Narco • Madeline Narco • Carol Narens • Dick Narske • Dennis Nash • Lisa Nash • Brian Nash • Peter Nash • Kim Nash • Morris Nathanson • Mario Natta • Gary Nel • Hugh Nellans • Charles Nelson • Ed Nelson • Eric Nelson • Ethel Nelson • Jim Nelson • Mary Nelson • Shelly Nelson • Ward Nelson • Jim Nelson • Margie Netzer • Marty Netzer • Allison Neumeister • David Neumeister • Annie

SEEDS AND STONES

When I was a child growing up on the south side of Chicago, my parents raised vegetables in a vacant lot across the street from our house. I remember one spring morning watching my dad prepare the ground for planting. I was fascinated by the rows of small trenches that he dug, and by the idea that a seed would grow into a plant that would produce corn or beans.

Later that day, in one of my mother's unused flowerbeds behind the garage, I dug my own trenches and planted small stones I had found in the alley. When my parents watered their garden, I watered mine. A few days later I noticed sprouts coming out of the ground in their garden. In my garden, I saw nothing except a few weeds.

My mother saw me behind the garage and walked over to see what I was doing. "Oh, you have a garden," she said with surprise. She asked me what I had planted. I told her about the stones, and that I was growing my own corn. She smiled and said, "Stones don't grow. Stones and seeds are different."

Sensing my disappointment, my mom and dad helped me dig up the stones and replace them with seeds. Green shoots were soon penetrating the topsoil, and I tended my garden until fall, when my parents took a picture of me with the corn we harvested.

In first grade, I learned about seed germination. I watched a lima bean, which I put into a jar with paper towels and water, develop a root system and sprout. Much later, in high school chemistry, I learned the difference between organic and inorganic—a distinction that echoed my earlier lesson about seeds and stones.

Recently, I was inspired to apply that same lesson to business organizations. After being part of many organizations, investing in many companies, and experiencing hyper-growth with one organization, I was struck by a dichotomy: **What distinguishes popular, fast-growing, or successful organizations from stagnant, bureaucratic ones?**

Thousands of articles and books have attempted to answer this question. Thousands of lectures and speeches have outlined factors that make organizations (business and otherwise) succeed; factors which include leadership, vision, technology, total quality management, flexibility, change management, integrated processes, continuous improvement, customer focus, product reliability, and service excellence. This list will no doubt continue to grow as new theories develop.

I suggest that all of the above factors are but part of the equation. There is something more—the difference between seeds and stones. As we move into a discussion of collective bandwidth in its most common form—organizational bandwidth—we will integrate a new distinction:the difference between organic and inorganic elements.

ORGANIZATIONS: PEOPLE AND STUFF

Every organization is comprised of organic and inorganic elements. Organic elements are living beings—people. Inorganic elements are "stuff" or "things." **People are the living, ever-changing, creative, organic elements that energize and animate the inorganic, non-living elements. Some organizations center on "seeds"—the people who infuse the organization with energy and vitality. But most business organizations center on "stones."**

Inorganic elements have no inherent energy, spirit, creativity, productive capacity, coordination ability, or potential to grow. Mission statements, concepts, ideas, policies, procedures, rules, and goals—all these are inorganic. True, all have been created by people but all are intended to support, enable, standardize, and channel human energy. By themselves, these things have no life.

Inorganic elements (like words, concepts, and ideas) are only meaningful when infused with the energy of people. Processes are created, designed, developed, executed, and interconnected by people. Purposes are created, articulated, agreed upon, and put into action by people. Products, programs, and services are created, designed, produced, sold, and delivered by people. Goals are established and achieved by people. Metrics or grades are determined and monitored by people. All of the above is also true about policies, procedures, and rules.

Inorganic elements limit and control people, unless they are purposefully configured to empower. When that happens, organizations are created in which the imaginations and creativity of people are boundless.

ORGANIC FOCUS = ORGAN-IZATION

Of the people, by the people, and for the people is a phrase in the United States' Constitution that embodies the spirit of our country. There is no more succinct language to sum up the opportunity created for us as Americans or the essence of who we are as a country. The period of American history that produced the Constitution demonstrates collective bandwidth—spirit, mind, emotions, senses, brain, and body of the colonists.

Of the people, by the people, and for the people also describes successful organizations. A business organization is comprised of employees, investors, and suppliers organized and lead by owners or leaders for the benefit of customers. In turn, customers provide benefits and income for the leaders, employees, suppliers, and investors.

Organic, by definition, is non-linear and alive. Organization occurs when the interdependent elements of people, purpose, processes, and goals act in concert to produce a result. What distinguishes an organization from a random crowd is the alignment of energy, an explicit or implicit focus on accomplishing the agreed-upon purpose or mission.

Clarity of purpose or vision creates an alignment of human energies and helps build the speed and momentum of people moving toward a shared goal. When people are able to animate the company purpose, their energy is unmistakable. When the collective bandwidth of people is aligned to benefit, create utility for, or bring value to others, the result is an extraordinary organization.

This distinction between organic and inorganic elements isn't recognized in most conversations about organizations. People may know on some level that these elements differ, but few act on this difference. Distinguishing these elements can increase awareness and participation, thus creating value.

It is the people in any organization—not the "stuff" — who create, sustain, and maximize value. By discovering and focusing on its organic center—people— energy is increased and collective awareness is enhanced. Human spirit can permeate the organization and create a culture of participation, enjoyment, discovery, initiative, service, creativity, effectiveness, passion, commitment, and satisfaction. All of these qualities create value and benefit for the members of the organization and its customers. The cumulative effect is higher performance and superior results.

Organization doesn't really accomplish anything. Plans don't accomplish anything, either. Theories of management don't much matter. Endeavors succeed or fail because of the people involved. Only by attracting the best people will you accomplish great deeds. In a brain-based economy, your best assets are people. We've heard this expression so often that it's become trite. But how many leaders really 'walk the talk' with this stuff? Too often, people are assumed to be empty chess pieces, to be moved around by grand viziers, which may explain why so many top managers immerse their calendar time in deal making, restructuring, and the latest management fad. How many immerse themselves in the goal of creating an environment where the best, the brightest, the most creative are attracted, retained and, most importantly, unleashed?

—Colin Powell

(The term "people centered" could be substituted for organic. But organic is a multidimensional word that may open up the mind and create more associations.)

In an organically-centered institution—an "organization"—people interconnect both with each other and all the "stuff," providing the energy that activates the interdependent elements of the organization. Purpose and vision align individual energies and set a pace at which those energies move toward results by transforming purpose into action. People create and produce products and services for customers. People—not stuff—create value, benefit, and satisfaction.

THE ROLE OF LEADERS

Leaders are the primary source of organizational energy. They are the Chief Energy Officers (CEO's) and, ideally, there are many in every organization. Through their actions, passions, attitudes, and commitments, they expand or contract the collective bandwidth of an organization. They are ultimately responsible for its energy field, environment, and culture.

Extraordinary leaders, through their own example, energize others to make contributions. By sharing their awareness, vision, commitment, and expanded personal bandwidth, leaders align the energy of all constituencies and weave in the inorganic resources to accomplish the organization's purposes. They demonstrate what's appropriate, and redirect and balance bandwidth energy—of the people, by the people, and for the people. They pass along power rather than hoard it for themselves.

Extraordinary leaders appreciate the need for an aligned, unified field of energy to successfully achieve organizational outcomes. They understand the delicate nature of organ-izations, continually sensing and respecting its interdependent, organic elements. They know how to use their power to guide, facilitate, empower, and inspire rather than manipulate, control, or rule. They are compassionate and serving, able to balance individual ego desires with the needs of their collective constituencies.

Leaders set and maintain standards for every facet of the organization. Leaders with broad bandwidth, and therefore higher awareness, will raise the organization's standards. Their principal focuses are people-related standards such as employee development and customer satisfaction (organic) which lead to higher financial standards (inorganic). Many leaders fall into the trap of focusing on financial results. Financial results are an outcome or by-product of the cumulative efforts of employees, suppliers, and customer satisfaction.

The most enduring quality of extraordinary leaders is their authenticity. At their cores, they are perceived as "real, straight, and truthful." This high bandwidth state can be sensed by everyone.

On the flip side, when leaders are self-absorbed or egocentric, members of the organization are unable to identify with them. People fear and resent being manipulated, degraded, or controlled. In many companies, there are too many "controllers." When leaders misdirect or misuse their power, resistance, resignation, and distrust will result. Unaware leaders often shift the organizational context from organic to inorganic. Dis-organization is the outcome.

The difference between "WE" and "ME" is also the difference between extraordinary leadership and unaware leadership. Extraordinary leaders lead from a context of WE. Self-confident and highly aware, they guide others to align their intentions with specific outcomes. Such leaders know their job is to mobilize, empower, and energize others.

When an organization operates on wide bandwidth, its constituencies are better able to confront and solve problems and seize the opportunities. Wide bandwidth employees respond positively to challenges, rather than retreat from them. Customers feel cared for and served, responding by continuing (or increasing) their demand for services and products. It is a self-reinforcing cycle. "We reap what we sow."

Companies are not the only place where leadership occurs. Parents lead organizations called families, creating the environment, which may range from loving to fear-filled. Clergy lead organizations called churches, synagogues, or mosques. They are responsible to co-create the environment with the members of their congregations. University presidents and principals are responsible for the collective energy fields of schools. Professors and teachers are responsible for the energy field of their classrooms. And so on.

ORGANIZATION WITH INORGANIC FOCUS = DIS-ORGANIZATION

Bureaucracy is a compound word formed from bureau—a chest of drawers; an agency; a government department—and cracy, which is derived from the Greek kratia, rule. Contrast these words to democracy which is derived from the Greek word demos: the people; government by the people directly or through representation; equality of rights, opportunity, and treatment.

Nowhere in the Constitution is the word bureaucracy used. But once its framers had

God gave me my money. I believe the power to make money is a gift from God . . . I believe it is my duty to make money and still more money and use the money I make for the good of my fellow man, according to the dictates of my conscience.
—John D. Rockefeller

finished their work, the spirit of the document began evaporating in the operational implementation and actions of the United States Government.

What happened in the transition from the Constitution to the implementation of a federal government? In short, bureaucracy prevailed. The perceived need to compartmentalize generated a government with many separate departments: the Bureau of Engraving, the Bureau of Indian Affairs, the Federal Bureau of Investigation, the Department of Justice, the Department of the Treasury, the Department of Defense.

In business, the overlay is similar: the marketing department, sales division, finance department, manufacturing division, service department. Specialization of labor developed to mass-produce products, and the prevailing interpretation of efficiency at the time was to departmentalize, to divide work into parts.

When an entity is rigidly structured around specialization and departmentalization, it is no longer an organ-ization. It is a dis-organization, the result of structure superceding people. **Disorgan-ization occurs when a company focuses on form over substance**, and it compromises the entity's innate ability to be creative, change quickly, and grow naturally. Dis-organization has historical roots. Organ-izations with hierarchical designs that emphasize "stuff" over people are a carryover from the monarchies and class systems that predominated in the last millennium.

Most organizations introduce the inorganic elements of policy and procedure to boost efficiency and standardize practices. Numerous approaches to performing repeated tasks can be inefficient, time consuming, and wasteful. So, at the beginning of the 20th Century, Fredrick Taylor introduced a scientific management approach and standardized labor practices. Initial gains in productivity were huge.

More recently, information technology was developed to enable and support business activity. But, many companies installed information systems that dictated rather than supported the workflow. Thus, standardization, hierarchical structure, and systems became the inorganic core of many companies, all in the name of organizational efficiency.

Most efforts to channel human productivity result in people being boxed into patterns of work behavior based on job description. Long-term growth, development, and retention of employees—a company's primary interface with their customers—take a backseat to control. There may be short-term gains, but workers are soon conditioned to not explore, question, discover, expand, or pursue their natural curiosity. This ultimately limits growth and development of the company.

Having the focal point be conceptual, or inorganic, is not conducive to generating high energy in an organization. Theoretically, the inorganic elements are designed to support people, not to replace or suppress them. Goals, processes, policies, procedures, and systems are powerful, and they can be used to encourage, support, or enable people. However, when this "stuff" is substituted for people and their human spirit, organizational contraction results.

Focusing on the inorganic is analogous to attending a concert only to read the sheet music; going to a basketball game and watching the athletes play computer basketball; sitting in a hotel room at Niagara Falls and watching a video of the cascading water—or having customer complaints handled by an automated phone system.

ORGAN-IZATION AND DIS-ORGANIZATION RELATE TO BANDWIDTH

Understanding the differences between organ-ization and dis-organization helps distinguish low- from high-bandwidth organizations. **Bandwidth is mostly organic. Only one element of bandwidth connects with the inorganic, and that is the mind.** All the "stuff" which dominates so many organizations results from the activity of the mind.

Low bandwidth companies (dis-organizations) resist change. Inorganic elements (non-organisms) cannot change without human input, but many people become fearful when seemingly permanent elements are changed. They are accustomed to being on autopilot, cruising through repetitive processes and procedures without awareness or thought.

Conversely, in high bandwidth companies (organ-izations) the goals can be changed at will by people who are responsible for a specific outcome. **A fundamental property of an organism (a living or organic body) is the ability to create and repeat change.** Change is natural when the focus is on customers, but difficult when the focus is policy implementation or enforcement. Customer service policies are useful tools, but when form prevails over substance, organic focus (serving customers) withers. Employees who are given the freedom to exercise their entire bandwidth create value. Customers, clients, or members receive service beyond their expectations, and the organ-ization flourishes.

Any company is a network of living relationships, either connected or disconnected. In an organ-ization, people are more often in the PRESENT MOMENT, connected through multiple bands of energy, and producing results for all. In a dis-organization, people typically connect only at the band of mind.

Ideally, the collective bandwidth of an organization creates a whole that is greater than the sum of its parts. This has been demonstrated in the most successful businesses, sports teams, science projects, medicine, and the arts. Human spirit makes it possible for a team to be focused, committed, responsible, supportive, and to produce extraordinary results. Attitude is synonymous with spirit, and is the framework from which actions and behavior flow. Spirit embodies synergy, momentum, and collective intelligence, resulting in flawless execution.

This graphic represents an organically centered organization. Typically an organization has four major constituencies, represented by the circles, which are interdependent elements of the whole. The human spirit connects people with purpose and processes to achieve the organizational goals in a changing environment.

AN ORGANICALLY CENTERED ORGANIZATION

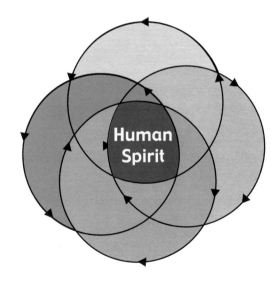

MALE AND FEMALE BANDWIDTH INFLUENCES ORGANIZATIONS

It is estimated that for more than three centuries men have held over 95% of all leadership roles in government, business, military, and education. In that 300+ years, the economy ran mostly on bodies—those of humans and beasts of burden. The body bandwidth dominated production.

Most organizations today are male-dominated, emphasizing the bands of mind and body. They are hierarchical systems, and they predictably generate inorganic elements such as plans, processes, products, goals, and technology. While these elements are necessary, organizations focused primarily in inorganic areas are compromised by their extremely low organizational bandwidth.

I have observed that, soon after a new business, concept or product gets off the ground in a male-dominated organization, bandwidth narrows to the predominant use of mind and body. Organizations with all male leadership tend to function with tense energy, under strong control. Organizations in which females have leadership roles tend to be more open, balanced, and progressive.

Certainly, gender bias has limited the full participation of women in society for more than 2000 years. The last 150 years has seen the women's movement (containing, among other things, the elements of universal suffrage, women's liberation, and the feminist movement) become a powerful sociological development. This movement has great momentum at the beginning of the 21st Century, and continues to alter the collective and organizational bandwidth of society.

Women naturally utilize the bands of emotion, senses, body, brain, and spirit, although they are often forced into "male" patterns in order to be successful in male-dominated arenas. As women gain fuller participation and power, the collective sensory, emotional, and spiritual bandwidth is expanding and balancing out the body and mind bandwidths.

As the influence of women grows, there is less competition and more cooperation within and between organizations (and countries). Missions, ideas, and challenges, characteristically male, harmonize more readily with listening, feeling, and relationships, which are characteristically female. Structures are becoming less rigid and controlling, more flexible and expansive. In time, giving and getting may even be reversed in order.

Emotions, senses, brain, and spirit generate innovation and growth, and more and more women are now demonstrating those capacities in the public arena. Not surprisingly, the service sector of high-tech industries (because they are newer) boasts the single largest percentage of women executives and business owners. **Increased participation by qualified women at every level of an organization can result in greater value and satisfaction for all constituencies.**

While customer-centered organizations are on the rise, managers of all types of organizations will benefit by looking at bandwidth, seeing if their organizations are operating on all channels. As human awareness increases and women continue to approach equality, men will find it increasingly difficult to satisfy their constituents while maintaining mind-based, command-and-control organizations.

A 1997 Gallup Survey of 55,000 workers found a strong correlation between financial performance and four attitudes:
(1) workers make a connection between their work and the company mission,
(2) they experience freedom to do what they do best every day,
(3) they believe their voices are heard, and
(4) they sense in their fellow workers a commitment to quality.

**Exercise**

Reflect on your experience with organization and dis-organization

Think of an important organization in your life. This could be your place of work or a business you frequent, such as a retail store or hotel. It might be a school or club, your church, synagogue, or mosque; or any organizational setting where you frequently spend time. Reflect on patterns of organ-ization or dis-organization you observe by answering the following questions:

- *What is your primary purpose for being affiliated with the organization?*
- *Is it easy to access physically? Do you have to go through gates or security guards? Is visitor parking closer to the entrance than employee or executive parking?*
- *Are the public areas as nice as the the private offices or areas?*
- *Is the receptionist friendly and attentive? On autopilot? Guarded?*
- *Is the facility user-friendly? Uncomfortably ostentatious?*
- *How does the physical space make you feel?*
- *Is it gender-neutral—inclusive of both men and women?*
- *What is the mood of the people you encounter?*
- *What does the body language of the people tell you?*
- *Are people in this organization present or in their minds?*
- *Do they focus on you or themselves?*
- *Do you get a helpful human being when you call?*
- *Do people respond quickly to your requests?*
- *Do you sense passion or commitment?*

Put your observations and reflections in writing.

Profile: Jack Welch

When Jack Welch became CEO of General Electric in 1981, he spoke about his vision and strategy during his first financial analysts meeting. He prefaced his speech with this definition of strategy: "Strategy is not a lengthy action plan. It is the evolution of a central idea through continually changing circumstances."

Welch declared, "GE will be No. 1 or No. 2 in every business we are in, measured by being the leanest, lowest cost, worldwide producer of quality goods and services or by having a clear technological advantage, a clear advantage in a market niche."

To achieve this central idea (vision), Welch proposed three intangible values:

1. Reality—Creating and developing an attitude which encourages people to see things as they truly are and to deal with what is, not what is wished or hoped.

2. Quality—Creating an atmosphere where every individual in the company is striving to be proud of every product created or service provided.

3. Human Element—Creating an atmosphere where people dare to try new things, knowing that the only limits on their creativity and drive (which will determine how far and fast they move within GE) are self-imposed.

Values one and three are the basis of individual and organizational transformation. Seeing and accepting what is constitutes awareness. Fostering the potential of people results in the development of their extraordinary natures.

Jack Welch effectively set the tone and context for GE in this powerful speech. He animated the vision and evolving strategy of GE by communicating it one-on-one and through his continuing development of people. Thousands of GE leaders were able to align employees to achieve his vision. After twenty years of creating collective awareness, Welch retired. After his farewell speech, he toasted GE senior leaders with, "Thanks for being so special. I love you all."

This profile was written by Gunnar Nilsson who is a shareholder and customer of GE.

CHAPTER VIII:
Organizations and Bands of Energy

Leadership in this new landscape is not about controlling decision-making... It's about creating the right environment. It's about enablement, empowerment... But the most magical and tangible and ultimately most important ingredient in this transformed landscape is people. The greatest strategy in the world, the greatest financial plan in the world, the greatest turnaround in the world, is only going to be temporary if it isn't grounded in people.
—Carleton Fiorina, President and CEO, Hewlett-Packard Company

Newman • Mark Newton • Chris Nichols • Herb Nichols • Steve Nichols • Peter Niemitz • Beth Niklas • Constance Nicklaus • Gunnar G. Nilsson • Vendla Nilsson • Petrus Nilsson • Borje Nilsson • Sonja Nilsson • Kenth Nilsson • Maila Nilsson • Jan Nilsson • Gerda Nilsson • Edith Nilsson • Signe Nilsson • Sofia Jonsdotter Nilsson • Jonas Nilsson • Emma Markstrom Nilsson • Jonas Gustav Nilsson • Erica Nilsson • Kirsten Nilsson • Laura Nilsson • Leo Nilsson • Ella Nilsson • Simon Nilsson • Bill Nissen • Pat Nissen • Phil Nixon • Jane Nohava • Shingo Nomura • Queen Noor • Chris Noon • Ulla Norberg • Herbie Norris • Carol Norris • Gerald Nudo • Britt Nystrom • Ron Obenauf • Cindy Officer • Jim Ogan • Britta Ohlson • Marten Ohman • Irene Ohman • Einar Oberg • John Oberg • Cathy O'Brien • Diane O'Connell • Denny O'Hara • Jim O'Keane • Sandy O'Keane • Tim O'Leary • Donald Olvigie • Bob Okita • Barta Andersdotter Olofsson • Enar Olofsson • Carol Olsen • Susan Olsen • Ken Olson • Michael Olson • Anna Kajsa Lindmark Olson • Per Olson • Amarta Lisa Johansdotter Olsson • Jan Olsson • Donald Olvigie • Ron Opper • Arlene Ores • Joe Ores • Dick Ores • Nancy Orlich • Andy Otting • John Osmanski • Arthur Oster • Betsy Osth • Eric Osth • John Osth • Lynne Osth • Andrea Owen • Owen Steve • Don Owen • Bud Owings • Carol Page • Joseph Parkander • Dorothy Parkander • Arnold Palmer • Coach Palmer • Catherine Parrish • Dov Parshan • Ellen Paseltiner • Scott Paseltiner • Don Pasquesi • Robert Pasqueti • Jim Passilino • James Patterson • Beatrice Paulino • Jon Paul • Susan Paul • Walter Payton • Ron Pearson • Sally Pearson • Charles Pechette • Malin Jonsdotter Pehrsson • Lars Pehrsson • Dick Pekofske • Jane Orr Peck • Page Pell • Van Pell • James Pellot • Gerald Penner • Larry Peoples • Javier Perez de Cuellar • Jack Peters • Cheryl Peterson • Edwin Peterson • Len Peterson • Les Peterson • Wallace Peterson • Andrea Petkevicius • Frank Petruzzo • Robert Piccirillo • Jimmy Piersall • Nelva Piersma • David Pilkington • Lisa Pilkington • Elkin Pincus • Sharon Pirchesky • Mel Pirchesky • Shelia Pizer • Howard Pizer • Mike Plunkett • Maja Pociecha • John Podmajerski • Thomas Podraza • Bernice Pollyea • Bill Pontikes • Ken Pontikes • Dennis Popp • Vicky Popp • Skip Porter • Dick Potter • Jack Powell • Randy Powell • Warren Power • Jim Powers • Pat Powers • Lloyd Powless • Morton Poznak • George Praggastis • David Price • Doris Pridmore • Jay Pridmore • Patsy Prince • Joe Priola • Phyllis Priola • Alex Priola • Carla Proffit • Robin Prokop • Donald Pryber • Roy Puccini • John Puotinen • Jim Purdom • Francine Purdom • Joe Purpura • Nancy Purpura • Stan Puttcamp • Dave Quade • David Quade • Kristen Quade • Pat Quade • Jim Quinlan • Bob Racz • Bob Ramsey • Barb Rock • Rose Rados • Viola Raguso • Al Randall • Joe Raver • Mike Ray • Tony Reaves • Marie Reed • Arlene Reid • Michael Reid • Brad

ORGANIZATIONS ALSO HAVE BANDWIDTH

The collective mind

Each of us is affected (programmed, actually) by the incessant chatter of our minds. Our histories, perspectives, habits, patterns, thoughts, and ingrained reactions largely determine who we appear to be and what we do. Organizations are programmed in similar fashion. The collective mind issues millions of thoughts, opinions, judgments, and ideas each day. Thoughts of unworthiness, ineptitude, and fear drain people of energy and perpetuate existing conditions. On the other hand, thoughts of contribution, service, and value energize and align people.

You've experienced the collective mind many times. Each time you visit a foreign country you experience the habits, patterns, and traditions ingrained in the culture. Advertisers and marketers strive to program the collective mind. Many companies have cultures to which employees are expected to conform. Fan clubs have strong opinions about their teams and their team's opponents. You may also experience the collective mind when working with a group of people to make something happen. Individual minds align, creating the focus and energy necessary to move a project forward.

An important function of the collective mind is it's capacity to link everyone together. Jargon, idioms, myths, goals, and values create the cultural fabric in families, companies, and countries. A mystic would say that there is no individual mind, only the collective.

The collective brain

As discussed earlier, the brain coordinates and integrates the six energy bands, and bandwidth manifests through language and actions. The collective brain coordinates the conversation and activity of a particular organization.

My experience with Southwest Airlines is an example. Within this "collective brain", gate agents are friendly and respectful. They handle check-in procedures quickly and courteously. I feel (emotion) served and cared for. The flight attendants have high energy (spirit), which is transferred through their smiles, humor, and attitudes. The employees appear to enjoy working with together. They seem to have transformed work into responsible "play."

In a company, the collective brain functions as network-based software, integrating and coordinating business and operational processes. Actual computer software assists, emulating that portion of the mind-brain oscillation effecting data transfer.

In contrast to the collective mind which is dominated and hardened by habits and assumptions from the past, the collective brain functions in the PRESENT MOMENT, free of historical constraints to generate new possibilities.

The collective emotions

Collective emotional bandwidth sets the tone or mood of an organization, helping outsiders to feel either welcomed and appreciated or excluded and suspect.

An organization's emotion band varies widely depending on its nature and purpose. Fan clubs are high-energy and emotional. Prison populations, on the other hand, exhibit low energy and high levels of fear and resignation. All emotions manifest on a continuum from connection to disconnection, from cooperation to competition.

Collective emotions in male-dominated organizations are often buried and can create apathy and resignation if not recognized and resolved. Contrast this with a Mary Kay Cosmetics convention, where emotions run high, associates are "turned on," and the resulting energy is channeled into generating sales. Acknowledging and supportive of each other, associates transfer this spirit of caring to their customer relationships.

Sororities, fraternities, high school clubs, fraternal groups like the Elks and Masons, and other social groups offer opportunities to be in relationship, and to channel spiritual, sensory, and emotional energies. Such organizations may have charitable and service programs, which extend the connectedness of the organization into the community.

You can learn much from observing the collective emotions of an organization and its constituencies. How do you feel when you participate in each of your organizations? Rewarded? Frustrated? Do you hear straight talk and candid feedback? Do you get as much as you give? How animated are meetings, parties, and events? How are outsiders treated?

The collective senses

Imagine a culture where people appreciate each other, listen respectfully, speak clearly, and respond appropriately to each particular situation. With some practice, you can tune into the collective sensory band of a team, company, or non-profit organization.

A few questions can guide your observation: Do you favor one store in a chain over another? Why? Is it because the employees notice your arrival, listen to your needs, and assist you more effectively? How attentive were the waiters in the nicest restaurant you've been to? Did you have to ask them to remove your plate or refill your water glass? Probably not. Are teachers at some schools better at sensing and addressing student needs than at others? In the meetings you attend, do people speak to be heard or just to hear themselves talk?

Dad believed in the dignity of the human spirit.
~Monte Schultz (son of *Peanuts* creator Charles Schultz)

The collective body

A collective body is a group of human bodies performing coordinated tasks in a work routine. On assembly lines, construction sites, retail stores, or restaurants, human bodies lift, carry, dig, and bend, creating products and delivering services as a collective body.

In churches, the collective body kneels in prayer and stands to sing. In a performance troupe, the collective body dances. In hospitals, the patients' collective body is in a very low energy state while the collective body of the staff is energetically engaged in a wide spectrum of physical activity.

During the last thirty years, the U.S. has experienced a significant shift from a labor economy to a service economy. Yet office workers still use their physical bodies to perform everyday tasks—keyboarding, walking, sitting—and their bodies experience work-related stress.

Stress is created when the unconscious mind has thoughts of overwhelm, disappointment, inadequacy, or performance deficiencies. These thoughts are transformed into the biochemicals of emotions (neuropeptides) and transmitted to the cells of the body. When thoughts and emotions are negative, bodily reactions such as stomach aches, ulcers, stiff necks, jaws, and shoulders, back pain, and chest tightness may result. If the organizational environment itself is negative, the stressful energy can engulf the people within. (Ghetto neighborhoods exemplify an organization engulfed in stressful energy.)

Many companies sponsor stress management or fitness programs to combat collective body issues. Safety is a major focus in most industrial organizations. Health club memberships are growing. A century of studies has chronicled more efficient and less physically damaging ways to use the human body, even at a keyboard. Collective body consciousness is on the rise, as evidenced by increasing awareness of nutrition, cholesterol, drug and alcohol treatment, alternative medicine, organic foods, and food labeling.

The collective spirit

Spirit is a collective phenomenon. It is an invisible energy, present everywhere and part of the fabric of the universe. Spirit does not have a specific location in the body, such as the heart or lungs. Rather, it is present in every living cell, enveloping and transcending the physical. Spirit animates our beings.

Spirit is an unmistakable stillness, joy, bliss, or energy. It is a state of pure potential and possibility, accessible by everyone. It is the source of human creativity and performance. By definition, spirit cannot be counted, weighed, measured, or registered on any device or instrument.

Have you ever walked into a Wal-Mart store early in the morning and observed the associates cheering? This is the lingering spirit of Sam Walton, who often made in-person appearances at his stores. Walton was able to demonstrate that spirit is not esoteric or obscure. At the outbreak of World War II, Franklin D. Roosevelt was asked whether major league baseball should shut down. He insisted that the games go on because they were vital to the American spirit.

Human spirit is the supply source for bandwidth. At the spiritual level, people innately know what is needed or wanted in any situation. It is the source of discovery, invention, and creativity, and the widest band of bandwidth. In fact, Spirit transcends the human domain, reaching into the eternal.

Spirit plays a unique and powerful role in organizations. My dictionary defines spirit as:

"An animating or vital principle held to give life to physical organisms; the activating or essential principle influencing a person; a special attitude; a lively or brisk quality in a person or a person's actions; life; intangible being; energy; vitality."

Taking a cue from this definition, I assert that the ultimate source of value in any organization—the animating or vital principle—is human spirit. Spirit transcends our minds and bodies, connecting people, fueling creativity, overcoming obstacles, and inspiring breakthrough performances. The presence of spirit connects us as human beings; even when we act as if we aren't connected at all.

Spirit can only be found in the organic elements of an organization. Thus the center (or nucleus) of any company must be human in order for it to grow and serve its constituents.

Spirit is contextual, an all-embracing attitude passed on from individual to individual. It gives each organization its unique culture or tone. Those who create that culture (leaders primarily, though each individual influences the culture to some extent) express spirit through their purpose, ideas, values, standards of performance, commitments, moods, and actions. This culture then shapes the actions and results generated by others within the organization.

As a summary of the meaning of spirit in organizations, consider some words from Albert Einstein, who wrote about the spirit of the times as: "An attitude or characteristic of a particular generation which is passed on from individual to individual and gives a society its particular tone. Each of us has to do his little bit toward transforming this spirit of the times."

To understand the role of spirit in organizations, just take the words "generation" and "society" in this quote and replace them with the word "organization".

CONVERSATIONS INFLUENCE ORGANIZATIONAL BANDWIDTH

As explained in earlier chapters, human bandwidth is expressed in conversation and action. In a similar way, collective bandwidth merges individual perspective and behavior into collective alignment through conversation and action.

Organizations are networks of conversations. Conversations are the most common form of interconnection. The purpose and configuration of the organization generally determines the dominant conversations. If an organization is goal-centered, conversations will be historically based, and focused on budgets and numbers. If a company is customer-centered, conversations will focus on customer needs, wants, complaints, and satisfaction. In a work environment, most conversations involve the sharing of information. Others involve requests, promises, judgments, evaluations, and opinions. Any of these conversations can create value—or waste time.

Conversations that generate new possibilities (generative conversations) produce value. Wider bandwidth expands creativity, and wider bandwidth is accessed in the PRESENT MOMENT. Imagine a group of scientists discussing ideas over coffee. Each has done research and is steeped in knowledge of the subject. Yet, during this group conversation, fresh nuances evolve as people offer different points of view. The outcome is often a breakthrough— insights that would probably not occur to anyone working in isolation. Synergy often yields new ideas or teases old ideas into breakthroughs.

Advances in science, technology, and business throughout the Twentieth Century flowed from these generative conversations (sometimes called brainstorming.) For example, an essential part of Albert Einstein's genius was his ability to advance his ideas within a network of conversations and relationships. Einstein, Niels Bohr, Robert Oppenheimer, Enrico Fermi, and Max Planck were all brilliant physicists in their own right. But collectively they advanced the science of physics through their generative conversations.

There are many other examples. NASA attracted preeminent individuals from various fields whose collective capacity resulted in the Mercury, Gemini, and Apollo manned space programs. Thomas Edison, Henry Ford, and Harvey Firestone engaged in generative conversations that advanced the fields of electricity and transportation. Based in part on momentum from these conversations, Edison founded General Electric, Ford the Ford Motor Company, and Firestone the Firestone Rubber Company.

Seventy-five years later, Bill Gates's and Paul Allen's generative conversations created Microsoft. Similarly, conversations between Steve Jobs and

Steve Wozniak led to Apple Computer. A culture of generative conversation is one reason why GE continues to be a leading US company after nearly a century.

Generative conversation prevails in many high-tech companies today. Technology, in particular, engages leaders, employees, customers, and suppliers in new thinking. Through their network of conversations, the high-tech industry has revolutionized business.

A generative conversation is high-bandwidth. Band integration produces a stream of creative insights and intentions. Generative or high-bandwidth conversations can be expanded beyond special teams into your entire organization. The power of this expansion lies in more broadly connecting the human spirit of people. **Significant value is created when people sense, feel, focus, think, and create beyond existing paradigms.** That value can be produced on a sustainable basis when you assemble people in nurturing environments that allow for full self-expression.

Effective brainstorming conversations occur in an environment that draws out all sorts of ideas (not just those which conveniently fit the mind band of the individual and company), and one where participants feel safe from criticism. It also helps when people are assisted to focus on their similarities and not their differences. Spirit is honored and organ-ization is supported.

When generative conversation is mixed with critical conversation, generative conversation stops. To avoid this, employ a two-step process. Step one: generate as many ideas as possible. Step two: filter the ideas in order to find a workable one. This process gives ideas time to flourish and to stimulate further ideas.

Everyone who is seriously involved in the pursuit of science becomes convinced that a spirit is manifest in the laws of the universe. A spirit vastly superior to that of man, and one in the face of which we, with our modest powers, must feel humble. —Albert Einstein

ACCESSING SPIRIT CREATES VALUE FOR ORGANIZATIONS

When people expand their collective bandwidth to connect at the level of spirit, the resultant energy benefits everyone within reach of the organization. They still experience the roller coaster ride—the ups and downs within their organization. Yet, when spirit is present, it is unmistakable.

Substance prevails over form. Passion is evident in the speaking, listening, service, creativity, and candor of the people. Focus is on producing results, not on who gets or takes credit. Innovation and development are expected and pursued. Creativity is never shut down; it is channeled to produce effective and efficient results. There is room for acknowledgment, sharing, contribution, joy, fun, and celebration. And when appropriate, there is room for disappointment, upset, frustration, and learning from mistakes.

Most American companies operate on narrow bandwidth. Short-term financial performance anchors the collective mindset, producing alternately good and bad results. Focus on inorganic elements cannot catalyze and align

employees, customers, leaders, and investors. **It is human spirit—passion, thinking, creativity, and committed action—that transforms a goal or process into sustainable value for all its constituents.**

INCREASE ORGANIZATIONAL BANDWIDTH ONE PERSON AT A TIME

Accessing an organization's human spirit is done person-to-person, through speaking and listening via the heart. Energy or spirit is reflected in attitudes, and our attitudes give rise to our actions. Selfish attitudes produce self-centered actions and ignore other people's needs. Serving attitudes seek to support others. Actions are always consistent with particular attitudes. As we become more aware, we realize that we have choices about both our attitudes and our actions.

When women and men who utilize greater bandwidth are recruited and developed, the collective bandwidth of the entire organization is expanded. This can only occur in organizations where leaders know that the company is "of the people, by the people, and for the people."

Human spirit is a deep well. . . . The idea flow from the human spirit is absolutely unlimited. All you have to do is tap into that well. —Jack Welch

If you did an "extraordinary people count" at Wal-Mart and K-Mart, you would understand why there is a vast difference in their market capitalization ($215 Billion vs. $5 Billion). Compare the number of exceptional or extraordinary people at Cisco and a bureaucratic organization. You will see substantial interconnection of people at Cisco and significant disconnection within and between many governmental agencies.

Anyone can boost—or zap—energy. Look at the energy level in your company. Who gives you energy and how much time do you spend with them? Who "zaps" your energy and how much time do you spend with them? The "boosters" and the "zappers" affect the energy of everyone in your organization. Imagine how this affects productivity.

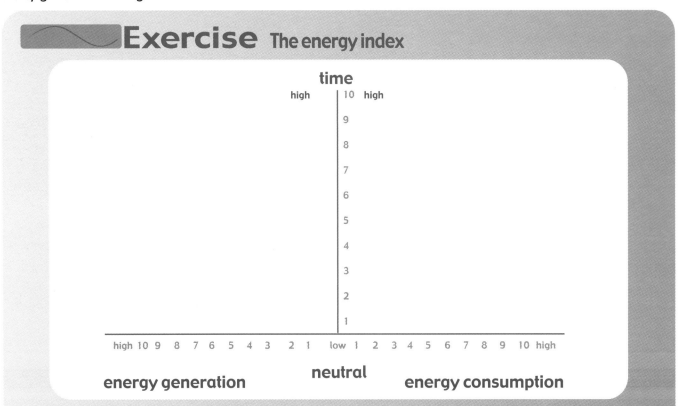

Exercise The energy index

1. *Make a list of the people with whom you interact frequently. Include colleagues, family, friends, and others.*
2. *Make a dot on the graph for each person, placing the dot appropriately in relationship to how much time you spend with each person, and how much energy he or she typically gives to or drains from you. Label each dot with the person's name. Reflect on your observations.*

# Exercise

Observe connections between your awareness, attitudes, and actions in organizational settings

The PRESENT MOMENT offers the opportunity to observe, examine, and change our attitudes. At any moment, we can shift our level of being simply by changing our focus of attention. The moment that we see our selfishness, we can release it. No one has to tell us how to change. We have the capacity to change immediately once we see ourselves directly and without judgment. This awareness translates spontaneously into new attitudes and new actions.

Ask yourself some questions:

Do I routinely experience people operating at low energy when I could help to unleash their energy?

When I become aware of people's true potential, do I continue to interact with them as I always have or as their potential?

What prevents me from helping other people to see and experience their inherent brilliance?

Am I willing to reach out—to infuse energy into my conversations and actions so people feel my support?

Am I committed to being present and keeping my commitments? How am I doing?

Record your answers to these questions in your journal.
Also record any new attitudes and actions that you would like to make part of your life.

The science of pure mathematics, its modern developments, may claim to be the most original creation of the human spirit.
—Alfred North Whitehead

Profile: Sam Walton

No one better personified the vitality of the American Dream in the second half of the 20th century than Sam Walton. At the risk of oversimplifying a rather complex business phenomenon, it can be said that the easiest way to grasp the essence of what Sam Walton meant to America is to read his ad slogan emblazoned on all those Wal-Mart trucks you see barreling down highways around the country: WE SELL FOR LESS, ALWAYS. Walton did not invent discount retailing, just as Henry Ford didn't invent the automobile. But just as Ford and his cars revolutionized America and its industrial model, Walton's extraordinary pursuit of discounting revolutionized the country and its service economy. Walton didn't merely alter the way much of America shopped; he changed the philosophy of much of American business, instigating the shift of power from manufacturer to consumer that has become prevalent in industry after industry. . . .

Once committed to discounting, Walton began a crusade that lasted the rest of his life: to drive costs out of the merchandising system wherever they lay—in the stores, in the manufacturers' profit margins and with the middleman—all in the service of driving prices down, down, down.

Using that formula, which cut his margins to the bone, it was imperative that Wal-Mart grow sales at a relentless pace. It did, of course, and Walton hit the road to open stores wherever he saw opportunity. He would buzz towns in his low-flying airplane studying the lay of the land. When he had triangulated the proper intersection between a few small towns, he would touch down, buy a piece of farmland at that intersection and order up another Wal-Mart store, which his troops could roll out like a rug. . . .

To his great delight, Walton spent much of his career largely unnoticed by the public or the press. In fact, hardly anyone had ever heard of him when, in 1985, Forbes magazine determined that his 39% ownership of Wal-Mart's stock made him the richest man in America. After that, the first wave of attention focused on Walton as populist retailer: his preference for pickup trucks over limos and for the company of bird dogs over that of investment bankers. His extraordinary charisma had motivated hundreds of thousands of employees to believe in what Wal-Mart could accomplish, and many of them had ridden the company's stock to wealth. It was the American Dream. . . .

There is no argument offered here that Sam Walton didn't clutter the landscape of the American countryside or that he didn't force a lot of people to change the way they made a living. But he merely hastened such changes. The forces of progress he represented were inevitable. His empowering management techniques were copied by businesses far beyond his own industry; his harnessing of information technology to cut costs quickly traveled upstream to all kinds of companies; and his pioneering retailing concepts paved the way for a new breed of "category killer" retailer—the Home Depots, Barnes & Nobles and Blockbusters of the world. This wave of low-overhead, low-inventory selling continues to accelerate. The Internet, in fact, is its latest iteration. One can only wonder what a young cyber Sam would set out to accomplish if he were just getting started.

Excerpted from *"Discounting Dynamo"* by John Huey (*Time*, December 7, 1998) ©1998 Time, Inc. Reprinted by permission.

CHAPTER IX:
Bandwidth is Connection

Today, all Western culture is going through a social transformation that is spawned by an ecological world view that recognizes the fundamental interdependence of all phenomena.   —Fritjof Capra

Reedstrom • Jerry Reinsdorf • Buddy Reisalt • Chuck Renderman • Joyce Renderman • Dan Reynolds • Gerry Rhoades • Ron Rhoades • Jeri Rhodes • James Ribbeck • Ronnie Rice • Bob Riesse • Don Riesse • Maureen Riley • Jimmy Riley • LuAnn Rickert • Lou Rissi • Gary Ritz • Barry Rivers • Bernie Rivers • Roland Rives • Dave Robbins • Hazel Robbins • Sandy Robbins • Jim Roberts • James Roberts • John Roberts • Mary Roberts • Russ Roberts • Ted Roberts • Dede Robinson • Fred Rockwood • Jolene Rockwood • Thomas Roets • Dick Rogers • Peter Rogers • Dennis Rogness • Fred Rolf • Wayne Rolfs • Adam Romeiser Sr. • Adam Romeiser Jr. • Harriet Romeiser • Adam Romeiser III • Ellen Romeiser • Emilie Romeiser • Lillie Romeiser • Clyde Rommey • Carol Rose • Curtis Roseman • Kenneth Rosenberg • Bob Rosenblum • Nancy Rosenblum • Gene Rosenfeld • Dan Rostenkowski • Howard Ross • Kelly Ross • Leslie Traub Ross • William Ross • Dana Rossmiller • Louis Rothbard • Cameron Rottler • Jeff Rovell • Greg Royer • Karen Royer • Neal Rubin • Marty Rud • Tom Rudd • Mark Rustvold • Chris Rugh • Chris Ruberg • Jim Ruberg • Cazzie Russell • Mel Rueppel • Mike Ryan • Margaret Sackley • Steve Sackley • Ryne Sandberg • Eunice Sandeen • Janie Sanders • Toni Sanders • Mary Sanders • Don Sandholm • Hilevi Sandland • Carol Sandland • Norman Sandland • Jim Sands • Marty Sandway • Rick Sandway • Joe Sangineto • Dan Santini • Toma Santini • Steve Sapkin • Susan Sarandon • Paul Sarris • Sophie Saroka • Hank Sauer • Frank Savarese • Carol Sawyer • Woody Sawyer • Galye Sayers • Keith Schaefer • Brian Schaenzer • George Schallman • Bob Scharfman • Robin Scheerer • Michael Scheisser • Bill Schick • Jim Schick • Jerry Schick • Renold Schilke • Richard Schluter • James Schmeltzer Jr. • Barbara Schmidt • Bill Schmidt • Denny Schmidt • Jennie Schmidt • Marty Schmidt • Pat Schmidt • Peter Schneck • Martin Schneider • Mike Schnitzler • Dayna Schoen • Richard Schofield • Dave Schopp • Linda Schopp • Paul Schrock • Jack Schuler • Ben Schull • Dick Schulter • Barbara Schultz • Bill Schultz • Bill Schultz • Ernie Schultz • Gerry Schultz • Niki Schultz • George Schroder • Michael Schumacher • Alan Schuster • Rick Schwartz • Joe Scully • Gideon Searle • Nancy Searle • Gregory Sears • Jim Sedlack • Jeff Seeley • Steve Seigler • Loren Semler • Paul Senegal • Glen Seno • Frank Sessa • Karl Sestalc • Randy Sergesketter • Estelle Setzer • Ike Sewell • Florence Sewell • Joseph Sexton • Munir Shaikh • Sophie Shaikh • George Shambaugh • Greg Sharpe • Michael Shapiro • Rick Shapiro • Stevie Shapiro • Ronnie Shadur • George Shambaugh • Bernie Shaw • Geoffrey Shaw • Jane Shaw • Don Shepard • Arnold Siegel • Bill Shield • Comfort Shields • Geoff Shields • Genie Shields • Fred Shoemaker • Jo Hardy Shoemaker • Larry Shoda • Bill Shreder • Dick Sigman • Michael Sigman • Bob Silva •

HISTORY IS OUR QUEST FOR CONNECTION

In the big picture, the human saga is a journey of increasing interconnectedness. Our historical quest is to connect in as many ways as possible. Seminal events in this quest have become the platforms of creativity, invention, and technological advances in all facets of human life.

Development of the boat and the wheel created opportunities for physical interconnection. Ancient people traveled long distances by dugout, and the Vikings rowed and sailed the oceans in their ships. Even today, 50% of the world's population lives within fifty miles of a major waterway or ocean. Wheels made possible every form of ground transportation—from the first crude cart to horse-drawn chariots to bullet trains.

In 1903, two bicycle mechanics, Orville and Wilbur Wright, claimed the sky as a medium of transportation, recording the first flight of a manned aircraft. Within a mere sixty-six years a Saturn V rocket launched astronauts on a journey to the moon. Land, water, air (and airways), and outer space all are now pathways of interconnection.

In the mid-1400's, collective knowledge and new information were available only to the privileged few. Johannes Gutenberg, a member of an aristocratic German family, invented a mold for moveable metallic type that could be combined with ink used by Flemish painters. His printing press made possible mass sharing of information and knowledge, and a more transparent interconnectedness was realized.

Years later, the telegraph, telephone, radio, television, and artificial satellite created new communication platforms which connected human beings.

Now, thanks to phone lines and wireless technologies, a person in Singapore can bid on a used computer being offered by someone in Hilton Head, South Carolina. The convergence of television, telecommunications, computers, and cable technology is the foundation of instantaneous communication across the world.

The World Wide Web is a hologram of interconnection, linking the digital, virtual world with the world of bricks and mortar. Companies are racing to invent, service, and expand this great interconnectedness. Software, portals, Web browsers and Web crawlers, online access, "e-tailers," virtual communities, content providers, e-marketers, e-zines, and digital infrastructures and exchanges are part of this wave of global interconnection.

As the Internet develops and grows, our perceptions of its uses will continue to expand. Learning, choice, creativity, exploration, and adaptability are some of the human capacities served or satisfied as we participate in this universal organization called the Web. Throughout the 550-year journey from printing press to Internet, mass-produced words and images have become the primary pathway to expanded interconnection.

A NETWORK OF LIGHTS

Imagine a hotel ballroom containing 500 light bulbs with just one bulb burning. Although the scene is nearly dark, that one light evidences the presence of electrical power. Connect another bulb to the same circuit as the lit one and two lights brighten the room. As each dark bulb is connected to the source of power, the growing network produces ever-greater light.

Now imagine that each bulb represents an individual in an organization, and that the organization is a network of lights. The energy and awareness of many is "turned-off" by fear. Those who regularly access their bandwidths via the PRESENT MOMENT burn brightly. What if each bright bulb could help connect another to a source of power, to the possibility of generating "light"—energy, enthusiasm, freedom, and capacity to create? Obviously, the light from such a network would be many times greater than that of several single individuals, however brightly they burned.

Carrying the analogy a little farther, we could say that most people lie on a continuum between unlit and fully lit. The average "bulb" might produce between 25 and 100 watts of light, with a few falling below 25 watts, some at 150, fewer at 300-watt people, and a few at 1,000 watts or more.

Imagine what could happen to the "candle power" of an organization if the light generated increased from 25 to 50 watts per bulb! Increasing the average wattage of 100 people by 150 watts would be exceptional, but increasing 25,000 people's wattage by only 25 watts would be transformational.

Take it one step further and try to imagine more than six billion lights in a network—one for each person on our planet. The potential for collective light increases exponentially as interconnection increases and more and more people expand their bandwidth.

TECHNOLOGY PROMOTES NARROW-BANDWIDTH CONNECTION

The paradox we face at the beginning of the Twenty-first Century is that while we are creating global interconnection, in many respects it is not "real." It only appears to be real. **What we primarily experience through television and computing is a disembodied technological connection at the level of the mind and brain.** Yes, other channels of human bandwidth are in play, but our electronic connections are one step removed from spirit, emotions, and senses. In other words, our global interconnection is one of constricted bandwidth.

Ironically, we are highly disconnected in some respects where we were once very connected. People move in and out of jobs, creating only short-term connections. (According to the U.S. Department of Commerce, the average job tenure for an American worker was 3.6 years in 1998.) They may live inches away from each other in adjacent apartments and never converse during the terms of their leases. Yet their apartments may be wired for high-speed Internet connection, and they may have laptop computers, Palm Pilots, VCRs, radios, TVs, land phones, cell phones, and fax machines. People may easily know all the family members on several different TV series, but not have a clue as to the name or story of the person living directly across the hall or the street.

In the developed world, electronic technology has aided our quest to be independent and self-sufficient. Increased mobility through global transportation, the creation of affluence for millions of people, the myriad of communication devices—these have created a global culture where physical proximity isn't necessary. People can "hole up" in their homes and cars, with little need for neighbors or colleagues. How often does a neighbor knock on your door?

According to industry sources the next phase of the Information Age within a few years will see more wireless phones than personal computers connected to the Internet. One effect of this development will be faster access to information and faster business transactions. E-commerce will move to another level. And, we will be faced with a new choice: What is interconnection without the bands of emotion, spirit, body, and senses? Can "virtual" interconnection nourish? Can it withstand conflict or neglect? What is lost when it becomes more expedient to speak to a voice-activated computer than to speak directly to your spouse, your friends, or your boss? What happens to our sense of community when it becomes more productive to leave a video-voice-mail message for your neighbor than to go next door and shake her hand?

In summary, we are capable of weaving a global electronic web that connects our outer selves without connecting our inner beings. We risk being in a relationship with a Hollywood movie set—a whole planet of single-dimensional, narrow bandwidth facades.

Inorganic connection is beginning to overwhelm fundamental human connection. We can welcome these forms of connection as means to serve human ends and solve many problems. But, let's not mistake technological bandwidth for the ultimate, inner, human connection. In moments of expanded awareness, especially at the band of spirit, we see that every human and every thing are interconnected. At the level of intelligence, matter, and energy, we are part of a whole that transcends the mind.

It is only when we see ourselves as part of a greater whole—a family, company, church, club, organization, neighborhood, community, city, continent, hemisphere, a member of the human race, planet Earth and the Universe—that we begin to realize the vastness of our potential as human beings.

OUR LIVES ARE LITTERED WITH DISCONNECTION

The term relationship is familiar to us in both concept and experience. Some relationships we inherit, as in family, others we choose, as in friendships. We categorize our relationships into family, social, business, mandatory, and discretionary, each with its parameters and interpretations. As a result, we have different standards of trust, respect, perceived value, comfort, feelings, and behavior across the range of our relationships.

This categorization (determined by mind) drives our interactions. While I'm not suggesting you interact with all people in the same way, I am suggesting that categorization of people and relationships discourages growth and development. Simply put, we assume that everyone was, is, and will continue to be the same. This is a form of disconnection.

We also live in the assumption that we are not connected. This is one of our greatest illusions. It defies the nature of the cosmos. Time and energy are wasted in the attempt to connect (or reconnect) when we are all already interconnected.

Young children know of this interconnection and live in this understanding, until some unfortunate episode occurs, or they begin to get the famous instruction: "Don't talk to strangers." Suddenly, they experience their first disconnections from the universe. From that moment, the child begins to categorize people into strangers and friends, bad people and good people. This process of differentiation through relationships soon extends to, "our state," "our town," "our school," "our grade," "my friends," "my girlfriend," and continues on throughout one's life.

During the teen years, disconnection often reaches new heights. Almost everyone experiences a certain amount of isolation, ridicule, embarrassment, loss of self-confidence, and loss of affection during these years. Some people are so affected that they begin a life-long pattern of being a loner. Others are fear aloneness and "must" be in relationship. Some erect elaborate internal layers of protection so as never to experience emotional hurt again.

The sense of disconnection occurs every day. No one listens as you speak up in a meeting. Their internal critics are working overtime, judging, evaluating, and criticizing. Your child tries to get your attention while you remain preoccupied and not present. You miss today's sunset. Customer dissatisfaction occurs. Suppliers break commitments. Workers are fired. Unions go on strike. Communication is incomplete and fraught with arguments and misunderstandings. Relationships change. Nations go to war. The landscape of life is littered with disconnection.

FULL BANDWIDTH REVEALS OUR ACTUAL INTERCONNECTION

Even after experiencing hundreds or thousands of disconnections, we can reawaken our understanding that everything in the universe is connected. We only have to widen our bandwidth.

You can begin by shifting to your sensory band. Go outside and look around. Notice that you are inhaling and exhaling the oxygen that surrounds you. Observe the sun, sky, clouds, wind, plants, birds, and animals; see how they are all choreographed elements of a single ecosystem. Then shift your attention to the man-made elements such as office buildings, homes, streets, and stoplights. Realize that all are organized to facilitate human activity. Get in your car and drive on the grid system of streets or interstate highways; all expressly designed to connect people. Make a phone call and marvel at how clear the transmission is, even when you call someone in London or Paris.

In an average day, as these examples demonstrate, interconnection is constantly present. However, it is transparent and taken for granted. As explained earlier in this chapter, most of the inventions and developments of the last six centuries have created more aspects of interconnection. The speed of technological interconnection can connect us at low bandwidth—or it can force us to awaken to the actual interconnection of everything.

Beyond technology is human spirit, the ultimate manifestation of interconnection. Spirit is woven into, under, and around each element of bandwidth. It is the transparent thread, mist, or space in which life and the universe occur.

Spirit is the band in which we can sense and feel our relationship to everything. Spirit is seeing the vast blue sky and the feeling part of the cosmos. Spirit is connecting with other people through laughter and tears. It is pure understanding, creativity, tenacity, love, straight communication, wholeness, and completion. We are born through the connection of male and female energies, and we yearn for connection to others all our lives. At the level of spirit, we satisfy that yearning.

In an expanded state of awareness, we can see that:

Every organization has the same universal core.

Human beings everywhere share the same desires for safety, material security, and love.

World religions have a common spiritual basis (we are all connected) and ethical imperative (treat others as you would like to be treated).

The universe is essentially comprised of energy, information and intelligence—not solid, separate objects.

From a DNA perspective, the six billion people on planet Earth are 99.9% the same.

The earth is a connected system of water, land, and air formations.

The galaxy is a vast array of stars and solar systems.

Contrast this with what we perceive in a contracted state of awareness:

Billions of competing organizations have little in common.

People live in different cultures, speak hundreds of different languages, and experience constant conflicts of interest.

The myriad of religions cannot reconcile with each other.

The universe is filled with separate objects with differing levels of mass.

Six billion people are separated by race, creed, geography, personality, and interests.

The Earth is a small, insignificant planet with a few continents strewn with oceans, lakes, and rivers.

Billions and billions of isolated stars and planets exist in the spatial void.

The difference between these two states is our willingness to enter the present moment via the gaps between our thoughts (see Chapters One and Six). **Until we experience the PRESENT MOMENT, we have no access to the true nature of people, of organizations, or of the complete, absolute, and permanent** interconnection of everything in the universe. By entering the present moment, we expand into the band of spirit.

Spirit is a space or way of being, which I can experience, but the moment I attempt to label or define it, its essence is lost. It is this infinite and inexpressible nature of spirit that creates adventure for some people and doubt for others.

Fortunately, it isn't necessary to capture spirit in words, formulas, or dogmas. Through practices that help us to access the PRESENT MOMENT, we can perceive spirit—the underlying connection of all things—for ourselves. (For more information on these practices, see Chapter 11.) Once we experience this level of interconnection, we can release our need to prove that it exists. We can live with the mystery.

Connection registers at the level of awareness. It leads us to make statements such as:

I felt or sensed something, even though I couldn't put my finger on it.

I don't know how I knew. I just knew.

The idea just came to me out of the blue.

I could feel the momentum change.

The energy in the room shifted as I began to speak.

We connected, and for the first time
he had a sense of who I really am.

What would it be like if you operated from a perspective of interconnection? What if you could look beyond "the optical delusion of people's bodies and minds" (Einstein) to their spirit, to that place where you can establish true connection? Few people sense this level of interconnectedness. Yet it is available to us at any moment, when we quiet our minds, awaken to our senses, allow our emotions, and expand into all of our bands of energy.

As we become aware of interconnection, we can release the need to classify events or people as "external" or "internal." When serving customers becomes the center of a business, it is no longer appropriate to talk about them as external entities. **If we see that all human beings belong to the same family, there is no longer any need to distinguish between friend and stranger, family vs. acquaintance.**

You can continue behaving as though you are disconnected, or you can accept interconnection as fact. If you can only imagine that you are connected to everything in the universe, you can experience the connection. As Walt Disney said, "If you can dream it, you can do it." To maximize the value for yourself and your organizations, heed the words of Buckminster Fuller: "We are not going to be able to operate our spaceship earth successfully, nor for much longer, unless we see it as a whole spaceship and our fate as common. It has to be everybody or nobody."

Stop reading for a few minutes. Close your eyes and take this journey:

Imagine that you are connected to everything in your immediate area. Now imagine being connected to everyone and everything in your company. Now imagine being connected to everyone and everything in your neighborhood. Expand your interconnection to the entire town or city in which you reside. Expand it to the State or Province. Go out to the borders of your country and imagine being connected to everyone and everything. Expand beyond your country to the entire world. Imagine flying around the world and being connected to everyone and everything. Now look up into the sky if you haven't already and imagine being connected to the stars and other planets, the galaxy, and finally, the universe.

 # Exercise

Take a look in the mirror

This exercise will allow you to become aware of yourself—specifically, your self-judgments.
(For a more detailed version of this practice, see the section on self-reflection in Chapter 11.)

STEP 1: To begin, simply look at yourself in a mirror. What are the first thoughts that come in to your mind?
Speak these thoughts out loud, no matter what they are. Keep speaking your thoughts as you continue
looking in the mirror. Do this for at least three minutes.

Observe the activity of your mind band. Many people who do this exercise find that they've plugged into
a stream of thought that offers constant self-criticism (I'm too fat. . . . I look old. . . . I can't stand to
look at myself. . . .).

STEP 2: This time, as you look in the mirror, make a conscious choice about how to use your mind.
State out loud what you like about yourself. It's ok if you need to think between statements. Most of
us are not used to speaking aloud our positive self-judgments. Do this for at least three minutes.

STEP 3: Finally, look into mirror and just be silent for a minute or two. Notice your breathing, and
release any thoughts that arise. See if you can get in touch with bands of energy other than your mind,
such as your senses, spirit, emotions, and body. Take a few moments to simply embrace the human
being you see.

You can also experiment with putting other people "in the mirror." Create a vivid mental image of a
key person in your life (or tape a picture to the mirror.) Then, speak or write the first thoughts that
come to mind about this person. Notice the role of these thoughts in connecting or disconnecting
with the person. Then repeat steps 2 and 3. Notice your sense of the person after you've completed
the exercise.

Exercise
Revealing your interconnections

Your mind has probably been asking, "Why are there names at the beginning of every chapter? Who are these people? What do they have to do with this book?" They are the names of some of the people with whom I have been connected. They include some of my ancestors, family, friends, acquaintances, teachers, associates, and neighbors from every era of my life. These people together with several thousand more not listed have been co-creators of and contributors to my earthly life.

Many have given me, and a few have taken, tremendous energy over the years. The same is true about me I have given energy and I have absorbed the energy of others. Regardless of our opinions about each other, we share an interconnection which has added energy to the world. Whether acknowledged or not, every network of relationship adds to the generational impact on society.

You will notice that the page at the beginning of Chapter 12 is blank. It represents space and possibility for new relationships which I have not yet co-created.

1. Over the next six months, make a list of all the people to whom you have been connected. You could begin with your family tree and build the list from there. Use your address book, Palm Pilot, Rolodex, yearbooks, photo albums, scrapbooks, membership lists, and memories as source documents. Notice what occurs as you write down the names. What was the predominant band on which you connected? (i.e. body, mind, emotions, brain, senses, spirit?)

2. Make a "future relationships" list of the people with whom you would like to be in relationship.

3. Make a list of people with whom you have connected at the level of spirit. Notice how you feel as you record these names.

4. Acknowledge your past, current, and potential interconnections. Consider acknowledging your connection to everyone and everything in the universe.

CHAPTER X:
Full Bandwidth is Co-creation

How old are you?

How long do you plan to live?

Are you afraid of dying?

Questions to ponder as you read this chapter.

We have only the world that we can bring forth with others, and only love can bring it forth.
—Humberto Maturana and Francisco Varela

Peggy Silva • Cliff Silverman • Curt Simic • Fred Simon • Melvin Simon • Rick Simmons • Chadha Singh • Dick Singleton •

Linda Skinner • Mike Sklar • Susan Sklar • Marylin Smilie • Ed Smith • Lindley Smith • Martha Smith • Alice Smith • Jan Smith

• Tyler Smith • Alison Smith • Kate Smith • Bruce Smith • Anne Smith • Peter Smith • Phil Smith • Jim Smith • Scott Smith •

Linda Smith • Maureen Sobeck • Harold Solomon • Ron Sonnenberg • Jan Solomon • Wally Soroka • Diane Spahr • Roy

Spahr • Alex Spanos • John Spasoff • Jody Speckman • Aaron Spencer • Pat Spencer • George Springer • Tad Springer •

Donna Stahl • Jim Stanhaus • Vicki Staples • Ralph Starenko • Marylin Starenko • Sally Stark • Larry Starkman • Dick

Starman • Gordon Starr • Lily Starr • Cobi Stein • Werner Stein • Jerry Steiner • Os Steinwald • Leo Stenz • Gary Stephans •

Karen Stephans • Earl Stevens • Linda Stevens • Dennny Stidham • Dorothy Stingley • Darlene Stewart • Al Stokely • Randy

Stokely • Lynne Stokely • Cheryl Stone • Chuck Stone • Lee Stopolus • Len Stopolus • Jim Stopolus • Channing Stowell •

Lynette Carlson Strand • Chris Stratton • John Strewe • Gene Strimling • Warren Strom • Faith Strong • Ruth Strong • Jim

Stuart • Diane Stuart • Bill Summers • Chris Summers • Mary Summers • Steve Summers • Mike Suthard • Cathy Suthard •

M.S. Swaminathan • Dennis Swan • Hjlmar Swanson • Elsie Swanson • Joe Swenson • Jerry Szarynch • Bill Taaffe • Fitigu

Tadesse • Ted Tannenbaum • Carole Tanner • John Tanner II • Penelope Taylor • Howard Teegen • PhilipTelleen • Sharon

Telleen • John Tellen • Marlis Tennon • Jenny Terrill • Dick Thain • Dorothy Thrap • Peg Thatcher • Bob Theer • Sue Theer •

Fred Thetford • Bob Thomas • Leonard Thomas • Sue Thomas • Jim Thompson • Marge Thompson • Jim Thorne • Jane

Thorne • Sara Thorne • Gerd Thour • Tommy Thour • Ray Tibbitts • Dave Tipton • Jim Toal • John Tobias • Dorthy Tobias • Ron

Tobias • Gary Tofil • Doug Toft • Mike Tomczak • Elin Svensdotter Torkilsson • Olof Torkilsson • Eric Tormoen • Al Toth • Lee

Traband • Les Traband • Denny Tracey • Ann Traub • Michael Traub • Thomas Tredway • Catherine Tredway • Bruce Trent

• Mickey Trent • Sharon Tribe • George Triezenberg • John Tschanz • Don Tuck • Lynne Tuck • Fred Tucker III • Fred Tucker

Jr. • Chris Tunney • Lenny Turelli • Paula Turelli • Herb Turetzky • Denise Turner • Virginia Turner • Bill Twist • Lynne Twist

• Hal Ulvestad • Pam Ulvestad • Bud Urban • Theresa Urban • Borje Vagenus • Gene Vandenberg • Jim Vanderhyde • Cathy

Vahey • Gerry Vahey • Jim Vail • Mary Ann Vail • Diane Vail • Debbie Valentine • Dorthy Valentine • Ron Valentine • Eduardo

Valdes • Bob Vancura • Greg Van Grinsven • Dave Van Singel • Paula Van Singel • Bob Vancura • Dennis VanderMeer •

Laura VanderMeer • Frans Van Oudenallen • Will Verity • Paula Verity • Jared Vegosen • Carol Veronie • Joanne Vetterick

A SURVIVAL MENTALITY MASKS OUR FULL BANDWIDTH

Death is a "high volume" thought, running unacknowledged through most peoples minds every day. What happens when you hear about a fatal accident? What thoughts and images raced through your mind when you learned of the terrorist attacks on the World Trade Center and the Pentagon? Why do you suppose so few people have annual physicals? What happens when you hear the "C" word (Cancer)? How many funerals or wakes have you attended? Do you believe in God? Jesus? Buddha? Lao-tse? Allah? Do you believe in reincarnation? Heaven? Hell? Everlasting life? Do these questions provoke discomfort or dissonance in your mind?

For most Westerners, death means the end of life. Death constitutes their greatest fear. Even those who believe in everlasting life would, if they had a choice, almost certainly choose life over death. Our unconscious minds are culturally programmed to avoid or deny this "dark side" of life. Yet, if we cannot accept death as a fundamental aspect of life, how can we fully live?

The eventuality of death is not usually at the forefront of our awareness. We tend to take for granted friends, families, jobs, our personal health and safety, and pretty much everything else. We assume that things will continue to go on just as they have, that life is an uninterrupted extrapolation of the past into the future. Coupled to that assumption is profound resignation about what's possible. We may think and say "That's just how it is," or "I can't really make a difference," or "What can I do anyway?"

Living on autopilot, we bury our fear, our low self-esteem, our bad habits, and other perceived "dark side" elements of our beings. We don't acknowledge negative or deep-seated issues. We hide behind facades, permitting others to see only what we want them to—either the all-positive "I've got it together" or the resigned "Life sucks."

The truth of these statements is born out in the faces around you in airports, office buildings, shopping malls, and city streets. Do they look truly happy? Do they make eye contact? What are their facial expressions? These are the faces of people who exist in their minds, on autopilot, just surviving. It is the look of low bandwidth.

Why does it take a close call, a serious illness,or accident, to wake us up to the gift of life? Perhaps it is because nearly all humanity exists in the same survival mode as it did 500 years ago. Living in fear or anxiety about what might happen next keeps us from moving beyond the limitations imposed by our historical and unconscious minds. Our survival mindsets effectively prevent us from leading fulfilling lives.

Preoccupation with national, as well as personal, safety is a strong element of the survival mentality. A mid-1990's United Nations poll revealed a single common issue among 187 countries in the world. The top concern, universally expressed, was security.

Defense is a leading budget item in many countries. Police, militia, and security forces account for a growing share of municipal, state, and corporate expenditures. The market for security systems and self-protection devices is gargantuan, fueled by constant media focus on the dangers of living in today's world. Sensational headlines and "news" programs target the unconscious mind, activating our fears over and over.

Thoughts of insufficiency, unworthiness, and low self-esteem are also survival based. For most of us, internal and external criticism has been in high gear since childhood. As previously discussed, early programming by external critics feeds the inner critic. This in turn sets into motion a lifelong pattern of unconscious criticism, the judging of self and others.

Survival behavior includes resistance to change, withdrawal, passivity, resignation, giving up, disease, cynicism, and pronounced aversion to risk.

All are low-bandwidth indicators. Other hallmarks of survival mode include self-centeredness and disconnection. Out of this defensive posturing, our personalities, habits, patterns, and relationships are formed and cemented. Our unconscious fears have us backing away from life instead of stepping into it.

EXPANSION AND CONTRACTION

Life, like bandwidth, is a journey of expansion and contraction. It is:

inhalation and exhalation
creation and destruction
contribution and self service
happiness and despair
passion and fear
love and hate
good health and disease
action and reaction
co-operation and competition
energy generation and energy expenditure
committed and non-committal
beginning and completing
outwardly-focused and internally-focused
responsibility and blame
growth and regression
success and failure
connection and isolation
birth and death

We spend approximately one third of our lives sleeping, a necessary contraction mode. On the other hand, surveys reveal that Americans spend over 50% of their "free" time watching television, a voluntary contracted activity.

Exercise

Expansion and Contraction

Ponder the following questions and jot your thoughts, reactions, impressions, and comments in your journal.

On an average day, how much of the time are you in an energy expansion mode?

How much are you in an energy contraction mode?

In what ways is work or school satisfying?

In what ways does it turn you off?

In what ways does your life afford you opportunities to contribute and grow?

In what ways do you feel stymied and stagnant?

How often do you give energy to others?

How often do you take energy from others?

What do you do with your "free" time?

EXISTENCE VS. LIVING FLAT OUT

Most of us merely exist. We populate the world like so many robots, walking the streets, riding in cars and buses, laboring in factories and schools, filling the churches, stores, offices, restaurants, and hospitals, enacting the rituals of eating, sleeping, earning and spending. We might see ourselves as cogs on the gears of society. By some accident of birth we appear, within the context of our families, neighborhoods, cultures, and countries, all of which seem to be "outside of us."

There is another, much more powerful way to view yourself and your place in the world. **You are an essential, living part of the universe, a microcosm of the unified field, containing unlimited potential and possibility.** Somewhere along the way, extraordinary people discover that the world emanates from within themselves, that they are perpetually choosing and creating their own experience. And, more significantly, these people know that their actions are linked to and part of a collective creation which is ongoing and includes all human beings.

Every living human being generates energy and adds it to the quantum mix of life on Earth. For a newborn baby it is breath and the possibility of a whole lifetime. For a dying person it is last breath and the possibility of life after death. Our every act of physical or mental labor concentrates and broadcasts energy into the universe.

Your life is the sum of your bandwidth. It is the expression of your mind, body, spirit, senses, emotions, and brain—and your moment-to-moment choices about consciously activating these bands of energy. **You are the sum of your bandwidth expressed in language, action, and being.**

> Our deepest fear is that we are powerful beyond measure. It is our light, not our darkness, that most frightens us. We ask ourselves, who am I to be brilliant, gorgeous, talented, and fabulous? Actually, who are you not to be? You are a child of God. Your playing small doesn't serve the world. There is nothing enlightened about shrinking so that other people won't feel insecure around you. We were born to manifest the glory of God that is within us. It's not just in some of us; it's in everyone. And as we let our own light shine, we unconsciously give other people permission to do the same. As we are liberated from our own fear, our presence automatically liberates others.
>
> —from Nelson Mandela's Inaugural speech as he adapted it from Marianne Williamson

THE UNIVERSE IS EXPRESSED THROUGH YOU

Each and every atom contains material from which the whole of the universe is continually reconstructed. Whether you look at the subatomic or the astronomical, all matter, energy, time, and space began with an infinitesimally-tiny single seed. Everything, even your own skin, bones, and blood, originated in that universal seed.

At birth you weighed maybe eight pounds. You cried as your raw little lungs inhaled their first air. Someone counted your fingers and toes and prayed that you were healthy. You were wiped clean of amniotic fluid and placed in your mother's arms.

Freeze frame! Here is where the distinction between merely existing and actually generating or creating the world is usually lost. Instead of seeing yourself coming through the birth canal, try to visualize the universe extending itself through your mother's energy field, pure potential transformed into a small body with a loud voice. You are a slice of the quantum energy field, containing within your DNA all the creative capacity of the universe. You came into being already connected to everything and everyone, a pure expression of joy, love, and creativity.

From the moment of your birth, you began to create the world from your perspective, perfectly correlated with the co-creative activity of the other billions of the world's inhabitants. It is perhaps a stretch to think that in your formative years you were capable of creating your own world, yet this is exactly what you did. You grew and developed in your own particular way, greatly influenced, of course, by genetics, parents, teachers, and community. Your self-expression was itself a stream of creative acts, unique and self-defining. Society resists these independent self-expressions, striving for conformity and compliance.

While birth and first breath are shared by all, each baby enters an environment that is significantly and involuntarily programmed by the people and conditions within it. As children, we are unaware that we are creating our reality in a context of cultural conditioning. Our societal programming continues unabated until we gain enough awareness to begin to intervene in the process. Unfortunately, most of us never really do intervene. We are asleep to the possibility that our lives are ours to create. We live on as low-bandwidth adults.

The good news is that we never lose our connection to the universe or our capacity for expanded bandwidth. At any time, we can begin to actively create the world from within ourselves. The possibility of creating extraordinary expression or contribution is always within—not "out there." We can transform from 50 watts to 100 watts or 300 watts, by our own creative acts. No one and no thing outside ourselves can do that for us.

The bottom line is we either allow other people and environmental factors to shape us into "human reactors," or we co-create a world calibrated by the level of our awareness and input from our fellow human beings. The higher our awareness, the greater the probability that we will convert our intentions into actions and results; that we will become the literal creators of our world. Creative action is born only of higher awareness, and higher awareness enhances the probability of serving and contributing to others.

BANDWIDTH IS CO-CREATION

In truth, we co-create the world with other human beings. **Co-creation occurs in the PRESENT MOMENT whenever we assert and integrate our basic human capacities in the process of living life.** By joining intention with action, we activate our senses, our imaginations, our communications, and our actions and interactions.

It is important to note that the energy of the universe is neutral. **It is through our intention and commitment that we create and shape the composition of the energy, positively or negatively.** Simultaneously, six billion other people are either consciously creating or unconsciously existing in their individual worlds. Our worlds interconnect with everyone else's. Our social lives are the co-creation or co-existence of the collective bandwidth in the communities, organizations, and countries, of which we are a part. Each of us expresses bandwidth individually, and our collective expressions of these universal bands of energy form the mosaic called the world.

People generally gravitate to the circles where they feel most connected. Thus, people who live more frequently in the PRESENT MOMENT will create a collective bandwidth that is more aligned, creative, and productive. People who are reactive, fearful, and dwelling in their minds 99% of the time will draw to themselves narrow collective bandwidth. If you view others through your historical mind, you will project your identity onto them, preventing their expansion. If, however, you view others as co-creators of your experience, you are more likely to see possibility instead of limitation.

Aware co-creation requires mutual respect. Conflict, at the individual or collective level, arises when one or both parties will not accept another's point-of-view. Einstein said, "Problems created at one level have to be solved at another level." Moving to another level allows us to enter the realm of "we"—to negotiate, to share a vision or common purpose, to co-create. This realm of "we" exists on the bands of spirit, emotions, senses, brain, and body. **Creating agreements at the level of mind often perpetuates conflict because intellectual understanding is insufficient to sustain cooperation, collaboration, and powerful interconnection. "A meeting of the minds" is a recipe for history repeating itself. A connection of spirit creates a new future.**

LOVE IS THE FUNDAMENTAL INTERCONNECTION

One of the most provocative studies into the nature of human beings was conducted by two Chilean biologists, Humberto Maturana and Francisco Varela. They suggested that the nature of organisms and cognition is to bring forth the world through the process of life itself. **"We have only the world that we can bring forth with others, and only love can bring it forth."**

Love is the most fundamental interconnection in the PRESENT MOMENT. It is the transcendent interconnection to ourselves, others, and God or Divine Spirit. Love is within each of us. It is the center of attraction and the primary source of energy in a human being. If you believe in God or a Divine Spirit, then you accept that we were "created in the image of the Divine and that God is love." If you do not, please consider it.

Through our unconscious minds and the illusion of individual bodies, we separate from each other and live, unaware, in a state of survival. Yet, love is like the sun. It radiates light and heat. Only the clouds of the unconscious mind obscure our interconnection.

It is never too late. Transformation is instantaneous. We can access our full bandwidth at any moment. And when we lapse back into the unconscious mind band, we can extricate ourselves the minute we recognize where we are. We can bring ourselves back to the PRESENT MOMENT.

"We hold these truths to be self-evident, that all men are created equal, that they are endowed by their Creator with certain unalienable Rights, that among these are Life, Liberty, and the pursuit of Happiness."
The Declaration of Independence

EXPANDING YOUR BANDWIDTH HELPS OTHERS TO EXPAND THEIRS

Access to your power and purpose begins with PRESENT MOMENT awareness and conscious choices. It involves discovering and developing your inner creative capacities, as well as telling the truth about your weaknesses.

Awareness, or "presencing" yourself, will alter your journey through life. If you are awake and aware, your focus, intention, commitment, and action will bring forth extraordinary contributions. You truly can create a shift in the collective energy field.

A great thing about expanding your bandwidth is the "spill over" effect. As you become who, in your heart, you desire to be, you more readily contribute your gifts to others. In so doing, you transform from ordinary to extraordinary. You expand from self-centered to other-centered. You become more and more connected. Your insights, actions, and service assist others to grow in their awareness.

Your life is a sacred manifestation of universal energy. Within you lies all possibilities of creation.

Your spirit is already connected to everything and everyone. In your full bandwidth, you can act to awaken thousands of others, and in the process, help to eliminate their suffering.

This is the true joy in life, the being used for a purpose recognized by yourself as a mighty one; the being a force of nature instead of a feverish, selfish little clod of ailments and grievances complaining that the world will not devote itself to making you happy.

I am of the opinion that my life belongs to the whole community and as long as I live, it is my privilege to do for it whatever I can.

I want to be thoroughly used up when I die. For the harder I work, the more I live. I rejoice in life for its own sake. Life is no "brief candle" to me. It is a sort of splendid torch which I have got hold of for the moment, and I want to make it burn as brightly as possible before handing it on to future generations.

—George Bernard Shaw

Exercise

Bandwidth imbalances

Ponder the following questions and jot responses in your journal. It's O.K. if your first thought about a question doesn't make sense. Write it down anyway and allow your insights to unfold over time.

Is there an imbalance in your bandwidth energy?

Are you letting the dark side of the mind cast shadows on your spirit, emotions, senses, body, and personal growth?

Are the unanswered questions or fears of your childhood co-piloting or automatically piloting your life?

Does fear have more influence in your daily life than love?

Does your unconscious mind, or the collective mind, exercise more power over you than God or a Divine Spirit?

Exercise

Move from sight to "in-sight"

Put on a blindfold for five minutes. (You can fashion a homemade blindfold from a towel or strip of cloth.) Then notice any sensations that come to the foreground, such as changes in your breathing or heart rate.

Remove the blindfold and reflect on your experience. For most people, sight is the primary player in their sensory band and creates a focus on the outside world. When you were blindfolded, did your other senses become more acute? Were you able to access your other bands of energy in the moment? Put your reflections in writing.

Do this exercise again, extending the length of time you are blindfolded to 15 minutes. Consider wearing it for a half-hour, an hour, or more. Ask a friend or family member to lead you by the hand for an outdoor walk while you're blindfolded.

Profile: Viktor Frankl

We who lived in the concentration camps can remember the men who walked through the huts comforting others, giving away their last piece of bread. They may have been few in number, but they offer sufficient proof that everything can be taken from a man but one thing: the last of the human freedoms—to choose one's attitude in any given set of circumstances, to choose one's own way.

And there were always choices to make. Every day, every hour, offered the opportunity to make a decision that determined whether you would or would not submit to those powers that threatened to rob you of your very self, your inner freedom; which determined whether or not you would become the plaything of circumstance, renouncing freedom and dignity to become molded into the form of the typical inmate.

Seen from this point of view, the mental reactions of the inmates of a concentration camp must seem more to us than the mere expression of certain physical and sociological conditions. Even though conditions such as lack of sleep, insufficient food, and various mental stresses may suggest that the inmates were bound to react in certain ways, in the final analysis it becomes clear that the sort of person the prisoner became was the result of an inner decision, and not the result of camp influences alone. Fundamentally, therefore, any man can, even under such circumstances, decide what shall become of him—mentally and spiritually . . .

One day, a few days after the liberation [from the concentration camps], I walked through the country past flowering meadows, for miles and miles, toward the market town near the camp. Larks rose to the sky and I could hear their joyous song. There was no one to be seen for miles around; there was nothing but the wide earth and sky and the larks' jubilation and the freedom of space. I stopped, looked around, and up to the sky—and then I went down on my knees. At that moment there was very little that I knew of myself or of the world—I had but one sentence in mind—always the same: 'I called to the Lord from my narrow prison and He answered me in the freedom of space.'

How long I knelt there and repeated this sentence memory can no longer recall. But I know that on that day, in that hour, my new life started. Step for step I progressed, until I again became a human being.

Viktor Frankl, psychiatrist, was a survivor of the holocaust and a prolific author. This passage is from his book, *Man's Search for Meaning: An Introduction to Logotherapy* by Viktor Frankl. © 1959, 1962, 1984, 1992 by Viktor E. Frankl. Reprinted by permission of Beacon Press, Boston

CHAPTER XI:
Being Present To Your Full Bandwidth

This chapter offers a sampling of practices which will increase
awareness and expand your bandwidth.

Please choose, modify, or create practices which will work for you given your age,
career, schedule, and desires.

Read this chapter early in the morning in a quiet place.

• Paul Vetterick •Marion Vetterick • John Vetterick • Gerry Vetterick • Rollie Vetterick • Ron Vetterick • Scott Vetterick • Stuart Vetterick • Bob Viner • Robert Vogel • Carl Von Medding • Ed Voss • Edwin Voss • Carolyn Voyles • Arlene Wahrry • Ken Walag • Glen Walbridge • Trisha Waldron • Charlie Walker • Barb Walsh • Charles Walsh • Jim Walsh • Frank Walter • Jim Walter • Johnny Wagner • Tommie Wagner • Jimmy Wang • Nancy Wang • Blake Wamester • Anna Ward • Dave Ward • Kristine Ward • Yoka Ward • Debbie Ward • Jack Ward • John Ward • Larry Warren • Angela DeJulio Warren • Rob Washburn • Al Washington • Ian Watson • Vicky Watson • Park Weaver • Bror Weberg • Eva Weberg • Joan Webster • John Webster • Roger Weiler • Arthur Weimer • Susan Weiss • George Weiss • Yon Wellerdeck • Arthur Weller • Peter Weller • Rolf Werner • Jane Wang Wesley • Roy Wesley • Barbara Wessel Weiner • Joe West • Monte West • Bob Whipple • Craig White • Dave White • Nancy White • Vanna White • Marie Wiborg • Roger Wiegard • Anders Wiking • Emily Wildhirt • Norman Wilkens • Bill Wilkinson • Mabel Wilkinson • Billy Williams • Chuck Williamsen • Freddie Wilson • Steph Wilson • Louis Winski • Carey Winston • Barry Winter • Don Wintrich • Tom Wintrich • Matt Wisemiller • Joan Witt • Kathy Witt • James Wittig • Mary Wittwer • Frances Wolf • Michelle Woller • Pat Wolsko • Peter Wolsko Jr. • Helen Wolsko • Tom Wolsko • Sue Wolsko • Pete Wolsko • Laura Wolsko • Chris Wolsko • Pauline Wolsko • Emil Wolsko • John Wolsko • Mary Ann Wolsko • Kirk Wolter • Mary Jane Wolter • Dick Wood • Doug Woodard • George Woodring • William Woodrow • Craig Wortman • Charles Wrobel • Ronald Wyatt • Melissa Wyers • Kelly Wynn • John Wynne • Ginny Yardley • Jenny Yardley • Jeff Yardley • StanYardley • Donatta Yates • Albert Yeatman • Kenneth Young • Karen Yuri • Laurie Zelino • Suzanne Zepf • Renae Zezulka • Sol Zisook • John Zonak • Charlie Zucker •

UNDERSTANDING BANDWIDTH THROUGH METAPHORS

Every aspect of our lives is generated from our bandwidth. Even though the world we are born into seems totally existent, and even when it seems as though life chooses for us, we choose our level of participation. Metaphors may help us see, feel, and distinguish bandwidth from other perspectives on life.

Recipes

Rice is the subsistence diet of hundreds of millions of malnourished and starving people in our world. Likewise, hundreds of millions subsist on a diet of mind-dominant recipes.

Most of us habitually use "mind" as the main ingredient in our recipes for daily life. The other bands (available in the PRESENT MOMENT) merely add flavor or spice to our steady diet of mind.

By consciously choosing the mix of ingredients, we create the recipes for our lives, a creation limited solely by our levels of awareness. Conceivably, all of the elements of bandwidth may be used interchangeably and in any proportions. Some days, our senses, emotions, and brain could be the main ingredients, with a dash or two of mind, body, and spirit. At other times, mind and brain are the main dish, seasoned with a teaspoon of senses, a shake of spirit, and a hint of body.

The essence of life is creation, not merely survival. Life offers us the possibility of being great chefs, or of settling for one bowl of rice after another.

Paint-by-numbers

As a child, did you do paint-by-numbers? Do you remember being admonished to "stay inside the lines?" Or that trees are not purple? Thus our unconscious minds were programmed for adulthood, limiting us to the policies, rules, and regulations of our social institutions. The bureaucratic practices of most mind-based organizations are an extension of paint-by-numbers. When adults (or children, for that matter) are treated as "mechanical doings" instead of "creative beings," their behavior and their beings change, becoming stunted and approval-seeking. Such behavior then carries across all facets of life and relationship.

Fire hydrant

Water gushing from a fire hydrant flows through a series of inter-connected pipes. These pipes may be many feet in diameter and be miles in length. They connect to pump stations, and eventually to a filtration plant that receives water from a lake or river.

The fire hydrant at the intersection of Manhattan Beach and Sepulveda Boulevards in Los Angeles, for instance, is connected by miles of pipe and aqueducts to the Colorado River, which flows from the Rocky Mountains. The Rockies, in turn, are provided with precipitation from the atmosphere.

So it is with human beings and bandwidth. Within our bodies lies the potential of unleashing our human spirits, which are already connected up to other people, to the earth, and to the Universe. Unlike fire hydrants, we don't need wrenches to open us. Our energy is available through the bands we always have on call. We only have to choose it. Just like the fire hydrant, however, our highest use and greatest value occurs in the PRESENT MOMENT.

Painting on a blank canvas

Innate creativity and connectedness naturally comes forth from people who are awake and aware. When you visualize an image and paint it spontaneously with your choice of colors, you are an artist. Your bandwidth is there, waiting for you to access it. Your life is there, waiting for you to create it. In the PRESENT MOMENT we are all artists.

David was already in the stone, waiting for Michelangelo and his carving tools to reveal him. God, Buddha, Lord Krishna, or creator exists in the PRESENT MOMENT. Conception is in the PRESENT MOMENT. Insight is in the PRESENT MOMENT. Sound, taste, and smell are in the PRESENT MOMENT. A heartbeat is in the PRESENT MOMENT. The PRESENT MOMENT is the blank canvas of life.

PRACTICES TO FACILITATE BEING PRESENT

Living on full or high bandwidth occurs when your senses are active, when you are in touch with your emotions and the sensations in your body, when you are aware of your breathing.

Being in the moment (living on high bandwidth) is the source of:

> Creativity
>
> Spirituality
>
> High quality of life
>
> Happiness
>
> High self-esteem
>
> Good health
>
> Courage
>
> Competency
>
> Feeling loved
>
> Contribution
>
> Nurturing yourself and others
>
> Loving yourself and others
>
> Connection with people
>
> Feeling acknowledged and appreciated

Before reading about the practices that follow, visualize your bands of energy by reviewing the graphic below. This graphic reinforces two key points. First, the mind band exists only in the past or future. And, you can access the other five bands by being in the PRESENT MOMENT—the focus of all the practices described in this chapter

PAST   PRESENT   FUTURE

spirit

brain

mind   mind

senses

emotions

body

Secondly, unless and until you act on your increased awareness you will only have great insights. Being extraordinary requires that you take actions which alter your behavior to be consistent with your increased level of awareness.

Take your time to read and experience this material. Experiment with the suggestions and use them as a basis for designing your own practices. Doing so could profoundly impact your health, happiness, and performance.

An intellectual understanding of this book is a good start, but it is insufficient to create the value intended. The following practices are designed to create an experiential knowing of what we have discussed. Beginner, intermediate, and advanced practices will offer multiple ways to access the PRESENT MOMENT, increase your awareness, and expand your basic human capacities.

BEGINNER PRACTICES

WAKING UP

Every morning, as your physical body awakens and you become aware of being awake, practice saying one of the following out loud:

THANK YOU!

THANKS FOR ANOTHER DAY!

THANKS FOR THE GIFT OF LIFE!

THANKS, GOD!

Then take fifteen seconds to notice what is happening internally and externally. Is your mind peaceful, are there a flurry of thoughts running through it?

Is your body stiff and sore or relaxed and loose? Do you feel rested or tired? Now, make a choice—get up or stay in bed. If you choose to stay in bed and your mind is racing, do some conscious breathing to calm your mind.

When you are ready to get out of bed, take three conscious breaths before your feet touch the floor. Feel your feet on the floor as you stand and begin to walk. Continue to breathe consciously and feel your body awakening as you begin to prepare yourself for the day. Experiment with staying present as long as you can. Notice when the mental "TO DO LIST" takes over and choose about that, too.

SELF-OBSERVATION

Self-observation, one gift of awareness. At any time we can hit the "pause button" and observe what is occurring with our mind, body, senses, emotions. We can indirectly observe our brain and spirit.

Mind

Mindfulness is the practice of being aware of your mind and what is currently occurring in it. Notice your thoughts. Notice your inner monologue of criticism and comparison—of self and others, of people and situations. Observe your mind in modes of fear, reacting, remembering, waking up from dreams, waking up with "to do" lists, daydreaming, and forgetting. Conscious observation slows down the mind and allows you to disengage from it. You begin to realize that you are not your mind. The practice builds upon itself-mindfulness engenders mindfulness and is ultimately very freeing

Body

Notice sensations, feelings, tightness, and energy in your body during the course of the day. Feel your feet on the ground. Feel your hands holding the steering wheel, your coffee cup, your child's hand. Notice your posture. When someone shakes your hand, feel it, maintain eye contact, and listen. Stretch your body consciously. Notice the contraction and expansion of your muscles.

Senses

Notice the smells in a room. Experience the scents outdoors. Savor your food and experience its texture as you chew. Feel the sun or wind against your face. Look at the sky, a building, a meadow, or a tree without thinking about it. Just look! Let the impressions come to you. Tuning into your environment is a useful prelude to tuning into people. Begin to notice how you filter your sensory impressions. Allow your senses to serve their purpose, connecting you to your environment and to others.

Emotions

Become aware of the patterns of your emotions. Notice the connection between mind . . . emotions . . . body. Let yourself feel what is occurring within you. Are you aware of the constant stream of emotions in your body? Recognizing and identifying your own feelings is the gateway to feeling what is happening with people around you.

Brain

For one hour, track and write down all of the actions coordinated in your brain, one after another—balancing, walking, keyboarding, recognizing, swallowing, and breathing. Become aware (and be astonished!) of the seamless, harmonious, and constant execution of thoughts, physiological processes, and task completions that your brain oversees and coordinates.

Spirit

Your spirit is always present. Your awareness of it varies, depending on the interference from your mind or the energy of others. Begin to observe your core essence. Spend more time in the PRESENT MOMENT. Notice when you feel peaceful, calm, empty, or joyful. What happens when you contribute, offer compassion, or serve? When are you most connected to others?

OBSERVE CHILDREN

Notice the uninhibited behavior, play, spontaneity, and creativity of young children. Ask a child to sing "Twinkle, Twinkle Little Star." Close your eyes and experience the extraordinary nature of a child. They are wonderful role models of complete self-expression and being free.

PRAYER

Prayer is conversation with God, Allah, or a Supreme Spirit. Prayer may take the form of petition, praise, thanksgiving, intercession, or a request for support. Pay attention to your prayers. Are they spoken from your mind or from your heart? Praying from the heart (or soul) brings you into the PRESENT MOMENT. Prayers of gratitude can help awaken you to your abundant blessings.

PRACTICE YOUR LISTENING AND SPEAKING

Although the topic of communication was addressed earlier, raising awareness of who we are as listeners and speakers is vitally important for bringing us into the PRESENT MOMENT.

Listening

Listening authentically—without a filter of judgment, opinion, or evaluation—acknowledges the speaker and his message. When we really listen, the speaker is received. Without listening there is effectively no speaking. True communication occurs only when there is a listener.

Chapter Five contained several paragraphs from a book by Brenda Ueland in which she eloquently captured the essence of full-bandwidth listening. To paraphrase one sentence, listening occurs when we are able to recreate the other person's speaking. Listening on full bandwidth means I am able to listen to you speak from your world, bring it into my world, and appreciate you for who you are and what you said.

When we filter or "go on autopilot" as people speak, we exercise a kind of control over them. When we interrupt or finish their sentences, we overrule them with our own opinions. Seeking agreement with our points of view and projecting our personalities and values onto others is another way that listening is compromised.

Mind-based interpretation (especially when overlaid with judgment, evaluation, and opinion) of spoken communication does not constitute true listening. True listening is a conscious gift, given to a speaker in the PRESENT MOMENT. It requires connecting our senses, emotions, and spirit with the speaking of another human being.

Speaking

Speaking evokes our world through language. It creates similar pictures in the minds of both the speaker and the listener (assuming a common language). For example, words such as sky, tree, car, plane, computer, house, or telephone create more or less the same instant, mental images for most people.

Speaking is a way to distinguish yourself and a way to share your being with others. Conversely, speaking can generate disconnections, misunderstandings, and problems. Thus, communication, both verbal and non-verbal, is both the creation and the responsibility of the speaker. Be aware of your words, tone of voice, body language, mood, and intention as you speak to others.

Most people broadcast from the channels of their unconscious minds, replaying communications that are consistent with their minds' identities. However they perceive themselves to be—"nice," "bright," a "follower," a "rebel," a "leader," "resistant," "detached," "polite," "passive," "aggressive," or any of a thousand other permutations—their communication springs from their identities. Because it is programmed mostly from the unconscious mind, speaking is derived primarily from the past, and sometimes from the future. Rarely is speaking sourced in the PRESENT MOMENT.

Many communications are about control, telling us what we can and cannot do. Control is a behavior rooted in survival. Typical bureaucratic speaking is not only controlling, it often evokes fear. Fear leads to contraction and disconnection. Were you embarrassed, upset, hurt, or irritated by someone who spoke to you today? People have been "talking down" to us since we were small children. We perpetuate the practice as adults, and not just with children.

Speaking is central to the constant changes taking place in relationships and in the world generally. It is often destructive. How many wars, strikes, deaths, divorces, and separations have been instigated through speaking? It is also generative. How many advances in civilizations have occurred through spoken or written symbolism?

When speaking from a context of creation, we naturally allow for the perspectives of our listeners. A multi-dimensional transmission of energy occurs with authentic speaking and listening. Rather than speaking to satisfy our own minds' incessant need to survive, we speak to the listening present in our intended audiences.

Expand your self-observation to include your speaking and listening throughout the day. Become aware of your listening in the following situations:

One-on-one
On the telephone
In a meeting
When you are peaceful
When you are stressed
With a friend
With someone you don't "connect with"
With a superior or authority figure
With children
With old people
With family members
At work
Socially
At home
In public places
Your internal monologue

For one day, record your observations three times during the day—preferably after lunch, after work, and before you go to bed.

On another day, turn your attention to your speaking. Become aware of your speaking in the above referenced situations and record your observations.

PHYSICAL ACTIVITIES

The following practices will bring you into the PRESENT MOMENT through body and breath awareness.

Walk

Walk in a quiet area and open up your senses. Feel your feet touching the ground and the sun or a breeze on your skin. Breathe consciously and notice what is happening in your body. This is not about exercise. It's about connecting to the PRESENT MOMENT.

Jog

Jog in a quiet place and again, focus on your body. Notice your feet hitting the ground, your muscles contracting and expanding, and your breathing. Notice the environment around you. Jog for a minimum of 15 minutes. When you finish, cool down and breathe consciously for five minutes.

Dance

Find a place with plenty of space where you can move unself-consciously. Play some fast music and dance "full out" for three or four songs. Let your body move any way it wants. (This is not ballroom-dance class or the prom!) Cool down and sit quietly for five minutes. Invite a partner who loves dancing to join in. For even more fun, go out dancing together.

Sing

Again, find a place where you can sing unself-consciously (the car is great). Put on some songs you know and belt them out. Even if you can't carry a tune, just sing. Sing from deep inside so that your whole body vibrates. The next time you're in a public gathering, really sing the National Anthem instead of just standing unconsciously.

Play an instrument

If you play a musical instrument, play a piece you know well enough to immerse yourself in it. Allow yourself to become one with the music.

Exercise

Over the last three decades, participation in sports and other physical activities by North Americans has increased significantly. Exercise is good for anyone who is not under specific medical restrictions. Moderate to strenuous physical activity elevates heart rate, clears and calms the mind, and deepens breathing. Consider committing to a consistent exercise program. It will reduce stress and bring you into the PRESENT MOMENT more often. Choose forms of exercise that you enjoy. Don't make it a struggle. A word of caution: Physical activity requires you to be responsible for your well being and adequately stretched or warmed up before you begin.

Tai Chi

Tai Chi is meditative exercise—a slow dance of repetitive, fluid, whole body motions. Like all martial arts, Tai Chi increases calmness, awareness, and energy flow.

Cheer

Cheer at a sporting event, parade or whenever appropriate. Yell from deep in your belly. Let it rip! This is a great way to release emotions.

Garden

If you enjoy plants or using your hands, this is a great way to connect with the earth in a simple and peaceful way.

Golf

Have you ever noticed the sparkle on a golf ball. Let your eyes connect with the sparkle as you address the ball. When you putt, connect again with the sparkle. Then, keep your eyes momentarily focused on the green after you putt and you will see a dark spot where the ball was. That spot is the residual image left by the ball, and your verification that you connected with the ball.

Clap

Consciously clapping your hands will bring you into the PRESENT MOMENT.

INTERMEDIATE PRACTICES

CONSIDER THE POWER OF BREATHING

We can access wider bandwidth through breathing. Breath is life. Breath links us to the universe. Everything is contained in a breath. In many languages, the words for spirit and breath are the same.

Breathing oxygenates our blood. Blood nourishes our cells, and removes waste products. Seventy percent of all metabolic waste is eliminated through exhalation!

Breath is our access to our bodies, feelings, brains, senses, and spirits. **Breathing with full awareness stills the mind, making it possible to enter the "gap" between thoughts.** As explained in Chapter One, entering this gap provides access to creativity.

For many people, the trauma of birth has a lasting impact on their breathing. At birth, we are forced to shift from the effortless experience of receiving oxygen through the umbilical cord to frantically breathing through the nose and mouth. The first rush of air into delicate lungs is painful, accompanied by a sense of panic. Our first breaths were quick and shallow. Many of us still breathe this way.

Throughout our lives, we experience emotional, physical, and mental problems that tend to confirm our initial experience of entering an unsafe, insecure world. "We store these traumas in our minds and bodies," says Caroline Myss, author of *Anatomy of Spirit*, "and they force us into behaviors of avoidance and fear instead of confronting or dealing with our life problems." **A basic knowledge of breathing helps us release such traumas, manage stress, and return to the PRESENT MOMENT.**

We breathe thousands of times each day. Yet for most of us breathing is a transparent, or unconscious, act. Thus we are disconnected from the present moment, the point at which we access our human spirit.

CONSCIOUS BREATHING

Conscious breathing dates back thousands of years. **When we pay attention to our breathing, we calm the mind and return to the eternal now, significantly increasing awareness, accessing inner stillness, and expanding our sense of what's possible.** When we are truly present to our breath, we can experience focused attention, relaxed alertness, greater creativity, and elevated levels of performance. Athletes often refer to this as entering the "zone."

Right now your mind's incessant chatter is competing with your spirit for your attention.

Conscious breathing will take you beyond your habitual stream of thought, providing access to your unlimited potential. Close your eyes, take some deep breaths, and begin to notice your breathing. You are entering the field of nothing—empty, peaceful, unknown, still, quiet, shapeless. It is waiting to be planted, fertilized, cultivated, and harvested by you.

Because potential and possibility are not tangible, visible, bankable, or easily defined, we are asleep to their presence. Possibility and potential are infinite, eternal, and only accessible in the PRESENT MOMENT. This sphere of higher intelligence, information, and energy is beyond the mind, one conscious breath away, waiting to be discovered and developed.

Our lives are comprised of an enormous string of moments. In each one, we can choose to design and create the lives of our dreams, or bounce around, reacting to upsets and problems, and going through the motions. Like all of us, extraordinary people have millions of unconscious, unproductive, frustrating moments, but they have also discovered the field of unlimited potential. Committed to exploring and expanding this field, they weave rich and satisfying lives.

As you practice conscious breathing, the gaps between your thoughts will begin to widen. Allowing more stillness. We have the innate

capacity to create new possibilities if we can enter the stillness in the gaps between our thoughts. **It is within this stillness that those new insights may appear.**

Becoming aware of your mind's patterns (your old, repetitive thoughts) and preserving new insights is very useful. Record both in a journal. **Acting on your insights is critical.** Begin this practice today. It is as simple as it sounds.

Consider, too, that every member of any organization—leaders, employees, members, guests, and customers—is breathing. This is the most basic commonality within (and between) every organization—people breathe! Imagine the collective effects for a group of people who breathed consciously once or twice daily to access their higher potential. Then imagine what could happen if these people consciously breath fifty or 100 times a day.

Everyone in your organization is only one conscious breath away from higher awareness and unlimited potential. If the dozens, hundreds, or thousands of people with whom you work or play would simply become conscious of their breathing, the resulting expansion of collective awareness, productivity, and connection would be astounding.

Conscious breathing can be practiced throughout the day by linking it to daily activities. For example, take three conscious breaths before you:

Get out of bed	Stop at a traffic light
Go to the bathroom	Eat something
Drink something	Open a door
Stand up or sit down	Answer the phone
Walk up or down stairs	Speak to someone
Go outside or come inside	Shift activities
Open or close a computer file	Say a prayer

Breathe in and breathe out—it's that simple. Conscious breathing is practiced one breath at a time. It nurtures our health on many levels. Our bodies release stress and tension. Our organs, muscles, and connective tissue receive cumulative benefits from improved circulation of oxygen and other nutrients. As we become more conscious and aware, we may find ourselves drawn to more nutritious food, or eating less food.

As mentioned earlier, conscious breathing also expands the gaps between our thoughts and extends our stay in the PRESENT MOMENT. When this happens, we become more alert and our senses open up. We hear sounds that we previously missed. We feel subtle sensations—fabric against our skin, or our fingertips touching glass. We more quickly sense the emotional states of others.

As this time between our thoughts expands, our "right-brain" capacities are free to be fully activated—expanding and exploring possibilities, inventing contexts, creating connections, converting intuition into practical action. In addition, our "left-brain" capacities to logically process information function with less interference from the incessant mind chatter.

Most importantly, conscious breathing allows us to access our spirit, connect with other people at this level, and unleash our unlimited capacities as human beings. This sets the stage for creating value with infinite return.

All these benefits can be summed up as follows:

Breathe in . . .
oxygen
compassion
listening without a filter
experiencing the actual situation
letting in new possibilities
sensing
seeing
energy
life

Breathe out . . .
letting go
carbon dioxide
discharging waste and toxins
freeing ourselves of our innermost fears
letting go of thoughts and stories
making commitments
speaking to be heard
releasing the past

PRESENCE YOURSELF

Practice being present to whatever is happening right here, right now. Actually be with what IS! Another way of saying this is "to presence yourself."

"Presence yourself" in your environment. Be with the energy of your community. Experience the roar of the crowd at an event. Feel your home. Is your bedroom restful? Is your desk chaotic? Immerse yourself in your outdoor space. When you are present to your surrounding environment, your senses, intuition and instincts are sharpened.

"Presence yourself" with other people. Feel the energy of people in a meeting. Be with the people you see walking down the street or riding an elevator. Experience someone's handshake. Shift into neutral and just feel their energy. Notice body language and movement. Open up. Make space for others to connect with you.

"Presence yourself" in nature. Walk in the woods or along a lake. Look at the landscape, first as a whole and then at the intimate detail of a leaf or the stem of a flower. Be with the ripple of the water. Feel the sun warming your face. Inhale the scents flowing from nature. Experience the beauty and interconnection of everything around you.

"Presence yourself" with food. Chew your food consciously. Feel its texture on your tongue and the roof of your mouth. Notice its movement as you swallow. Savor the flavors and smells. Notice the coolness of water as it glides down your throat. Being conscious of what you put into your mouth is a great way to lose weight, as is discovering which foods replenish your energy and which ones deplete it.

BODY SCAN

Once a week, set aside ten minutes for a body scan. Sit in a comfortable, quiet place with your spine erect. Start at the top of your head and consciously scan each part of your body down to your toes. (Energy primarily enters your body through the head. Your feet ground you to the earth.) If you notice anything unusual, go back to the sensation and focus on it. If the feeling or sensation does not diminish, it may be a signal that something is out of balance. If it persists, treat it or seek treatment. The body scan is a useful, early warning system for your health and well being.

BEEPER

A beeper can be set to beep every ten minutes as a reminder to bring yourself into the PRESENT MOMENT.

GIBBERISH

Gibberish is incoherent or unintelligible babble. Nonsensical sounds emitted from the mouth, such as AH WA DAH NANA BA OH YO DO MO EN YA, gibberish clears the mind simply and effectively. Especially valuable during a hectic or busy day, babbling for five minutes in a private place releases energy. Blood rushing to your head, or your face getting hot, signals the release.

Another variation of gibberish is external monologuing. Words are actually spoken but very rapidly in a stream of consciousness. In this way, the mind's internal monologue is exaggerated and externalized.

RECOGNIZE CONTEXT

Context is a physical, psychological, emotional, or spiritual space in which things occur or exist. It is a paradigm or a "way of being," a hidden or transparent framework for human activity. Context is the energy field within which a person lives. Usually programmed by a person's unconscious mind, it can also be consciously created by choice or through states of awareness.

Knowing or establishing context is invaluable to powerful speaking and listening. A first step is to ask, "What is the context in which I live my life?" You might respond, "leader," "nurturer," "capitalist," "lover," "musician," or "explorer." Or you might say "wise, "creative," "empowering," or "skeptical," "anxious," "fearful," "resistant," or "angry." You could be any of the above, depending on the situation, and there is a dominant context that is a defining characteristic of your bandwidth.

Become aware of the overarching feelings and attitude that are behind your self-expression and actions. What do people say about you? What kind of feedback do you most often get? There is probably a common thread running through what you sense and what others say. That is the current context of your life.

Start using your full bandwidth or awareness to observe the context in which others live. What underlies or surrounds their speaking, expression, and actions? What is the context from which their speaking and behavior emanates?

Being aware of context offers deep insights into other human beings. It takes practice, and it is a very practical way to employ higher bandwidth in communications and relationships. For example, speaking from a context of suggestion to a listener whose context is one of openness will be productive. Making demands when a listener is fearful will likely increase the fear and and create a "disconnect" in the communication.

Awareness is an expansion or shift of context. Problems, issues, and resistance often disappear when the context expands or shifts. Such shifts can reveal the whole rather than one or some of the elements.

At the end of this chapter, there is a quiz that will give you an instant experience of discovering context.

SELF REFLECTION

This exercise may seem strange at first. It is powerful. Every morning, stand in front of a mirror, and have the following conversation out loud with yourself. (It might be useful to have a note pad or journal nearby.)

How do I feel today? Animate your response.

What do I intend to accomplish today? Speak it!

Am I really committed to what I just said?

Do I have any undelivered communications to anyone? Speak them!

If so, will I deliver them?

Do I want to acknowledge someone today? If so, who, and what will I say?

Then consider:

I am responsible for and create the outcomes of my life today.

ACKNOWLEDGEMENT

One of the simplest and most profound ways to show appreciation, recognition, and gratitude is simply to acknowledge. Acknowledgement is a communication that empowers or gives energy to both the speaker and the listener.

Acknowledgement transcends the mind and usually involves the senses, emotions, spirit, and body. Acknowledgements bring us into the PRESENT MOMENT. When someone looks you in the eyes and says "thank you" from their heart, something happens inside you. You come alive, if only for just a few seconds.

Experiment with daily three-part acknowledgements. Acknowledge others. Acknowledge yourself. Acknowledge God or the Divine. Do this from your heart so that all three feel your appreciation.

COMMITMENT

Committed speaking is a powerful way to confront and manage your mind. The unconscious mind is random and nonspecific. Commitment creates clarity and focus,

Committing means promising to fulfill on something in the future, often with only partial information and substantial uncertainty. Consider marriage vows or having children. A specific commitment is promised or implied "for life."

Commitment is "being your word." It is doing what you say you will do, no matter what. Commitment is composed of integrity, intention, and responsibility. Promise only what you intend to follow through on. Don't promise what you don't want to do. Don't promise merely to please someone. LEARN TO SAY NO!

It is only in exceptional moods that we realize how wonderful are the commonest experiences of life. It seems to me that sometimes these experiences have an "inner" side, as well as the outer side we normally perceive. At such moments, one suddenly sees everything with new eyes; one feels on the brink of some great revelation. It is as if we caught a glimpse of some incredibly beautiful world that lies silently about us all the time.

—JWN Sullivan

ADVANCED PRACTICES

MEDITATION

All meditation involves conscious breathing over an extended period of time. In a typical meditation, a person sits quietly in a comfortable position with spine erect, eyes closed, and consciously breathes. In some practices a mantra, a pleasant sounding word or a phrase of scripture, is silently repeated. As one continues to sit, the rate of breathing and oxygen intake decrease. Blood pressure and heart rate fall. The "parade of thoughts" is noticed, allowed, and let go. There is nothing to do.

Many problems can be solved by becoming aware of the thoughts that perpetuate them. This is mindfulness. Consciously letting these thoughts go will break up the mental habits that keep problems in place. It may take many attempts, but with awareness and consistency, we can release thoughts we don't want.

YOGA

Consider experimenting with blending movement with meditation through practices such as Tai Chi (described previously) and yoga. Yoga is a Hindu system of mental and physical exercises designed to achieve spiritual insight and tranquillity. Most varieties incorporate bodily postures and breathing techniques. Improved health is among the many benefits of yoga.

Thousands of books and tapes have been created on meditation and yoga and several are listed at the end of the book.

SUSTAINED SILENCE

During the next month, plan to spend an entire morning (or afternoon or evening) without speaking. This will likely require some alterations in your daily routine—as well as some explanation beforehand to your family and friends about what you're doing.

At the end of the time period, write in your journal about your experience. What connections did you observe between your external silence (lack of speaking) and your interior silence (the activity of your mind band)? When did your stream of thoughts increase? When did they decrease? What feelings did you have about not speaking?

Another possibility is to try this exercise when you are away from home, for business or for pleasure. Then, if you choose, try it in the context of your regular day.

Consider doing this exercise again when you can extend your period of silence to an entire day.

SHIFT FROM ME TO WE

When we "wake up" (to our full bandwidth), we naturally come from an attitude of serving. When we shift from self-absorption to empowering and supporting others in high collective bandwidth, we become extraordinary. We transform the energy of relationships, organizations, and communities.

Regardless of title, there are service-oriented elements in virtually any job. The worker's attitude plays a big role in generating the experience of being served or cared for. Obviously, serving others is not confined to a job. It is fundamental to who we are as human beings. It is the essence of being a loving parent or a great leader. Experiment with an attitude of service.

Connecting with people and serving from the space of spirit is not commonplace. Huge opportunities exist in which to expand and practice serving within our families, jobs, charities, and service organizations.

FORGIVENESS

Unresolved incidents can affect people's self-esteem, relationships, and performance for the remainder of their lives. Carrying resentment and trauma can be debilitating. **Resentful thoughts and feelings are stored in the historical mind and in the cells of the body.** A prolonged attachment to trauma and frustration may sometimes manifest as illness or disease.

Resentment is ego-based. The mind is attached and wants to "get even." It wants special consideration. Specifically, the mind is locked into a context of victimization. Often resentment is imbedded in an episode that occurred when the person was very young and did not possess the mental, physical, or emotional capacity for self-defense. Because the trauma is retained in the mind and body, a similar episode often will trigger the reaction of the initial event.

Caroline Myss said, "Forgiveness is the most powerful thing we can do, but it is very unappealing to the mind." The mind is survival-based. It will do all it can to protect and preserve its judgments and opinions, including those which support a victim-based identity.

Forgiveness is giving up resentment or feelings of ill will toward a person, family, group, company, or country that has hurt, traumatized, embarrassed, insulted, or somehow victimized another person or people. Colin Tipping, in his book *Radical Forgiveness*, created the distinction of "radical" and "mock" forgiveness. "Mock forgiveness holds on to victim consciousness...but still has great value in its own right...Radical forgiveness goes to the very core and brings about transformation."

We like to take credit for the good while blaming the bad on some external factor or person. This is another trick of the subconscious mind. Compassion for ourselves and others is not mind-based. It is spiritual. Forgiveness is the ultimate juxtaposition of the unconscious mind and spirit. We can only forgive in the PRESENT MOMENT. When we know that we create and/or co-create all of the events of our lives, we can take full responsibility for them.

Forgiveness is one of the most powerful gifts of high bandwidth. Look into your heart and spirit to see if you are willing to forgive yourself and whoever else your mind says has hurt or victimized you.

A BREAKTHROUGH PROCESS

Breakthrough thinking is the focused generation of new ideas and possibilities. The human spirit is the source of breakthrough because it is linked to the universal field of intelligence, information, and energy.

We have all experienced random breakthrough thinking—those ideas that come "out of the blue" while shaving, driving, showering, or lying in bed. The following process helps to set the stage or create the environment for more specific breakthroughs. It can be used with a specific project, to solve a particular problem, or to generate new possibilities.

Experiment with the following process:

Be in the PRESENT MOMENT or the gap between thoughts—use breathing, meditation, silence or any method you choose. Speak a commitment or intention into the "gap" and be specific. Release the outcome. Do not push for a result. Allow the universe or Quantum Field to produce the result. Listen actively and attentively for a signal or the idea.

A good time to do this is right before you go to sleep or when you are in a peaceful state such as after meditation or exercise. Ideas, thoughts, and signals often occur upon awakening. Sometimes, the ideas come a few days later. You can repeat the process nightly, keeping paper and pen by your bed, and paying close attention. Strange as it may sound, it works!

This graphic summarizes the breakthrough process.

Field of information, intelligence, and energy

QUIET FOCUS — SPEAK INTENTION — LET GO OF OUTCOME — IDEAS PRODUCED — ACTIVELY LISTEN

The Universe

Exercise

Context Quiz

What is context of all these phrases? Notice how discovering the context enables the translation of the content. Translate each sentence into a commonly known phrase.

Vintage bituminous sovereign.

Siblings traversing an elevation.

Venerable lady occupying a domicile
    designed for pedal adornment.

Emaciated fellow who viewed with disdain
    any form of set.

The feline pet and the Stradivarius.

Double Mary Tyler Moore, exceedingly obstinate.

Embryo situated on a retaining edifice.

Ebony four-legged fabric source speaks out.

Miniature muncher crouching at the intersection
    of two lateral surfaces.

Dairy product consumer demonstrating
    an unreasoning fear of arachnids.

Rodent scaling an antique timepiece.

Female scholar followed persistently by
    a young member of the ovine family.

Feather-brained boy who encountered an
    itinerant baker enroute to an exposition.

A trio of rural rodents afflicted with
    vision deficiency.

United Kingdom's historic transportation span
    in a state of collapse.

◠ Exercise

A vision of my life

The following exercise requires you to imagine your future specifically, and to create from the future into the present. It is NOT intended to be a retrospective look, or a creation of the future as an extrapolation of the past.

In your journal or on a separate sheet, answer each question. Add your own questions, as necessary. Design a life that is satisfying, productive, and fulfilling. When you determine who you choose to be and what you choose to create with your life, you significantly increase the probability of achieving it.

The finished questionnaire can become a blue print from which to create a future in accordance with your vision and purpose.

1. *I plan to live until age*
2. *My principal contribution to the world will be*
3. *My health during my life will be*
4. *I expanded into high bandwidth at age*
5. *My extraordinary career moments will be*
6. *My extraordinary moments as a spouse will be*
7. *My extraordinary moments as a friend will be*
8. *My extraordinary moments as a parent will be*
9. *My extraordinary moments as a change agent will be*
10. *The real value of my life will be*
11. *I learned from being present that*
12. *I had major wake up calls at ages*
13. *When I confront risk, I will*
14. *The key relationships I establish will be*
15. *To continue my personal growth and development during my life time, I will*
16. *In order to create balance in my life, I will*
17. *My primary commitments in life will be*
18. *My vision for my life including my family and career will be*

Wait a week or two, then review your comments, add to them, and incorporate new insights. Are all of your answers consistent with or supportive of one another? How can any conflicts be resolved?

Wait a few more weeks and return to this exercise, reading your plan as if it were written by someone else. Reflect on the kind of person who would write this vision. Doing so will give you new ways in which to look at and think about yourself. Record your insights and observations.

Now, act on your vision.

COMMIT TO PRACTICE

You can read this entire book, including the last few pages and probably get several new insights. You may even experience a transformation. But that is of no lasting value unless you act upon what you have read and experienced. Unless you commit to one or more practices to alter your awareness, nothing sustainable will occur. Until you act on your insights or sustain a transformation, your mind will regain its long-term control over you and none of this will make a difference. As a way to keep accessing your full bandwidth on a regular basis, please consider making a commitment to one of the practices described in this chapter or another one that will work for you. This is for you!!

I, _____,

PROMISE MYSELF AND

_____

THAT I WILL PRACTICE _____

_____

_____

_____

_____

TO ACCESS THE PRESENT MOMENT

AND MY HUMAN BANDWIDTH.

Signed _____

Dated _____

CHAPTER XII:
Unleashing Your Human Spirit

No one can flatter himself that he is immune to the spirit of his own epoch, or even that he possesses a full understanding of it. Irrespective of our conscious convictions, each one of us, without exception, being a particle of the general mass, is somewhere attached to, colored by, or even undermined by the spirit which goes through the mass. Freedom stretches only as far as the limits of our consciousness.
—Carl Jung

People I have yet to meet . . .

AN INVITATION

Because expanding into your bandwidth is a process, an ongoing journey, this book has no conclusion. Instead, I again offer an invitation. Consider utilizing your expanded bandwidth to make a difference for your family, community, company, organization, or wherever you choose to invest your life. You have the opportunity to live an extraordinary life, no matter how old you are.

Living an extraordinary life (being a highly aware human being) occurs when you discover, develop, and then contribute your expanded human bandwidth to the world. This book focused primarily on discovering and developing the capacities of humans and organization, and while the written word may serve as a guide, life is the ultimate laboratory. But self-awareness alone will not result in being extraordinary.

Yes, self-awareness prepares you for the journey of an extraordinary life. You create and express your life as part of the constantly changing mosaic of the world. But manifesting who you really are occurs when you go beyond yourself (your unconscious mind) and co-create your world with your fellow human beings, in a context of connection, compassion, love, and contribution. When we express and act through broad band-width, with the intention to benefit others, we are in the territory of extraordinary. We are sharing our gifts. We are connecting at the level of spirit.

Human spirit is the infinite and eternal aspect of human bandwidth, the source and space of interconnection. Spirit is the expression of oneness with everything and everyone. It is our link to the divine, where duality does not exist. In spirit there is only oneness.

Human spirit is the synthesis of the individual with the universal. Collectively, we bring forth our lives. Life is concurrent moments of now, now, now. Responsibility, contribution, permission, and sharing are inherent aspects of conscious co-creation. The PRESENT MOMENT is our portal to spirit, to the infinite and eternal field of pure potential and possibility.

THE LANGUAGE AND ACTION OF HUMAN SPIRIT

Each of us is a thread in the organic fabric of planet Earth. Our ongoing migration toward interconnection is an outward manifestation of the already present, indivisible connection of spirit.

How many words in the English language begin with co-, col-, com-, or con-? These prefixes denote "with, together, or joint." Cooperation, collaboration, conversation—all such words connect us as human beings, co-existing and co-creating the world, exemplifying the oneness of human spirit.

Our spirit can be unleashed through all forms of expression—struggles, confrontation, compassion, learning, skills, love, creativity, compromise, acceptance and commitment. Whether connection occurs individually from the outside in or inside out, a major shift is occurring in the collective consciousness of the world. (This book is intended to accelerate this shift.) By discovering, developing, and contributing your capacities in your own way, with your own style, you increase the level of awareness in the world—one person at a time. As you expand your bandwidth and effectively use the power within you, you contribute to the expansion and growth of the world or universal organism.

VOLUNTARY UNLEASHING OF HUMAN SPIRIT

It seems, unfortunately, that the collective unleashing of human spirit most often occurs in the midst of war, accidents, or other emergencies. Can we generate our human spirit as a way of life, rather than solely in response to tragedy?

For an answer, we can look to nature, where physicists see a unified field of matter and energy. Balanced harmony occurs naturally, perfectly correlated to the needs of all species. Although periodically skewed by disturbances such as floods, earthquakes, and fires, the predominant energy of nature is generally constructive and supportive.

We humans, in contrast, have altered the natural flow of life. The unconscious actions and automatic-pilot reactions of our dominating minds suppress and cover up our spirit. Nevertheless, spirit resides within us, waiting to be unleashed.

As you choose to more frequently move into the realm of broad bandwidth and spirit, you will see a difference in your communication, action, and output. In your growing awareness, your outputs will begin to have more value and greater impact. You will learn to recognize people who zap your energy. You will consciously choose whether to continue contributing to them, or to confront them with your realizations, or to change your relationship in some other way.

Of course, you will periodically go unconscious and disconnect from those around you. From time to time you may react to circumstances automatically and draw down someone else's energy. We all drift into our historical minds. Don't be too critical. Just be aware as you move in and out of the PRESENT MOMENT. Reconnect with yourself and others. Remember your essence. How quickly you return to the here and now will determine the quality of your life.

In every moment, we are either giving or taking. Just as our awareness is a gift, keeping the energy flowing, our non-awareness is a gift also. Noticing when we go unconscious, and about what, is instructive, and it reminds us to wake up and return to the PRESENT MOMENT.

COLLECTIVE CONTRACTION AND EXPANSION OF BANDWIDTH

Throughout the Cold War era, the collective mind tended to focus on political stability, economic expansion, and the development of new products, services, and technologies. The United Nations, NATO, and the Warsaw Pact, motivated by fear of nuclear war, successfully prevented another global conflict. The standard of living, as measured by socio-economic data, in the developed countries steadily improved, and with it came the concept of "life style." The majority of people in developed countries now say that their quality of life is "acceptable" or "good."

This is in spite of the fact that several dozen wars are being fought simultaneously around the globe. More people are now dying of hunger-related disease, starvation, malnutrition, and inadequate medical help than in 1945, during the final convulsions of World War II. Divorce rates exceed 50% in the US and Europe. The percentage of people attending churches, synagogues or mosques has declined. Security is the foremost concern of all the countries of the world, and national defense constitutes the largest budgetary expenditure for nearly every developed country.

Awareness of self and the world is low. Fear overwhelms love. Disconnection overshadows connection. Habit outweighs creativity. Personal comfort trumps compassion. Human spirit is generally suppressed and disconnected, dragging emotions, conscious mind, senses, brain, and body down with it. It seems that we have only improved our standard of existence, not our standard of living.

Collective contraction

On September 11, 2001 the world witnessed dramatic examples of radical contraction and expansion of collective bandwidth. In less than an hour (four discreet moments, actually), 19 men altered the collective psyche of practically the entire world. Three airliners, each fueled for a trans-continental flight, were crashed into office buildings filled with people. A fourth plane crashed into the ground in Pennsylvania. Over 3,000 people died.

Many of us found it difficult to grasp and process these unprecedented events. American minds could only conjure memories of a vaguely similar occurrence—the attack on Pearl Harbor. The collective mind was horrified and shocked. Senses were inundated with visual and audio stimulation, from media reports and personal conversations in which emerging details of the tragedy were shared and reiterated. Thus was the contracting experience of the observers.

Collective expansion

What happened at "Ground Zero" in New York and the Pentagon that day was a global wake-up call. For those on the scene, spontaneous physical action occurred in the PRESENT MOMENT: running, jumping, falling, dodging, bumping, shoving, stumbling, rolling, carrying, dragging, hurting, shouting, crying, screaming, and choking.

People heard, smelled, saw, and felt explosions, vibrations, debris, fire, ash clouds, heat, and the faces and bodies of other people who were caught in the mayhem. A huge range of emotion occurred simultaneously in the people present. Brains orchestrated all bands of energy. Their unconscious minds stopped their internal monologues. (Often in emergencies, the mind stops broadcasting.) People were totally present to what was, and tens of thousands of people were able to exit the buildings and the area very quickly.

Fire fighters, police, rescue workers, and volunteers poured into the buildings to save others, placing their own lives at risk. Strangers carried each other down forty, sixty, eighty flights of stairs. Prayers were said. Hands were held. People hugged and cried. They pulled each other out of danger. Ordinary people transformed into heroes.

In those successive moments of now, each of the people caught up in the tragedies acted from a deep, natural knowing. Courage, caring, and spontaneous constructive action emerged, all attributes of heroism and human spirit.

Passengers on the fourth airliner, some of them aware of what had occurred on the other hijacked planes, and sensing their imminent deaths, attacked the hijackers and forced the plane to crash. Boarding the plane earlier that morning, they were ordinary people. They became extraordinary with "Let's roll!" giving their lives so others might be saved.

As news and images of the tragedy circulated, something very powerful unfolded. The human spirit in hundreds of millions of people all over the globe responded. There came another wave of spontaneous heroic action. No debate was needed. There were no mental log jams. Hundreds of thousands of people, in the military, civil defense, FAA, the Administration, Congress, and government at all levels, moved into action to protect the public and prevent further destruction. Foreign governments responded in similar fashion.

The combined heroic efforts of people, both on the disaster scenes and far away, saved thousands, perhaps hundreds of thousands, of other lives. An unmistakably focused and coordinated PRESENT MOMENT energy connected people worldwide. Business CEOs, interviewed on TV, revealed their humanness. Race, age, ethnic origin, religion, and gender were no longer divisive. For a short while, the transcendent and true nature of people became visible. For a time, all were one—in spirit, action, life, and death. September 11th was living (and dying) proof of the broad bandwidth potential of all human beings.

Post Mortem

Then came the aftermath. The heroes were buried. Thousands of families waited and prayed for lost loved ones, many of whose bodies were never found. Some whole companies, having lost all their employees, ceased to exist. Intellectual, emotional, and creative energy was depleted, creating a profound, long-term impact. A New York Times headline from September 18, 2001 read, "Stress from attacks will chase some into the depths of their minds, and stay." It goes on to say, "For some, the ultimate legacy of last week's events will be memories that gradually turn malignant, as dangerous as any cancer."

September 11th was a watershed event for the collective mind. Already in place subconsciously, fears about survival and physical safety permeated our consciousness. The same terrible images and conversations were replayed again and again. Many people decided to fly less frequently, or not at all. Skyscrapers, once beautiful architectural treasures, are now imagined as targets. Sports stadiums, amusement parks, large arenas-anywhere that large numbers of people can gather—trigger thoughts of danger. Our fears were amplified by the media, which incessantly repeated each nuance of the horror, postulating future terrorist incidents, and raising the spector of chemical, biological, or nuclear weapons being employed against our cities.

Researchers who study the psychological impact of war, torture, violent crime, terrorism and natural disasters say that what stirs them is not the debilitating effects of such tragedies. It is rather the resilience of the human spirit revealed in them. September 11th illustrated an unleashing of human spirit unparalleled in its breadth and depth of connection and caring in this generation.

We were all presented with clear choices in the aftermath of the attacks. Will we be free or will we be captives of the fearful thoughts and images involuntarily flowing through our minds? Will we live our lives from a context of possibility or one of avoidance? Will we be students of love or disciples of fear?

Living or sleeping?

The mission of terrorism is the polar opposite of the freed human spirit. Terrorism is designed to generate intense fear. Its purpose is to drive people out of high bandwidth and into the depths of their unconscious mind.

How terrorism will alter the behavior of citizens into the future is unknown. Mourning knows no right formula for the families, friends, and associates of the people who were killed. The survivors, rescue workers, government workers, military service personnel, and members of the community experienced unprecedented trauma, shock, and disbelief.

The communities of New York City and Washington, D.C. were dramatically changed for at least the short term. World-wide, airlines and related travel services suffered significant declines. The status quo became more ambiguous.

As aware human beings, we have a choice. We can unconsciously succumb to the fear generated in the individual and collective mind. This has happened repeatedly throughout the Twentieth Century, in the terrorism of Stalin, Mussolini, Hitler, Pol Pot, Idi Amin, Mao Tse Tung, and Saddam Hussein, to name just a few. They kidnapped, murdered, tortured, imprisoned, starved, and terrorized entire populations, effectively freezing the individual and collective mind in a state of fear.

We have another choice. We can choose to shift the energy of the world away from fear and disconnection toward constructive action such as love, caring, and interconnection by invoking our Human spirit.

Morrie Schwartz offered millions of us a loving wake-up call and a template by which to live life. Jon Hobart and my wife Jan offered me personal wake-up calls. You and I can seize the day and the moments of now and now and now. Or, we can be seized by the events of the day and miss the PRESENT MOMENT. Wouldn't it be great to really wake up at age twenty instead of forty, or fifty, or eighty, or never?

Waking up to life and all its possibilities can be as invigorating or as unsettling as the sound of an alarm clock. Staying awake requires that we get up and get going. Apathy, resignation, anxiety, and fear keep us in bed or locked indoors. Why stay in bed, waiting to die? Are you willing to let your unconscious mind dictate the terms and conditions of your life?

The invisible, razor-thin line between human spirit and the unconscious mind is still a mystery to most people. High bandwidth and low bandwidth are but a moment apart—the PRESENT MOMENT.

EPISODES OF UNCONSCIOUS MIND OR HUMAN SPIRIT?

Following are a few additional episodes which illustrate both the power of the human spirit and the influence of the unconscious mind.

During the 600's A.D., Islamic Arabs conquered the Holy Land. Four hundred years later, Turks took control and interfered with Christian pilgrims seeking to visit. As a result, a series of Christian military expeditions were undertaken during the 10th, 11th and 12th centuries The original purpose—to reclaim the rights of Christians—was eventually supplanted by the quest for wealth, power, and new land.

A thousand years later the Middle East is still entrenched in conflict. Sensory perceptions are filtered by historical paradigms in the unconscious mind. Collective fear suppresses collective bandwidth. Low collective bandwidth permits the perpetuation of hatred and violence, resulting in disconnection and continuing strife.

All the battles fought over the last 3,000 years reveal a fairly consistent pattern. The suppressed emotions of male-dominated societies are triggered in individual and collective minds, and physical bodies release this tension (also known as rage, hatred, torment, craziness) on other human beings, often in the name of that culture's deity.

After each war, a choice is made—either to resolve and reconnect through forgiveness and generosity of the human spirit or to negotiate mind-based peace accords (which deal with the form of issues but rarely get to the heart). Typically, when the latter path is taken, the unconscious, mind-driven cycle of suppressed emotions and physical explosions begins anew.

In 1620, a band of English Protestants seeking to worship as they chose, risked their lives in a trans-Atlantic voyage to what is now Plymouth, Massachusetts. The Plymouth Colony exemplified the human spirit. Their commitment, courage, perseverance, creativity, suffering, and hard work in an unknown and sometimes hostile environment served as a model for future generations. Their commitment to achieving religious freedom personifies expanded human bandwidth. Conversely, their religious persecution of both the indigenous Americans and later newcomers to America, is an example of how the unconscious mind will perpetuate the violence from which the spirit sought to be freed.

The Marshall Plan, under which America financed the rebuilding of Europe after World War II, is another example of expanded collective bandwidth. Extraordinary creativity, focus, investment, physical labor, and interconnection of spirit created a new Europe.

Reconnection naturally occurs in the face of adversity. A common illustration of this is siblings who fight unmercifully among themselves until an outside threat is perceived. Then they instinctively form a unified front.

Natural disasters generally don't afford much time to think, much less to squabble. People just do whatever is required of them to help one another. The aftermath calls forth our co-creative natures, working in partnership to heal wounds and rebuild lives and communities.

Sudden illness, accident, or other intense stress will often signal a choice point for individuals, a crossroads of narrow and broad bandwidth. A heart attack is a terrible experience, yet it may be the wake-up call that saves that person's life, granting instant awareness of unexpressed emotions, eating and exercise habits, stress levels, and perhaps, family genetics.

The 2002 Winter Olympic games saw the United States garnering an unprecedented number of medals—a total of thirty-four compared to the previous record of thriteen. Could there be a connection between the US athletes' stunning performance and the cohesive spirit of the country following September 11? Was being on "home turf" an added factor?

Hundreds of thousands of examples of expanded bandwidth occur every year. Breakthroughs in technology, relationships, medicine, and courage occur daily. The human aspects of these events turn up in heart-warming stories of regular (extraordinary) people in *Chicken Soup for the Soul* or *Reader's Digest*. But most go unnoticed.

And then, there are people who, perhaps while reading a book like this one, or watching a movie, or jogging along a beach, or listening to the words of a friend, will catch a glimpse of what it means to be human. They see their connection to the wider field of human possibility and potential. They get a taste of their expanded bandwidth. In time (after dozing off and waking up over and over again), they choose to consciously grab on with both hands and to co-create their world for what remains of their lives.

Exercise

Life's wake-up calls

Fear can serve as a wake-up call, jolting us out of unconsciousness. What thoughts rush through your mind when you drive by an accident, or hear an ambulance, or read about a tragedy? What feelings accompany those thoughts? How is it when you visit someone in the hospital? What happens in your mind and body when you are the one being admitted?

WE HAVE A CHOICE

An emergency, a tragedy, or some other stimulus is not required in order to tap into our human spirit—that mysterious, precious, invisible essence connecting us all. It is always there, just like the blue sky beyond the clouds, available and accessible. It always will be. Spirit is who we are when we come into the PRESENT MOMENT—pure potential and possibility.

But we tend to cover up who we are, and thereby forget. Our minds distract us, disconnecting us from our true essence and from each other. The western world continues to emphasize the growth of the intellect. Our true essence is hidden under this focus on the mind and brain bands of energy. But the human spirit awaits, like the proverbial candle, its light hidden beneath a bushel basket.

As each person realizes that who she is is full band-width led by the infinite band of spirit, the world is transformed. Perhaps the awesome, worldwide display of human spirit in response to September 11, 2001 was not a temporary phenomenon, but the beginning of a new era of expanded bandwidth. Full bandwidth can be activated by our choices and through our commitments to contribute to one another. One person at a time, we can help to shift the focus from form to substance, from reaction to action.

Life is truly lived from the inside out. It is about body, e-motions, senses, and spirit. Yes, it's also about mind and brain. Life is creation. Life is participation—singing the songs, experiencing the thrills, tasting the salt of our tears, and making the choices that build our world. Life, fully lived, is a game played on the field, not in the stands.

WHO DO YOU CHOOSE TO BE?

Experiencing high bandwidth, that space in which we are our most creative, passionate, and connected—to ourselves, to others, and to God or a Divine Spirit, is the most profound discovery we can make. The ultimate personal conflict is between the unconscious mind and the human spirit. In other words, it is between low and high bandwidth, being ordinary or extraordinary, existing (even worse, resisting) or creating, and living in the past and the future as opposed to living in the PRESENT MOMENT.

Discovering who you really are and creating a vision for your life is the threshold of freedom. Now, you have choices. You can consciously determine your pathways, your commitments, your actions, your attitudes, and your connection to your fellow human beings.

Continued growth and development is a crucial aspect of discovering your true essence. Discovery without development is merely insight—useful, but not necessarily transformational. Presencing one's self takes practice and full participation in life. Claiming authorship of your life and taking responsibility for your actions is a natural consequence of awareness. Increased expansive and connective actions are powerful outcomes of development.

Contribution is another powerful outcome. Contribution is giving to and sharing with others, requiring the release of your ego (your mind-based identity). It encompasses being a team player, cooperating, collaborating, and co-creating. The purest energy, the energy of empowerment, flows through you when you share your skills, competencies, knowledge, and caring with others.

ACCESS YOUR FULL BANDWIDTH NOW

The end of this chapter brings us full circle.
As T.S. Eliot wrote:

> We shall not cease from exploration
> And the end of our exploring
> Will be to arrive where we started
> And know the place for the first time.

In short, we have come back to you. You are your bandwidth capacities. You create and express yourself individually and in co-creation with other human beings.

Throughout this book, I have endeavored to:

Awaken you to your true nature;

Reveal your bandwidth as innate capacities waiting to be unleashed;

Demonstrate that you are a creative being, suppressed by your mind and ultimately by the collective mind;

Propose that you create your life from love;

Suggest that you can do and be whatever you can imagine;

Give you the access point to your bandwidth—the PRESENT MOMENT;

Have you experience the mystery, power and value of being present;

Encourage you to speak, listen, and act in the PRESENT MOMENT;

Increase the probability of your converting intentions into results through higher awareness;

Help you realize your always-existing connection to other people and the universe;

Support your expansion from "me to we";

Inspire your contribution of your full bandwidth to the world;

Encourage you to trust in God / Divine Spirit;

Recommend an attitude of gratitude and acknowledgment of others;

Communicate that we are the world.

Whether in a dorm room, an office, on the factory floor, a hospital bed, a retirement village, at home, or on a city street, all your bands of energy are available, waiting to be activated. You have untold capacity on tap in the PRESENT MOMENT, and millions of present moments remaining to be experienced in your lifetime.

In each and every PRESENT MOMENT lives the possibility of being exceptional. In each and every PRESENT MOMENT lives the opportunity to access our true nature. Our human spirit is always there, waiting to be liberated. There are no exceptions. It is simply a matter of getting beyond the life-long programming of the unconscious mind and the manifestations of that programming which hold us back from fully participating. Stringing together more and more moments of now, now, now, and now increases the probability of an extraordinary life.

The infinite and eternal PRESENT MOMENT is the ultimate fertile field of pure potential, freedom, and full bandwidth. And you, my friend, are a microcosm of that field!

Welcome! We are the world.

May you go forth into the world,

experiencing yourself as a fully alive human being—

deeply connected to self, to others, and to the Divine Spirit,

expressive, creative, and contributing.

Recommended Reading

BOOKS & ARTICLES

Albom, Mitch. "*Tuesdays with Morrie*", New York: Doubleday, 1997.

Byrne, John A. "*Jack*", Business Week, June 8, 1998, p. 90.

Campbell, Joseph with Moyers, Bill. "*The Power of Myth*", ed. Betty Sue Flowers, Doubleday, New York 1988.

Capra, Fritjof. "*The Tao of Physics*", London: Flamingo, 1976.

Champy, James, and Michael Hammer. "*Reengineering the Corporation*", New York: Harper Business Publishers, 1993.

Chopra, Deepak. M.D. "*Quantum Healing: Exploring The Frontiers of Mind/Body Medicine*", Bantam Books, 1990

Collins, James C., and Porras, Jerry I. "*Built to Last*", Harper Business, New York, 1994.

Covey, Stephen R. "*The 7 Habits of Highly Effective People*", New York: Fireside/Simon & Schuster, 1990.

Czikszentmihalyi, Mihalyi. "*Flow: The Psychology of Optimal Experience*", Harper Collins, 1991

DePree, Max. "*Leadership is an Art*", New York: Doubleday, 1989.

Flores, Fernando, and Terry Winograd. "*Understanding Computers and Cognition*", Norwood, New Jersey: Ablex Publishing Corporation, 1986.

Folsing, Albrecht. "*Albert Einstein*", New York: Viking, 1993.

Frank, Philipp, "*Einstein, His Life and Times*", New York: Alfred A. Knopf, 1947.

Frankl, Viktor E. "*Man's Search for Meaning*", New York: Touchstone, 1959.

Greene, Bob. "*Hang Time*", Doubleday, 1992.

Golas, Thaddeus. "*The Lazy Man's Guide to Enlightenment*", Salt Lake City: Gibbs-Smith Publisher, 1971.

Goleman, Daniel P., "*Emotional Intelligence*", Bantam Books, 1997.

Greenleaf, Robert, "*Servant Leadership*", Paulist Press, New York, 1977.

Heckler, Richard Strozzi, "*In Search of the Warrior Spirit*", North Atlantic Books, Berkeley, 1990.

Heerman, Barry. "*Building Team Spirit*", McGraw-Hill, 1997.

Heidegger, Martin. "*On The Way To Language*", Harper & Row, 1982.

Huey, John. "*Sam Walton, Made in America*", New York: Doubleday, 1992.

Jackson, Phil, "*Sacred Hoops*", Hyperion, New York, 1995.

Kabat-Zinn, Jon, "*Wherever You Go, There You Are*", Hyperion, 1994.

Kegan, Robert. "*In Over Our Heads*", Harvard University Press, Cambridge, 1994.

Klein, Eric and Izzo, John. "*Awakening Corporate Soul*", Fairwinds Press, 1998.

Lowe, Janet. "*Benjamin Graham on Value Investing*", New Delhi: Vision Books, 1994.

Maturana, Humberto and Varela, Francisco. "*The Tree of Knowledge*", Shambhala, Boston, 1991.

Mukherjee, Rudrangshu. "*The Penguin Ghandi Reader*", New Delhi: Penguin Books, 1993.

Myss, Caroline. "*Anatomy of the Spirit*", New York: Harmony Books, 1996.

Peck, M. Scott. "*The Road Less Traveled*", Simon & Schuster, New York, 1978.

Penick, Harvey. "*Harvey Penick's Little Red Book*", Simon & Schuster, 1992.

Peters, Thomas and Robert H. Waterman Jr. "*In Search of Excellence*", New York: Harper & Row Publishers, 1982.

Ramo, Joshua Cooper. "*Person of the Year*", Time, December 27, 1999, 50.

Remen, Rachel Naomi. "*Kitchen Table Wisdom*", New York: Riverhead Books, 1996.

Ruiz, Don Miguel. "*The Four Agreements*", Amber-Allen Publishing, San Rafael, 1997.

Rumi, Jelaluddin, "*The Essential Rumi*", Translation by Colman Barks, with John Moyne, Harper, San Francisco, 1995.

Senge, Peter et al. "*The Fifth Discipline: The Art and Practice of the Learning Organization*", Currency/Doubleday, 1994.

Sheehy, Gail. "*New Passages*", New York: Random House, 1995.

Shoemaker, Fred. "*Extraordinary Golf*", Perigee, 1997

Sloman, James. "*Handbook for Humans*", Tiburon, CA: Ocean Blue Publishing, 1998.

Strauss, William, and Neil Howe. "*Generations*", New York: Quill-William Morrow, 1991.

Thich Nhat Hanh. "*Peace is Every Step: The Path of Mindfulness in Everyday Life*", Bantam Books, 1992.

Tipping, Colin C. "*Radical Forgiveness*", Marietta, GA, Global 13 Publications Co., Trust, 1997.

Tolle, Eckhart. "*The Power of Now*", Novato, California: New World Library, 1999.

Wheatley, Margaret J. and Myron Kellner-Rogers . "*A Simpler Way*", San Francisco: Berrett-Koehler Publishers, 1996.

White, Michael, and John Gribbin. "Einstein, A life in Science", New York: Dutton Books, 1993.

Wing, R.L. "The Tao of Power", London: Thorsons, 1988.

Zajonc, Arthur. "Catching the Light", Oxford University Press, New York, 1993

Context Quiz Answers from page 179
1. Old King Cole
2. Jack & Jill
3. The Little Old Woman Who Lived in a Shoe
4. Jack Sprat
5. The Cat and the Fiddle
6. Mary Mary Quite Contrary
7. Humpty Dumpty
8. Baa Baa Black Sheep
9. Little Jack Horner
10. Little Miss Muffet
11. Hickory Dickory Dock
12. Mary Had a Little Lamb
13. Simple Simon
14. Three Blind Mice
15. London Bridge

To offer feedback about your experience of this book
or for further information, please e-mail
gunnar@human---bandwidth.com

To order additional copies
of this book, please e-mail
orders@rapidcreekpublishing.com